Paper, Ink, and Achievement

Paper, Ink, and Achievement

Gabriel Hornstein and the Revival of

Eighteenth-Century Scholarship

EDITED BY KEVIN L. COPE AND
CEDRIC D. REVERAND II

Bucknell | UNIVERSITY
UNIVERSITY | PRESS
LEWISBURG, PENNSYLVANIA

Library of Congress Cataloging-in-Publication Data

Names: Hornstein, Gabriel, 1935–2017. honouree. | Cope, Kevin Lee, editor of
  compilation. | Reverand, Cedric D., editor of compilation.
Title: Paper, ink, and achievement : Gabriel Hornstein and the revival of
  eighteenth-century scholarship / edited by Kevin L Cope, Cedric D Reverand II.
Description: Lewisburg, Pennsylvania : Bucknell University Press, [2020] |
  Includes bibliographical references and index.
Identifiers: LCCN 2020004896 | ISBN 9781684482511 (paperback) |
  ISBN 9781684482528 (hardcover) | ISBN 9781684482535 (epub) |
  ISBN 9781684482542 (mobi) | ISBN 9781684482559 (pdf)
Subjects: LCSH: Hornstein, Gabriel, 1935–2017. | English literature—18th century—
  History and criticism. | Scholarly publishing—United States—History—20th
  century. | England—Intellectual life—18th century. | Enlightenment.
Classification: LCC PR442 .P37 2020 | DDC 820.9/005—dc23
LC record available at https://lccn.loc.gov/2020004896

A British Cataloging-in-Publication record for this book is available from the
British Library.

www.bucknelluniversitypress.org

Distributed worldwide by Rutgers University Press

Manufactured in the United States of America

Contents

PART III
Re-evaluating Literary Modes

Preface: Gabriel Hornstein
(1935–2017)

Cedric D. Reverand II

Abraham's Magazine Service, better known in modern times as AMS Press, was originally in the business of acquiring old books, serial publications, and newspapers and then reselling them. As Gabriel Hornstein, who became president of AMS around 1969, once explained to us, the press would get a complete run of, say, an out-of-print scholarly journal, then locate academic libraries that, because of an oversight, budget constraints, or different priorities, had failed to subscribe to the journal when it was originally published. Once AMS found a critical mass of libraries that needed to fill that gap, it would secure the rights, reprint the journal run in facsimile, and sell it to the libraries. Often the publication in question was in the public domain; when one company announced it was going to reprint such a work, competing companies, by gentleman's agreement, backed off. While this was a healthy business model, with several major reselling companies churning out reprints for many years, by the early 1970s academic library purchasing tapered off, most likely because there were far fewer gaps to be filled, thanks to the efficiency of publishers like AMS, which, in essence, were rendering themselves obsolete.

Starting in the 1970s, Gabe, as he was known to his friends, began doing something different: AMS Press started publishing original scholarship. And for some reason, Gabe focused his attention specifically, although not exclusively, on the so-called long eighteenth century (he also published an important Dickens bibliography as well as *Emblematica*, a scholarly annual that kept the study of Renaissance emblems alive for many years). He established AMS Studies in the Eighteenth Century in 1970, which went on to publish over seventy original scholarly monographs, including books on literature, women's studies, science, history, psychology and literature, philosophy, religion, theory, and the publishing trade. In the 1980s, AMS Press also began to publish scholarly annuals, growing to seventeen in total, most of which Gabe initiated, after lining up an appropriate editorial team. The following AMS Press annuals deal with the eighteenth century, each of them containing about fifteen essays and running from two hundred to four hundred pages:

Age of Johnson
Eighteenth-Century Novel
Eighteenth-Century Thought
Eighteenth-Century Women
Religion in the Age of Enlightenment
1650–1850: Ideas, Aesthetics, and Inquiries in the Early Modern Period

But there is more. Gabe also seemed to be in the habit of bailing out universities that, for one reason or other, could no longer sustain certain scholarly projects. In 1946, a handful of scholars founded the Augustan Reprint Society, which reprinted facsimiles of eighteenth-century texts; the editorial work was done by UCLA faculty members, and most of the facsimiles were based on texts from the William Andrews Clark Library, which issued over a hundred titles, until 1990, that is, when the program was transferred to AMS Press, which went on to print a further sixty titles.

In 1922, *Philological Quarterly*, at the University of Iowa, started publishing an annual bibliography of eighteenth-century scholarship, at first edited by the great R. S. Crane, running to about forty pages and sandwiched into the July issue of *PQ*. Initially, this covered just English literature, but gradually added philosophy, science, religion, arts and crafts, and continental background, doubling in size by the end of the decade. An important breakthrough, however, came with the establishment of the American Society for Eighteenth-Century Studies (ASECS) in 1969; the founders decided that ASECS would be multidisciplinary. In part this was a response to what was already happening, but it also accelerated the move toward scholarship in the field covering more disciplines and becoming international. While the bibliography for 1969, ASECS's inaugural year, ran to one hundred pages; by 1970 it was two hundred pages, at which point it filled an entire, fat issue of *PQ*; then three hundred pages by 1971; and by 1974, at a hefty four hundred pages, it started to overwhelm *PQ*.

Gabe took over: the bibliography for 1975, now titled *ECCB: The Eighteenth-Century Current Bibliography*, was published by AMS Press, which continued annual volumes right through the bibliography for 2009 (published in 2013). What began as a small bibliography covering just English literature grew to an enormous multidisciplinary bibliography, with six-hundred-page volumes, and what was once compiled by one, then two editors, eventually employed up to thirty contributing editors. Instead of gentlemen scholars patiently sorting three-by-five cards, everything was now being integrated and assembled by a multicomputer system, staffed by graduate students, assisted by a computer programmer, occupying several offices at Louisiana State University. A field that began modestly, by covering just English literature, now covers every imaginable discipline, which reflects what is happening across the field: for example, all the major scholarly journals focusing on this period, including *Eighteenth-Century Studies* (the official journal of ASECS), *Eighteenth Century: Theory and Interpretation*, and *Eighteenth-Century Life*, are multidisciplinary.

ECCB is an extremely important tool for Enlightenment scholars. While most English literature scholars rely on the venerable *MLA International Bibliography*, now available online, that only covers literature, and although the Modern Language Association would be loath to admit it, its bibliography has always had substantial gaps. *ECCB*, by contrast, is closer to complete; not only does it cover a wide range of disciplines, beside just literatures, but it is also a "critical bibliography," that is, it contains not just a list of titles, but also book reviews and, for a long time, even article reviews. It has been a standing joke in the field that what we call a "current" bibliography has never been current; it has tended to lag four or five years behind. But this is because the editors needed time to find and order the books, then submit them to reviewers, who are spread across the world; the reviewers needed time to write the reviews, and then it all had to be collated and proofed. What *ECCB* lost in timeliness was more than compensated for by breadth and depth of coverage.

Along with the Augustan Reprint Society titles, AMS Press also published a facsimile of Samuel Richardson's *Clarissa* (1748). This was part of what was called the Clarissa Project, spearheaded by Jim Springer Borck at Louisiana State University (who, from 1980 to 1993, was also the general editor of *ECCB*). Borck gathered up a team of major Richardson scholars, and then applied for a National Endowment for the Humanities (NEH) grant to produce a complete, variorum edition of *Clarissa*, to be followed by eight supplementary volumes, containing commentary and restored passages, then critical essays on *Clarissa*, beginning in Richardson's time, and going right to the present. As Borck explained in his grant proposal, *Clarissa* has long been regarded as a key text in the history of the novel and, increasingly, as an important text for feminist scholarship. "Everybody writes about it," Borck explained. "But nobody can actually read it," since no complete text was available. The NEH was not persuaded, in good part, one expects, because of the size of the project—*Clarissa* is longer than all of the Jane Austen novels combined (one of the NEH panelists implied as much when he snidely likened Borck to Cecil B. DeMille). This was simply too big for the U.S. government to handle. So Gabe stepped in. Although his edition was not the variorum text originally intended, and the eight following volumes ended up as one volume of contemporary Richardson criticism, it was nonetheless the only complete text of *Clarissa*, a facsimile of the third edition, in eight, handsome, maroon volumes (the Penguin paperback, edited by Angus Ross, although it could serve as a doorstop, is based on the first edition and is thus about a hundred pages short). As we recall, the list price for the eight volumes was $750, and since few major research libraries had a complete text of *Clarissa*, and no library had a text that could be checked out, AMS Press made a killing. Gabe was returning to AMS Press's original business model of finding libraries with gaps and filling them with a facsimile reprint.

We do not know why Gabe gravitated toward the eighteenth century; we'd like to think he was attracted by the intelligence, wit, charm, and cultural sophistication of eighteenth-century scholars. But, of course, it wasn't only that. Gabe loved books, especially old books. His AMS Press books were handsome, cloth-covered volumes in solid, rich, "library" colors (red, blue, green)—no tawdry dust jackets—beautifully printed on cream-colored, archival stock, with title and author information embossed in gold foil on the cover and spine. They seemed designed to be lined up in serried ranks on dark, oak bookshelves. It makes sense, then, that Gabe would be interested in the period that saw the birth and phenomenal rise of what became the modern book printing and selling industry. But why did he bother doing this at all? At the 2001 ASECS conference in New Orleans, Doug Canfield asked him that very question: "Why do you do this?" Gabe replied, "I know how to make books. I know how to market books. That isn't enough."

It would be hard to think of any other single person who has had such an impact on the field of eighteenth-century studies, not merely presiding over the enormous expansion of scholarly coverage in the field, but, in many ways, making it possible. So far, we've mentioned just the publications. We haven't mentioned the people, the editors, the book authors, the article writers, literally hundreds whose scholarship Gabe published, including the contributors to this volume (and its editors as well). He jump-started careers, revived careers, sustained careers, and he did this for nearly fifty years. Gabe knew how the academic world worked. He knew that reappointment, tenure, promotion, salary increases all depended on publishing; we were doing what our universities wanted us to do and what our jobs required. Yet, as a businessman, he also thought he was getting a good deal: highly skilled, free labor. He was putting out book after book, and he never had to pay us royalties. Thus, while we were extremely grateful to him, he was equally grateful to us, and he showed it. Whenever Gabe attended an ASECS convention, he would round up twelve, fifteen, eighteen of his authors and invite them to dinner. In later days, when we had the internet, Gabe would search out restaurants in advance, select one, and then print out the menu and wine list. At the Richmond ASECS conference in 2009, as we recall, he had three limousines take a dozen or so of us to a posh restaurant; before we could order our food, he pulled a copy of the wine list out of his breast pocket and ordered six bottles of a French Bordeaux (he was on that section of the menu where the prices were in the three-digit range). Midway through the meal he ordered six more, of a different French Bordeaux, a bit richer (always go from the medium-bodied wine to the full-bodied wine: never the other way around). Gabe always enjoyed the company and could be depended upon for making some shrewd, sardonic observations on the state of the profession. A lavish meal was the least he could do for his authors. And he worked the room. He wanted to publish more scholarship on war. Whom do we suggest he should contact? One of us was now on the editorial board of *The Scriblerian*. Was there any possibility that he could become the publisher? How? Manuel Schonhorn, a fellow New Yorker who knew Gabe for decades (and who is a contributor to this volume), described what was special about Gabe: "Gabe's belief in sound scholarship and his untiring support of and respect for his authors should have been the model for the industry. We should remember his graciousness, his generosity, and his genial conversation to all of his authors when they visited New York or he attended conferences. He was a host in this age of absent civility that cannot soon be replaced." This is not how scholars are accustomed to being treated. As one of our party once remarked, university administrators often seem to regard professors as necessary nuisances who need constant monitoring. And on those rare occasions when administrators feel inclined to celebrate some scholarly accomplishment with a catered reception, what we can generally expect is the best wine you can get in a box.

The scholars who worked for Gabe genuinely appreciated both his support and interest, but also his hospitality. As we expected, we had no difficulty at all finding scholars who wanted to contribute to this volume since there were so many who were beneficiaries of Gabe's patronage. But the relationship works both ways: it was the productive scholars, including those in this volume, who made AMS Press an important, influential source of eighteenth-century scholarship. Three of us published monographs or scholarly anthologies with AMS Press (Cope, Philip Smallwood, and Reverand). Five of our contributors are the general editors of AMS Press annuals: Cope, *1650–1850: Ideas, Aesthetics, and Inquires in the Early Modern Period*; Brett C. McInelly, *Religion in the Age of Enlightenment*; J. T. Scanlan (coeditor), *Age of Johnson*; Susan Spencer, *The Eighteenth-Century Novel*; and Linda Troost, *Eighteenth-Century Women*. Both David Venturo and Manuel Schonhorn have edited texts for AMS Press—in Manny's case, that meant serving as one of the editors of the authoritative Stoke-Newington Defoe edition. And although Kevin Cope took over the editorship of *ECCB* when Jim Springer Borck died, Cope's work as a contributing editor to the bibliography started nearly thirty years earlier, which is also true of James E. May, Reverand, and Venturo.

While we are glad we can celebrate Gabe's accomplishments and produce yet one more example of the kind of scholarship he loved and nurtured, we also reflect on his career with sadness, not just because he died but also because his passing may mark the end of an era. When he died, and his heirs decided to file for bankruptcy rather than continue AMS Press, we lost our Maecenas, and our field lost a major publisher. This may well be the end for *ECCB*. Immediately, seventeen scholarly annual editors started scrambling to find new publishers. A few authors whose works were officially "forthcoming" when Gabe died—at least two of whom already had page proofs—have struggled to find new publishers. As it so happens, the last book AMS Press published, just a few weeks after Gabe's death and days before the company declared bankruptcy, was *An Expanding Universe: The Project of Eighteenth-Century Studies: Essays Commemorating the Career of Jim Springer Borck*, edited by Cope and Reverand—Gabe had called us and asked us to put this anthology together. It seems appropriate that the last volume AMS Press published was in effect Gabe's own tribute to one of the many scholars he admired and supported. It seems equally appropriate that we return the tribute, and especially appropriate that it be published by Bucknell University Press, which, under the directorship of Greg Clingham, has also been a major publisher of multidisciplinary scholarship on the long eighteenth century. Gabe, we think, would have been pleased.

Paper, Ink, and Achievement

Introduction

Kevin L. Cope

Uplifting adjectives such as "metaphysical," "transcendental," or "Olympian" may seem ill suited to the inky, oily, mercantile world of type fonts, bindings, burins, quoins, paper, signatures, presses, and distributors that accommodated the thoughtfully easygoing but occasionally obstreperous Gabriel Hornstein. A learned gentleman who loved to lease limousines and who talked more about Marco Polo or Tiffany designs than about ledgers or inventories, Gabe might seem too refined for the book factories yet too worldly for the contemplative ethers. Publishers, whether peddlers of sensational stories such as the Augustan Nathaniel Crouch or the modern Rupert Murdoch, or whether imperial presences such as Benjamin Franklin, Robert Maxwell, or Joseph Pulitzer, share with Gabriel Hornstein one characteristic: a paradoxical mixture of engagement and disengagement. Intensely committed to highly speculative particular projects—a one-off book, magazine, or pamphlet is always an unpredictable investment—publishers are more likely than most executives to converse, meddle, or interact with laborers on the production line. On the other hand, publishers stand in the same relation to finished compositions as a philosopher stands in relation to the orbit of Pluto or the anatomy of a bumblebee. A bit more than a step beyond direct experience, publishers look on their releases from a distance, as they are worked and reworked by authors, editors, subalterns, and craftsmen. The president of a car company may occasionally turn a wrench or modify a design, but a publisher cannot write books and has few options other than seeking, urging, explaining, and promoting.

The contrasts in the publisher's role were especially salient in the career, mien, and occasional adventures of Gabriel Hornstein, who, by telephone and occasionally email, monitored the world from his electronic Parnassus overlooking the Brooklyn Navy Yard; those who experienced his hours-long telephone calls marveled at his apparent readiness to chat with his authors and editors, oblivious to the distinction between the time in New York and the time, say, in Germany, when he would make his call. He seemed to delight in the most minute details of book manufacture, and, somehow, he could always get wind of a promising but obscure project by a downtrodden professor in a tiny, distant college, all in time to turn a forlorn manuscript into an honorable publication.

The peculiar role of publishers poses a special challenge to editors seeking to assemble a commemorative collection of essays. Publishers have no scholarly record that would allow for the consecration of the volume to this, that, or the other academic discipline, yet publishers produce more scholarly volumes than any savant. Through their annual performance reviews and productivity metrics, colleges and universities recognize professors' finished works. A publisher, especially an interventionist such as Gabe, exercises his or her greatest influence during the conception and development of emerging projects. That influence, moreover, is diverse. A mindful publisher must think of individual projects in relation to series, sets, and the full suite of press offerings. This ability to conceive, influence, contextualize, and distribute a wide but not altogether shapeless body of work would have been recognized by encyclopedists such as Diderot; by museum founders such as Elias Ashmole or Sir Hans Sloane; and, most of all, by Enlightenment publishing colossi such as Leipzig's Moritz Georg Weidmann or Holland's Abraham Elzevir. It is less easy for researchers to recognize this multifaceted talent today, when scholars planted deep in academic monoculture flourish far afield from academic presses, and when most of those presses operate more like conglomerate corporations than like patrons of learning.

By celebrating the life and career of Gabe Hornstein, this volume aspires not only to award overdue acclaim to an academic publishing magnate, but also to give shape and substance to an inadequately studied aspect of academic life and of the archaeology of knowledge: the process by which a publisher guides and contours research. Although this Festschrift seems to cover a world of topics—if not from China to Peru, then at least from Soho to Kyoto—the arrangement of the volume resembles a navigable river with many diverse channels carrying Gabe's influence. An ingenious reader can follow a course downstream through the volume, which opens with Part I, "On Publishing," a trio of essays on the first and foremost component of Gabe's or any other press impresario's life. Next comes Part II, "Neglected Authors," an area of special interest to AMS Press, which routinely published research on topics with small audiences. Part III, "Re-evaluating Literary Modes," follows from the preceding discussions of both publishers and neglected authors. Authors, after all, fall into neglect by writing in modes that no longer command mass attention and that therefore lose their appeal to publishers. The genres examined by the essayists in Part III—ferocious religious propaganda; epic; urban pastoral (and a bit of scatology); visionary, prophetic verse—circulated around the core of long-eighteenth-century literary and publishing culture. Today, however, these vibrant forms have either slipped in popularity or been relegated to the professional suburbs of subspecialties and background studies, an edgy world that Gabriel Hornstein enjoyed visiting. Gabe delighted in modes and genres with varying audiences, such as the once wildly popular but now nearly unknown corpus of emblem books, or bibliographies, like *ECCB: The Eighteenth-Century Current Bibliography*, which AMS Press published annually for over thirty years, which might be consulted once in a decade, but which also might lead to somebody writing a prizewinning book.

Relentlessly searching for studies on abstruse topics that might attract some overlooked readership—in his ingeniously idiosyncratic pursuit of what we now fashionably call "diversity"—Hornstein cultivated an audience that reached from the undergraduate classroom to the scholar's carrel and on to the colosseum of popular culture. He made the rounds of the book clubs, the church groups, the business associations, and the Michelin-starred restaurants. For business reasons, Gabe remained secretive about his distribution methods, yet was never without a new anecdote about a Japanese industrialist or European collector or independent scholar-enthusiast who relished his books. And then there is the clearest demonstration of the popular appeal of Gabe's press: the prodigious day when AMS Press, moving to its new headquarters in Brooklyn, set out its surplus, backlist books in the literary equivalent of a Manhattan dumpster, whereupon so many book scavengers emerged from the Big Apple's boulevards that the event drew top coverage in no less than the *New York Times*. Scholars writing for this celebratory volume commemorate Hornstein's enthusiasm for the novelties and extremes of data delivery. Their essays throw into relief Gabe's success in distributing rigorous scholarship, success that would be the envy of many university presses. All of the essays celebrate the moving of "copy" into ever more diverse audiences and ever more expansive territories.

Thinking of the volume less as a static structure than as a river allows us to see the currents or meanders in the course of Gabriel Hornstein's career. We can follow the myriad ways in which study of the long eighteenth century coevolves with the publishing industry. Rolling on from "On Publishing," we diverge into one rivulet, "Neglected Authors," that, owing to Gabe's special interests, underwent an inundation: a flood of support that washed away the bad habit, in universities, of granting scholars more credit for studying putatively major authors than for opening new channels of inquiry. The high tide of AMS Press books and articles on allegedly minor authors changed minds and relocated the crest of the scholarly wave. Gabe's enthusiasm for the obscure deserves more credit than is commonly given for the unparalleled success of long-eighteenth-century scholars in recovering and recuperating noncanonical authors. The "Neglected Authors" rivulet flows in another direction, toward "Reevaluating Literary Modes," an area of study that also reached a high-water mark during the Hornstein era. Mixing and mingling, these two eddies in the river of Gabriel Hornstein's influence provide a case study of the way in which a publisher's interest can create interacting specialties and new areas of inquiry. Even a quick scan of the topics of AMS Press books—the Bodleian Library catalog alone lists nearly eight hundred AMS Press imprints in its physical holdings—reveals a veritable "who's who" of "who was once" but "who was not always" and yet "who could be" among the genres.

Pointing up Gabe's ability to bring neglected literary and cultural traditions back to the center of attention, such library inventories also indicate "who might be revived by an AMS monograph": topics such as Oriental tales; Ovidian imitations; memoires of Enlightenment grandees; verse exposition; diaries; allegory; sensationalism; medical poetry; alchemical literature; revenge tragedy; even the history of eighteenth-century studies societies, bibliographies, and institutions. Long before canon expansion became the rule of the academic day, Gabe's interests led inventive scholars to consider how obscure authors and underappreciated modes contribute to the distribution—the publishing—of information. Thus, Leah Orr's study of the prescience and the power of eighteenth-century publishers when it came to forming new literary canons (chapter 2) could equally well describe the twentieth- and twenty-first-century career of Gabriel Hornstein, as could Brett McInelly's research on the co-opting of the periodical press into a vitriolic religious controversy (chapter 7). McInelly and Orr demonstrate how minor authors, evolving genres, and the publishing industry whirled out toward unexpected, sometimes unwilling audiences. Similarly, Manuel Schonhorn's study (chapter 6) draws on a mode, satire, that, over the centuries, undergoes extraordinary vacillations in its reputation among critics, a mode that has long been under scrutiny among those who worry about its snarling, deprecatory, devilishly disrespectful ways, and yet also a mode that has risen to the uppermost heights of popularity. The fluid structure of this volume helps us to understand how Gabe's choice of publishing projects created a reciprocal interest in overlooked authors and in modes with fluctuating reputations; how that interest flows into both the classroom and public discussion; and how all of this feeds back into the publishing industry and its audience-development programs. Both the arrangement of the volume and the essays in it elucidate how exchanges between scholars and presses generate enduring traditions within scholarship— say, the long-running AMS Press interest in the religious subcultures of several periods. The volume also shows those traditions turning, twisting, and otherwise transforming, whether by invoking a search for other "neglected authors" or by exposing the turbulence in mainstream scholarship.

AMS Press, under the direction of Gabriel Hornstein, was, if nothing else, plentiful. The contributors to this volume are continuing that tradition of largesse, exploring a profusion of topics and discovering the full extent, impact, and longevity of debates, discussions, and inquiries that began in but continued well beyond the Enlightenment. The categories that define the sections of this volume provide one way of seeing the symbiosis among these essays, but it is worthwhile to reflect on the many other ways that these essays illuminate one another. Brett McInelly's essay on anti-Methodist propaganda (chapter 7) and Susan Spencer's study of the outer circle of Japanese literary culture in Osaka (chapter 4) both illustrate the creation of special audiences. One thinks of Gabe's resurrection of the audience for Samuel Richardson's *Clarissa* or of his preservation of a readership for some of Daniel Defoe's least-remembered works.

Together, the Spencer and McInelly essays show how special-interest publishing kept easily neglected dissident, distant, subjugated, or colonial populations at the center of attention in the reading public. Despite striking differences in subject matter (genial patron publishers and the catch-as-catch-can world of early fiction collections and their marketing), the essays of J. T. Scanlan (chapter 1) and Leah Orr (chapter 2) demonstrate the unstoppable vitality of long-lasting eighteenth-century modes, personae, and ways of life, such as the blend of modern commercialism and antique noblesse oblige that percolates through publishing dynasties, or the durable pugnacity of publishers ready to cash in on the popularity of a new literary mode that may not enjoy the highest esteem of the would-be intellectuals of the day. Another provocative juxtaposition involves James May (chapter 3) and Linda Troost (chapter 5), both of whom implement interesting approaches to gender studies. May investigates what might be described as the "feminist print-shop picaresque": the adventures of women who took charge of major publishing houses after having stumbled into the trade owing to the loss of a husband. Meanwhile, Troost rejoices in the career of Frances Brooke, whose imagination outpaced her sense of oppression as she smashed not only gender stereotypes but also national identities, genre rules, and neoclassical norms—who produced fantastic operas with settings and stories spanning continents, social class, ethnicity, and economic status. In the essays of David Venturo (chapter 8), Philip Smallwood (chapter 9), and Manuel Schonhorn (chapter 6), we see the many guises taken by the past as it pushes its way into the present and future. Venturo reviews Swift, not merely as a satirist but as a writer wrestling with the epic tradition, and wrestling, as well, with "cousin Dryden," whom he could never quite get out of his mind; in a daring act of anti-sans culotterie, Smallwood reveals the secret Augustan hiding inside William Blake's revolutionary commentary and poems; and Schonhorn relishes the vitality of the imagined past, uncovering a hitherto neglected source that Pope, and to some extent Swift, relied on, the Renaissance Stoic Justus Lipsius.

These and many other connections readily arise from a set of essays that, centrifuging their way into a widening world, spin out from the energizing life of Gabriel Hornstein. Like Schonhorn's Justus Lipsius, who put the world together out of adages and anecdotes, Gabe delighted in the big picture available to a publisher surrounded by a panorama of books and authors, but he also reveled in the unassembled jigsaw puzzle of the past. Among the many things that he enjoyed being, Gabe was first and foremost an avid collector: a sponsor of multitudinous volumes of essays; a recurring publisher of periodicals; a gatherer of offbeat, extraordinary, and invariably luxuriant experiences; and a maker of connections. He amassed valuable bits and pieces and had confidence that his friends in academe would fit them together. Talents like Hornstein's seldom appear in the lists of criteria for promotion and tenure at institutions of higher learning, but they are what keep the academy running and, as the astounding output of AMS Press clearly proves, are what instigates new understandings of cultural history. In both organization and content, this volume lauds a publisher who habitually, heroically, and single-handedly joined together persons and projects, who, by routinely linking the traditional with the unexpected, gave the expansive discipline of eighteenth-century studies both the genial personality and the refreshing abundance that make it the most delightful and inventive of intellectual pursuits.

PART I

On Publishing

CHAPTER 1

Raising the Price of Literature

THE BENEFACTIONS OF WILLIAM STRAHAN
AND BENNETT CERF

J. T. Scanlan

"But, Spick and Span I Have Enough"

When modern, commercial London emerged in full during the first decades of the eighteenth century, booksellers and printers claimed a place near the heart of it, not far from newly rebuilt St. Paul's Cathedral. Like other shopkeepers in the area, these purveyors of print increasingly became adept at stimulating, satisfying, and sometimes degrading the public's "hunger for actuality," as John Richetti has put it.[1] At a time when satiric expression actuated the leading writers of the day, some of the more discreditable tradesmen in books inevitably appeared in some of the greatest poetic satires in English. In fact, I suspect most readers of any of the elegant volumes of eighteenth-century scholarship bearing the AMS imprimatur can probably quote from memory more than a few derisive lines on some of the colorful figures of the publishing world.

> Some Country Squire to *Lintot* goes,
> Enquires for SWIFT in Verse and Prose,

writes Swift in his own mock-celebratory *Nachleben*, "Verses on the Death of Dr. Swift, D.S.P.D."

> Says *Lintot*, "I have heard the Name:
> "He dy'd a Year ago." The same.
> He searcheth all his Shop in vain;
> "Sir you may find them in *Duck-lane*:
> I sent them with a Load of Books,
> Last *Monday* to the Pastry-cooks.
> To fancy they cou'd live a Year!

I find you're but a Stranger here.
The Dean was famous in his Time;
And had a Kind of Knack at Rhyme:
His way of Writing now is past;
The Town hath got a better Taste:
I keep no antiquated Stuff;
But, spick and span I have enough."[2]

Alexander Pope, Swift's comrade in literary arms, was more outrageous in his blasts against such people. In book 2 of *The Dunciad Variorum*, for example, Pope has the Queen of Dulness celebrate the "great Tibbald" by proclaiming "high, heroic Games," which draws a large turnout of "true dunces."[3] Along with authors, "Stationers obey'd the call" (2:27). The competition, evidently, was fierce.

But lofty Lintot in the circle rose;
"This prize is mine; who tempt it, are my foes:
With me began this genius, and shall end."
He spoke, and who with Lintot shall contend?

Who, indeed, could rival Bernard Lintot, the successful, stout bookseller of Fleet Street?

Fear held them mute. Alone untaught to fear,
Stood dauntless Curl, "Behold that rival here!" (2:49–54)

And off they go, in a mock-heroic race, with Edmund Curll taking an early lead over "huge Lintot." Although a quarrel had cooled the good relations Pope once had with Lintot, Pope, like others, thought Curll a menace to intellectual society. Respecting the scatological suggestions in Dryden's *Mac Flecknoe,* Pope has Curll slip and fall in a lake of crap left by one "Corinna," a Curll author.

Obscene with filth the Miscreant lies bewray'd,
Fall'n in the plash his wickedness had lay'd. (2:71–72)

Pope dismisses Curll in the succeeding couplet as a "caitiff Vaticide" (2:73–74), that is, a despicable murderer of poets. For Swift and Pope, the booksellers and publishers of the eighteenth century were responsible, at least in part, for "a new Saturnian age of Lead" (2:26).

Do we think of the business of publishing and bookselling differently today? Perhaps less so than we might suppose. In the mid-1980s, Martin Amis in *Money: A Suicide Note* presented the marketing guru John Self, who exults in the new intellectual geography of London. "There used to be a bookshop here, with the merchandise ranked in alphabetical order and subject sections. No longer. The place didn't have what it took: market forces. It is now a striplit boutique, and three tough tanned chicks run it with their needy smiles. . . . You get the idea?

My way is coming up in the world."[4] Amis, alas, was prescient, for the literary dystopia he presents actually came to life in Manhattan in the decade or so after *Money* was published, when many of the famous bookshops along Fifth Avenue—Brentano's, Scribner's, Doubleday Book Shop, Books & Company—closed. The story isn't much different in university towns today, one might argue. How could it be otherwise when campus bookstores operating under the aegis of the university itself (or Barnes & Noble) seem increasingly willing to replace shelves of books with shelves of university iconography? Even the best independent bookshops in college towns—Literati in Ann Arbor, Atticus in New Haven, Porter Square Books in Cambridge—have expanded their wares well beyond books, as they adjust to the "disruption" of Amazon and the like.

According to this gloomy line of thought, the book is first and last a product, and the prospects for the dissemination of all but the most popular of ideas are dim. As Colin Robinson argues in an arresting contemporary update of Swift's words:

> The accumulated effect of Amazon's pricing policy, its massive volume and its metric-based recommendations system is, in fact, to diminish real choice for the consumer. Though the overall number of titles published each year has risen sharply, the under-resourcing of mid-list books is producing a pattern that joins an enormously attenuated tail (a tiny number of customers buying from a huge range of titles) to a Brobdingnagian head (an increasing number of purchasers buying the same few lead titles), with less and less in between.[5]

When the advertising and selling of ideas ceases to be distinct from the selling and advertising of Brobdingnagian blueberry muffins and new apps for a cell phone, the mind of the public gradually, almost unnoticeably, withers. And the result is often a defensive nostalgia for an idealized past. Peter Mayer, of Overlook Press, comments on his own work in books in this vein. "I grew up in a world in which many parts together formed a community adversarial in a microcosmic way but communal in a larger sense: authors, editors, agents, publishers, wholesalers, retailers and readers. I hope . . . that we do not look back one day, sitting on a stump as the boy does in Shel Silverstein's *The Giving Tree*, and only see what has become a largely denuded wasteland."[6]

But then there's the example of Gabe Hornstein, living and thriving in a world of ink, paper, and print during the very years that so worry Colin Robinson and Peter Mayer. Gabe's confident presence, along with his many benefactions to the community of scholars and readers of eighteenth-century literature, suggests that the seductive, apocalyptic narrative of the attenuation of reading and writing may not capture the whole truth. In fact, printing, publishing, and bookselling have always been financially risky enterprises, and while times are indeed tough these days for the humanities in the United States, there is much evidence in the past to support an alternative, more uplifting, narrative—a story of lasting literary friendships, principled publication, and supportive, comic bonhomie among authors and those who help them get their works into the hands of readers. Literary history is replete with examples of publishers and booksellers who joined forces with writers to keep at bay the ever-present forces of Dulness, a reality that literary critics, especially those who have come of age in the shadow of the New Criticism with its classroom focus on "the text itself," naturally tend to underestimate. And the publication of a Festschrift for Gabe Hornstein is as good an occasion as any to revisit a couple of these relationships.

Two such figures whose lives and efforts could animate an alternative, hopeful narrative are William Strahan (1715–1785), Samuel Johnson's printer and friend, and Bennett Cerf (1898–1971), the irrepressibly enthusiastic native New Yorker who founded Random House, who helped strengthen the quality of American middlebrow reading in years following the Second World War. Each in his own way—one during the eighteenth century and one during the mid-twentieth—anticipated some of the more laudable aspects of Gabe's career. Their contributions, or more broadly their benefactions to writers and readers, should remind us that the nexus between writing and publishing is often much less adversarial than such great writers as Swift and Pope have encouraged us to believe.

"I Was Bred a Bookseller, and Not Forgotten My Trade"

William Strahan worked with many leading authors in the eighteenth century, including Edward Gibbon, David Hume, Tobias Smollett, and Adam Smith, but he is probably most famous for his association with Samuel Johnson, and for good reason. Robert DeMaria Jr. has convincingly argued that Samuel Johnson lived a buried, somewhat unrealized life as a scholar, modeling many of his projects along the lines of the works of such towering European intellectuals as the Italian humanist Angelo Poliziano (1454–1494) and the Dutch scholar and poet Daniel Heinsius (1580–1665).[7] But unlike specialized scholars working "under the shelter of academic bowers," Johnson viewed himself as one of a legion of London book people.[8] And so it should come as no surprise that the initial business relationship Johnson had with the printer William Strahan developed into a strong professional friendship that lasted to the end of Johnson's life. Johnson respected and depended on Strahan in various ways throughout his life of writing, and his close connection to Strahan is a tribute to the camaraderie between authors and those who help authors get their works into print.

Strahan first came to know Johnson in the early 1750s, when Johnson was well into his work for his *Dictionary*. Even then, they had much in common. First of all, they had come to London at roughly the same time, and they were neighbors. In his teens, Strahan was apprenticed to a printer in Edinburgh, but by the late 1730s, when Strahan was in his early twenties, he moved from Scotland to

London, got married, worked with the booksellers Andrew Millar (1707–1768) and Thomas Cadell (1742–1802), and set up shop in an alley off Fleet Street. In 1748, Strahan moved to No. 10 Little New Street, just off Shoe Lane. The distance between No. 17 Gough Square, where Johnson lived and worked on the *Dictionary*, was at most a five-minute walk. While Johnson may have chosen the Gough Square house at this time of his life in part to be near Strahan, they both shared the assumption that their work demanded that they live where they did.[9] Perhaps to a degree we still don't fully comprehend, this neighborhood, made up to a significant degree of authors, lawyers, printers, and booksellers, all engaged in the common enterprise of using print as the means of intellectual and cultural enlightenment, has much to do with the intellectual intensity of eighteenth-century writing and thinking. The people who set up their working lives in this area thrived in part because of their proximity to one another. They knew one another, and they influenced one another, often for the better. Strahan and Johnson are representative in this way. The simple literary geography of London in the 1750s is a first indication of why Johnson and Strahan got on so well with one another.

But they had much more than a neighborhood in common. In addressing or commenting on works of the intellect, the two used very much the same prosaic in-house language of printing, binding, and bookselling, a lexicon that reflects the respect each had for the other's work. The son of a Midlands bookseller, Johnson, by background, experience, and temperament, was incapable of romanticizing any dimension of the making of books, from the moment of their composition to their final resting places on shelves. During the 1750s, he wrote bracing essays in *The Rambler* on the vainglory of authors, and even noted the disquieting effect of a library, where "mighty volumes, the works of laborious meditation, and accurate enquiry, now scarcely known but by the catalogue" are "treasured up in magnificent obscurity."[10] Although less pugnacious, Strahan evidently thought of books with a similar clearheadedness. He had the perspective of a tradesman, thoroughly invested in all aspects of printing, especially the financial aspects. As J. A. Cochrane writes in an exhaustive study of Strahan's practices as a printer, "We are fortunate in having a detailed record of Strahan's business life. From 1739 he kept meticulous accounts of his expenses and receipts." Cochrane quotes to great effect a mid-twentieth-century commentary on Strahan's account books:

> They were kept with such scrupulous care that Strahan must always have been aware of his precise financial position, so that he could both allow for the disadvantages of the long credit he was generally obliged to give and of the uneconomically large editions that he sometimes had to print, and also take the fullest advantage of the friendly, well-organized trade and of a reading public that was continually increasing.[11]

Although their contributions to the making of books differed in kind, Johnson and Strahan shared a similar no-nonsense outlook.

The broadly pragmatic and empirical attitude they shared enabled Johnson to write with precision on various aspects of Strahan's trade, as occasions presented themselves. One of the earliest letters from Johnson to Strahan, in March 1753, is in essence a proposal for a "Geographical Dictionary." Johnson writes in the legal-financial language they both knew well, commenting on the difficulties he would likely encounter in obtaining sources. Points 3 and 4 are especially telling:

3. As it is certain that many books will be necessary the Authour will at the end of the work take the books furnish'd him in part of payment at prime Cost, which will be a considerable reduction of the price of the Copy. Or if it seem as You thought yesterday no reduction, he will allow out of the last payment fifty pounds for the use of the Books and return them.
4. In two months after his first demand of books shall be supplied he purposes to write three sheets a week and to continue the same quantity to the end of the work unless he shall be hindered by want of Books.[12]

As contemporary scholars have increasingly come to understand, Johnson's writing, from his earliest work for the *Gentleman's Magazine*, is heavily dependent on other publications, and by the 1750s Johnson well knew the difficulties he would have in obtaining the proper sources for this project on geography. The geographical dictionary never came to fruition, but the letter nonetheless reveals Johnson's sensitivity to the specific costs a printer might foresee or be forced to bear. And Johnson characteristically sets for himself a tough goal, in the language of a printer: "three sheets a week." The entire performance, at first glance merely contractual, suggests the difficulty of drawing a line too sharply between Johnson's ideas and how those ideas might get into print.

In a letter to Strahan written later that year on the specifics of the making of the *Dictionary*, Johnson uses similar language in addressing the concerns Strahan evidently had in trying to transform into print the slips of paper on which Johnson and his amanuenses had defined and illustrated words. In the letter, Johnson tries to explain how the problem emerged in the first place.

It proceeds from the haste of the amanuensis to get to the end of his days work. I desired the passages to be clipped close, and then perhaps for two or three leaves it is done. . . . But . . . I could never get that part of the work into regularity, and perhaps never shall. I will try to take some more care but can promise nothing, when I am told there is a sheet or two I order it away. You will find it sometimes close, when I make up any myself, which never happens but when I have nobody with me, I generally clip it close, but one cannot always be on the watch. (*Letters*, 1:73)

Johnson is completely comfortable with all the in-house language: the discussion of leaves, sheets, and some being "clipped close." The letter is also notably devoid of multisyllabic diction or literary allusion. There is no "Johnsonese" here. And Johnson's attention to the financial implications of minor revisions after submission continues in later letters to Strahan. In 1774, Johnson became involved in the possible renovations of Lichfield Cathedral, and he wants to soften some of the strong opinion in what he had earlier written. "In one of the pages," Johnson begins in his letter to Strahan,

> there is a severe censure of the Clergy of an English Cathedral which I am afraid is just, but I have since recollected that from me it may be thought improper for the Dean did me a kindness about forty years ago. He is now very old, and I am not young. . . . Can a leaf be cancelled without too much trouble? Tell me what I should do. I have no settled choice, but I would not refuse to allow the charge. To cancel it seems the surer side. Determine for me. (*Letters*, 2:156–157)

Johnson took Strahan's advice and revised the passage.

By this time, Strahan and Johnson had come to know one another fairly well. So naturally their letters addressed matters others than writing and printing. They write about politics and the press, especially after Strahan had become a member of Parliament in 1774. We should bear in mind, too, that, according to a letter from Francis Barber, Johnson's servant, which Boswell includes in the *Life of Johnson*, Strahan had come to see Johnson shortly after Johnson's wife Tetty died in 1752, an undeniably tough time for Johnson, among other tough times for him during the 1750s.[13] Regardless, Johnson's correspondence, like some of his correspondence with booksellers, is notable for its uninflected saturation in the language of ink, paper, and print. His correspondence with Strahan substantiates what Johnson famously wrote in 1779 to Thomas Cadell, when complaining about the inapt binding of a particular work: "I was bred a Bookseller, and have not forgotten my trade" (*Letters*, 3:159).

It was in part because Johnson was so close to the people associated with London printing and bookselling that he called upon them for various reasons. As we've seen, he often borrowed books from them, including material from Andrew Millar and even from Strahan's wife.[14] More significantly, when Johnson was arrested for debt in March 1756, he famously went to another man who made his name first in printing and afterward in novel writing, Samuel Richardson. It is often forgotten, however, that in the letter requesting the money from Richardson, Johnson writes that he thought first of two other men of the book trade. "I am obliged to entreat your assistance, I am now under an arrest for five pounds eighteen shillings. Mr. Strahan from whom I should have received the necessary help in this case is not at home, and I am afraid of not finding Mr. Millar" (*Letters*, 1:132). Richardson evidently sent six guineas. And more famously, when

Johnson first learned that his mother was seriously ill at age ninety in early January, he wrote first, with some emotion, to his mother—"The account which Miss gives me of your health, pierces my heart. God comfort, and preserve you, and save you, for the sake of Jesus Christ"—and later sent her twelve guineas. But he was pressed for money at this time, and one week after writing to his mother, he wrote to Strahan. The letter is well known because of what Johnson proposes, but it is typical of the letters he wrote to Strahan.

> When I was with you last night I told you of a thing which I was preparing for the press. The title will be The choice of Life or The History of —— Prince of Abissinia. It will make about two volumes like little Pompadour that is about one middling volume. The bargain which I made with Mr. Johntson [a London bookseller] was seventy five pounds (or guineas) a volume, and twenty five pounds for the second Edition. I will sell this either at that price or for sixty, the first edition of which he shall himself fix the number, and the property then to revert to me, or for forty pounds, and share the profit that is retain half the copy. I shall have occasion for thirty pounds on Monday night when I shall deliver the book which I must entreat you upon such delivery to procure me.

And he adds as a postscript, "Get me the money if you can" (*Letters*, 1:178–179). Strahan was happy to oblige.[15]

Like any friendship, the literary-professional friendship Johnson experienced with Strahan had moments of tension. For example, Johnson had been particularly supportive of Strahan's son George when he decided not to join the family business, as his father had hoped. Johnson encouraged the young's man's interests in scholarship and learning, which ultimately led to his becoming a vicar in Islington. The relation between George and his father was further strained when George didn't manage his money well. Johnson, somewhat caught in the middle of these family matters and undoubtedly supplied with only a partial understanding of them, tended to side with the son. In fact, by the end of his life, Johnson had developed an independent friendship with George. As his will states, Johnson bequeathed to George "Mill's Greek Testament, Beza's Greek Testament by Stephens, all my Latin Bibles, and my Greek Bible by Wechelius."[16] Certainly Johnson's inclination to help George is understandable, especially when one takes into account the significance of Johnson's religious convictions, especially in his later years. But overall, the strained relationship between William Strahan and Johnson at this time did not represent the many respectful associations they experienced with one another during more than forty years in the book business.

Indeed, the high regard Strahan had for Johnson was especially important to Johnson as Johnson grew older, when his career was, by his own estimate, winding down. In 1777, Strahan joined Cadell and the bookseller Thomas Davies—at whose shop on Russell Street Johnson first met Boswell—to propose that Johnson supply the prefaces to an elaborate edition of English poets, a somewhat hastily planned scheme of a consortium of London booksellers and printers. Today, the *Lives of the Poets*, as Johnson's contribution to this publishing venture is popularly known, remains perhaps Johnson's most enduring work of critical prose, notwithstanding what Johnson said about its composition: he wrote it, he claims when evaluating himself on Good Friday in 1781, "in my usual way, dilatorily and hastily, unwilling to work, and working with vigour, and haste." As Johnson declined in late November and early December 1784, Strahan continued to be an important figure in Johnson's life. In early December, Johnson went see Strahan briefly in Islington, just north of London, where Johnson hoped to escape the foul air of London. The brief visit helped, at least temporarily. The last two letters Johnson wrote were to William Strahan, both inquiring about his pension. Strahan had long ago helped Johnson with financial matters, serving at times essentially as his banker. Johnson's friend and printer served in a similar capacity in the last days of Johnson's life. Strahan himself died less than a year later, on 9 July 1785.

The literary friendship between Johnson and Strahan, both among the most important and influential figures in the London literary and intellectual world from the late 1730s to the early 1780s, was one of mutual respect, to be sure. But as Johnson's own letters testify, at the core of their friendship stood a successful businessman's benefactions to an often struggling, hardscrabble author. And those benefactions helped Johnson complete his projects, and in some cases present to the "common reader" some of his best work, including the *Dictionary* (1755), *Rasselas* (1759), his edition of Shakespeare (1765), and the *Lives of the Poets* (1759). Johnson was grateful for Strahan's help, as were many of Strahan's literary acquaintances, including David Hume. As Cochrane writes, Strahan's "friendships on the whole ring true and do not appear to have been mere business civilities" (119). To Johnson, Strahan's support was both professional and enabling. The different tasks and predispositions of the printer and the author caused little conflict for the two of them, and I suspect that is because, from Johnson's perspective at least, the two tasks were not as distinct from one another as we tend to believe they are now. As J. D. Fleeman has noted, "Of all the multifarious influences upon works of literature, perhaps the least romantic is that of the economics of the . . . book trade. Yet the literary student ignores it at his peril."[17] This is especially relevant to the study of Johnson and his works, I think. Strahan, perhaps the most significant printer of his time, helped nurture and shape Johnson's own ideas about writing, and Johnson's pungent, reassuring, and inspiring words on the life of writing are a tribute to both their friendship and the collaborative nature of writing and printing and the literary camaraderie that characterized the eighteenth-century book business in general.

"When People Are Decent Things Work Out for Everybody"

William Strahan, though sometimes stubborn, did not become the public figure that some of his contemporaries in printing and bookselling became. The same cannot be said for Bennett Cerf, the cofounder of Random House, one of the great publishing houses of mid-twentieth-century New York. During his heyday in the 1950s and early 1960s, Cerf was a shameless bon vivant, a "man about town" who basked in his celebrity as a star on the postwar hit television show *What's My Line?*[18] He was immediately recognizable: he spoke with a high-pitched, nasal New York accent, was a natty dresser, and wined and dined his friends in both publishing and entertainment at his country house at the crest of a hill on Orchard Street in tony Mount Kisco, in Westchester County, New York. He wrote egregiously popular joke books, at a time when humor, as a kind of writing, was in fashion. He appeared in glossy magazines advertising L&M cigarettes and Hertz rental cars. A color drawing of him, featuring his wry smile, appeared on the cover of *Time* magazine in December 1966. When asked years later how he, a publisher, emerged as a star of a television game show, he said, "I loved it from the start because, as I've told you again and again, I have a streak of pure ham in me, and this appealed to every part of it. Within about six weeks, I was a national figure. As a publisher nobody knew who I was."[19]

But within the American literary world, everybody knew who Bennett Cerf the publisher was. And as legions of authors and readers have testified, Cerf did much for authors, for readers, and for American cultural life in general. It's easy to understand why he meant so much to so many. From his earliest moments in publishing, he was a champion of good writing. In 1925, he and Donald S. Klopfer bought the Modern Library and expanded its influence. "There were no paperback books in those days," wrote Cerf. "We had the only cheap editions of *Moby-Dick*, *The Scarlet Letter*, *Dorian Gray* and all the modern classics. The Modern Library was used in every college."[20] In 1927, he and Klopfer were chatting in their modest New York office with Rockwell Kent, who had gone to Columbia with Cerf and who had illustrated some of their early publications. "He was sitting at my desk facing Donald," writes Cerf, "and we were talking about doing a few books on the side, when suddenly I got an inspiration and said, 'I've got the name for our publishing house. We just said we were going to publish a few books on the side at random. Let's call it Random House'" (65). Thus was born the publishing house that brought James Joyce, William Faulkner, Eugene O'Neill, Sinclair Lewis, Robert Penn Warren, Truman Capote, and Dr. Seuss, among many, many others, to everyday American readers.

As any list of Random House authors would suggest, Cerf liked nothing more than to land an important new manuscript by an important American writer. And he supported and defended his writers, in both good times and bad. Though Cerf certainly enjoyed the social whirl of midcentury Manhattan, he is yet another example of a shrewd and successful businessman who helped many people in the book world, broadly conceived, throughout his long life in publishing. As he wrote of a deal that emerged between Random House and the then fledgling Book-of-the-Month Club regarding an illustrated edition of *Moby-Dick*, "Everybody was being decent, and when people are decent things work out for everybody. That has been my theory all through life. If you're making money, let the other fellow make it, too. If somebody's getting hurt, it's bad, but if you can work a thing out so that everybody profits, that's the ideal business" (74). Like Strahan, Cerf understood his trade first and foremost as a business, a job centered on financial speculation—on risk. And curiously enough, Cerf had just the right background and education for such work. He was born in Harlem in a solidly middle-class Jewish neighborhood in 1898. His father was a lithographer who had once had a tryout with the Brooklyn Dodgers. Cerf himself was a big baseball fan as a kid—and a so-so student as a teenager. He wanted to go to college at Columbia, but by his own admission he knew he'd never be able to master Latin and Greek, then required, and so he took some courses in the extension school, got a little extra academic coaching, and discovered to his delight that Columbia's journalism school did not require those languages. All he needed to do was pass an algebra test: "But I flunked. I simply couldn't do it. So I took an exam in free-hand drawing," which gave him a credit, and then he sat for a French exam, which he just barely passed. So off he went to the nearby university (12).

At Columbia he wrote some humor pieces for two campus publications, the *Jester* and the *Spectator*. He became the editor of the latter, and after graduating he went to work at a brokerage house in Wall Street in the early 1920s—at just the time Wall Street was booming. He was successful there. His friend Donald Klopfer, a recent college grad from Williams, worked at the same brokerage house. Cerf had also stayed close to a friend from Columbia, Dick Simon, who was working in publishing, and Cerf liked to talk about Simon's good job, always "moaning" about not being in publishing himself. When Simon quit his job to go into business with Max Schuster (another Columbia grad), Simon spoke to his boss about his friend Cerf. Simon commented on Cerf's background and interest in journalism. And a short while later, Cerf left Wall Street for the book business.

In recounting these times, Cerf liked to claim, "I was the one who loved books" (25). But his time on Wall Street had given him real experience in understanding financial risk and speculation. And he capitalized on what he knew: he made for himself a fair amount of money in the stock market. He also inherited $125,000 after the death of his mother, who died when Cerf was sixteen. As a young New Yorker in the 1920s, then, Cerf had enough money to propose to his friend Klopfer that the two of them, in the manner of Dick Simon and Max Schuster, go into business together. Klopfer, initially hesitant, came up with his share of the money—"He came from a well-to-do family, so it wasn't too hard," writes Cerf—and together they bought the Modern Library (54). As Cerf reports, "Modern Library was a roaring success, and the money was rolling in" (63).

Cerf definitely enjoyed the world of the public cultural life of Manhattan, especially the theater. (He was delighted to publish Eugene O'Neill, though he didn't much care for him personally.) But as his early adulthood suggests, Cerf was primed to be an astute businessman, and he maintained his keen business sense throughout his long career in the book business. Like Strahan, Cerf was meticulous in documenting expenses. Also like Strahan, he thought carefully about how the social pressures of the day affected the business of books. Cerf expanded his enterprises many times in part because of his perceptive analyses of the real-world conditions facing publishers. One needs only to recall the upheavals and transformations in American economic and social life before, during, and after the Second World War to grasp the significance of Cerf's focus on the possible relations between such changes and the book business.

A good introduction to his admirable business acumen may be found not in his somewhat chatty memoir *At Random*, drawn from a recording for an audio archive on notable New Yorkers, but in his wartime letters to his partner, Donald Klopfer, who had enlisted in the Army Air Corps after Pearl Harbor—at age forty!—and then spent two and half years as an intelligence officer for a B-24 bomber group. The letters these two sent to one another are beautifully treasured up in an elegant little volume published by Random House in 2002, *Dear Donald, Dear Bennett*.[21] The dust jacket features photo cutouts of the two of them, each smoking a pipe, with Donald in uniform and Bennett holding a book.

Donald wrote Bennett many letters on just how the war, from his vantage point, was actually conducted, many of which speak to the youth and inexperience of many who fought. "These crazy kids don't know what the hell it's all about and when they start to take up 18 tons and 4000 h.p. it aint safe!," Donald wrote (72). Bennett, perhaps with a touch of wit, responded with an update on the precise expenditures of Random House on paper. Paper was in short supply during the war, and Bennett's letter, like many uplifting letters from the home front, accentuated the positive, to quote a wartime song, but Bennett's letter did so by means of specific financial facts.

> This is just to tell you that we fixed up an agreement yesterday designed to net us additional paper for between 400,000 and 500,000 flats [juvenile books]. It was worked with a guy named J. A. Richards, president of J. A. Richards, Inc., publishers, Minneapolis. . . . There is 110 tons of paper involved and the fee we are paying Richards for "supervision" is $13,200.00, or at the race of 8¢ for every pound of paper used. (73)

Other letters from Bennett to Donald address other specific financial matters, from the possible purchase of other struggling publishing houses to how well this or that book was selling. Never far from his mind was the pricing of new books.

> Our present plan is to bring out four or five of these Illustrated Modern Library editions for Christmas. . . . Each book will be boxed. Some of them will be illustrated in color and some in black and white. The price will be either $1.25 or $1.45. The art work for each book will average us about $1000.00. After this expense is written off, the books will actually only cost us between 8¢ and 10¢ a copy more than the regular Modern Library. I am very anxious to hear your reaction to the idea.
>
> There is a lot of to-do about what titles we should select to start the series, but Confucius, Brothers Karamazov and Pickwick Papers will certainly be three of them. The other two will be selected from Don Quixote, Emerson, Longfellow, Candide, and Whitman. I am very anxious to have your opinion of all this. (81)[22]

Like Strahan, Cerf apparently kept close watch on financial matters, and although he typically couched his obvious concern for his friend's proximity to the blunt violence of war in the breezy, upbeat, language of noncombatants, the main message in most of these letters is a statement to his business partner on the monthly "figures," which he was pleased to report were almost always very good.

As the list of authors in that last paragraph suggests, Cerf's letters to Klopfer also help explain how American "middlebrow" readers developed a taste for the "classic" writers we now associate primarily with university education. To be sure, the great expansion of higher education after the war, stimulated in part because of the Servicemen's Readjustment Act of 1944—the legendary G.I. Bill— occurred at just the time "great books" courses at Columbia University, the University of Chicago, the University of Michigan, and other large and distinguished universities were flourishing. Certainly, this minor cultural revolution had a profound influence on what America read.[23] So did that long shelf of *Great Books of the Western World*, published by *Encyclopaedia Britannica*, in 1937, and championed by such figures as Mortimer Adler, author of the 1940 best seller *How to Read a Book*.[24] But Cerf and Random House's contributions to the development of the taste of American readers should not be underestimated. It's notable, too, that Cerf's motives have not the least tincture of the self-improving high-mindedness one associates with midcentury university great books courses, Western Civ programs, and other discussion groups and outgrowths concentrating on what University of Chicago president Robert Maynard Hutchins in an opening essay to the *Britannica* publication termed, with memorable grandiloquence, "the great conversation." Cerf, operating from entirely different motives, published Aquinas and Cervantes and Shakespeare because he thought people would like to read them. With illustrations by Rockwell Kent, he thought such volumes would sell.[25] And he was right.

The war was especially significant to Cerf, for during it he further developed his keen understanding of what and how people read. Of course Cerf was quick to publish books with a direct connection to the war, like Richard K. Tregaskis's *Guadalcanal Diary* (1943), a memoir by a marine featuring honest, straightforward language. The book itself is a beautiful artifact of its time: the memoir is wrapped in a fitting olive-green jacket, with the title printed in a large brightyellow font resembling handwriting. The bottom of the front jacket is equally meaningful: full block letters, in the same bright yellow proclaim, "A RANDOM HOUSE BOOK." Thoughtfully designed for a wartime audience, the volume features a double-sided, slick-photo frontispiece, which on the verso side features the U.S. Marines' anchor and eagle, and on the recto side, opposite the title page, a picture of "Maj. Gen Alexander A. Vandegrift and the author." The scene in the picture is informal, even uplifting and positive, at least given the obvious subject of the book: Vandegrift and Tregaskis sit on a makeshift bench, while Vandegrift, who is smiling broadly, reads a handful of seemingly handwritten pages, with Tregaskis sitting to his left. The entire scene confirms the authenticity of the words on the page—and their humor. General Vandegrift, a highly respected officer who won both the Navy Cross and the Medal of Honor, led, in 1942, the First Marine Division in Guadalcanal, where American forces achieved one of their first important victories on the ground in the South Pacific. As Cerf often reported in his letters to Klopfer, such elaborately conceived volumes were profitable.

But more important to him was the expansion of reading in America during the war, which he connected to the restrictions on certain kinds of purchases—the wartime "rationing." As he explains in *At Random*,

> Publishing during the war was not just a matter of bringing out war books. It was also business as usual—in fact, more business than usual. We soon found out that gasoline rationing and the military pre-emption of space on trains and planes made travel extremely difficult, so that many people even found it impossible to get to the movies very often (and of course there was no television). So people stayed home and read books, and the market expanded tremendously. The Book-of-the-Month Club, for example, more than doubled its membership during the war, and *Reader's Digest* doubled its circulation. (170)

While in his memoir Cerf emphasizes his new "sideline" writing columns and such, these were good times for Random House, as the letters to Klopfer prove. And Cerf's authors, who continued to produce, reaped the benefits. In other words, Cerf's reliable interpretation of the reading public, his willingness to think carefully about it and to try to reshape it for the better, and, overall, his commitment to wartime readers in general led to real benefactions for his legion of writers.

Random House authors appreciated what Cerf did for them. Sinclair "Red" Lewis was one who profited significantly during the later years of his career because of Cerf's thoughtfulness. When Henry Maule, one of the senior editors at Doubleday, was "asked to retire" in his early fifties (!), Cerf hired him at Random House, and Maule brought to Random House Sinclair Lewis, who, by the early 1940s, was perhaps past his prime. Cerf had known Lewis in the 1930s: "I thought he was a difficult man and a habitual drunkard, but I liked his books. . . . His last book for Doubleday, *Bethel Merriday*, in 1940, was by his early standards a failure" (145). But Cerf stuck with him. Lewis continued to produce, giving to Random House in the 1940s three now long-forgotten works, *Gideon Planish*, *Cass Timberlane*, and *Kingsblood Royal*. The last two, while hardly up to the standards of *Babbit* and *Main Street*, were best sellers. Lewis had by now split from his first wife and attached himself to "an eighteen-year-old would-be actress Marcella Powers," whom he sometimes introduced, according to Cerf, as his niece. Their relationship didn't last. If Cerf was unimpressed with Lewis's personal life, he was undaunted in his decision to work with Lewis. "We published Sinclair Lewis for the rest of his life, and though he could be extremely touchy and irritable, both Phyllis [Cerf's wife] and I became very fond of him. He was a lonely man and his loneliness came mostly out of his own doing" (145). As time went on, Lewis's submissions got worse. Shortly before he died in Rome, Lewis revised a draft of his last work, *World So Wide*, which Random House published after his death. Cerf thought the revision was worse than the earlier draft. Cerf's words on Lewis's later years are typically direct and exhibit his unblinking understanding of the realities of publishing. But they also express his concern for his authors, and his generosity.

> Here was a case of a man who kept on writing too long. His last two works were dreadful and should never have been published, but how can you stop a once very successful author from writing if he wants to continue? . . . Reviewers often blame publishers in these situations, saying that we have done an author a disservice by not turning down this or that book. But anybody who knows anything about the literary world should know that if we reject a manuscript by an author with a big reputation, somebody else will publish it, and we will destroy our relationship with the author even if it has been a close and long-standing one. (147)

That last sentence delivers a good sense of Cerf's commitment to his authors. In tough times, Bennett Cerf stood by them. And they appreciated him for that.

Another author who liked Cerf's work was William Faulkner. Cerf first landed Faulkner as an author when Random House merged with the publishing company Smith and Hass. The first book Random House published by Faulkner was *Absalom! Absalom!* in 1936. Random House published everything by Faulkner after that, doubtless in part because Faulkner liked his relationship with Random House. Cerf loved publishing Faulkner, though like Lewis, Faulkner could be tough to deal with on occasion. But what really impressed Cerf, and what helped Faulkner get especially good treatment from the people at Random House, was Faulkner's deference to his publisher.

> William Faulkner had a firm belief that the author writes the book and the publisher publishes it. He would bring in a manuscript, and I'd say, 'Bill, do you have any ideas about the book jacket and the advertising?' Bill would say, 'Bennett, that's your job. If I didn't think you did it well, I'd go somewhere else.' The result was that Faulkner got more attention in our office than most others, perhaps to prove to him that he was right in trusting us. (129)

Here is yet another example of the author and the publisher cooperating, to the advantage of both. Both have a sense of the each other's duties, and as was the case with Strahan and Johnson, Cerf and his colleagues at Random House did that little bit extra on the behalf of the author.

Probably the most widely known act of benevolence Cerf performed for an author and for literature generally is his unwavering support of James Joyce and the American edition of *Ulysses*. The genesis of the Cerf's involvement in this influential legal case is typical of him. A lawyer friend of his, Max Ernst, one day told him that "the banning of *Ulysses* was a disgrace." Cerf took Ernst out to lunch, and proposed a deal: "If I can get Joyce signed up to do an American edition of *Ulysses*, will you fight the case for us in court? . . . We haven't got the money to pay your fancy prices. . . . We'll pay all the court expenses, and if you win the case, you'll get a royalty on *Ulysses* the rest of your life" (90). Ernst agreed—"Ernst said, 'Great, great.' He loves publicity just as much as I do!" (90)— and afterwards Cerf wrote to Joyce in Paris, addressing the letter to Shake-speare and Company, the bookshop on the Left Bank where Joyce spent time. Eventually, after Cerf met Joyce in Paris, the challenge to American obscenity law began, as expected. Ernst won the case, a subsequent appeal was denied, and in 1934 Random House published an American edition of *Ulysses*. The Random House volume included Judge Woolsey's opinion, featuring his immortal words on the novel: "a sincere and serious attempt to devise a new literary method for the observation and description of mankind" (93). To be sure, the lawyer Max Ernst deserves much of the credit for bringing to Joyce a new American reader-ship. But it was Cerf's social skill—his way of bringing people together in a com-mon enterprise—that led in part to the legal triumph. It is characteristic of him that the decisive moment in this episode takes place over lunch.

"If There Is One National Flower in Book Publishing, It Is the Martini"

Yes, the publishers' lunches. Cerf enjoyed—and arranged—plenty of those lunches, and the important and protracted discussion about books that often took place at those lunches sometimes ended only with the surprising recognition that it was time for dinner. As I've tried to suggest, the literary world was the better for it. In our nostalgia for these supposed halcyon days, however, we may be seduced to believe that the end of such lunches has killed off the benevolent publisher. Deferent to sales of books driven by Amazon and other distributors' "metrics-based recommendations systems," we worry that the book industry has given new life to the tenuous relation between the publisher, who focuses on the bottom line, on the one hand, and the author, the "artist," as well as the readers, who just want to read good books, on the other. But as I have tried to show, an attractive nostalgia for the past shouldn't lead us away from understanding that publishers and authors play for the same team, if at different positions, and William Strahan and Bennett Cerf are good reminders of that fact. Al Silverman, a longtime fixture of New York publishing who held important posts first at the Book-of-the-Month Club and later at Viking/Penguin, speaks with a compelling autobiographical flair in his study of leading American editors and publishers from roughly the 1940s to the early 1970s, *The Time of Their Lives: The Golden Age of Great American Publishers, Their Editors and Authors* (2008). But he doesn't indulge a tempting explanation of why this golden age ended. After commenting in his introduction on how "exhilarating" it was for so many to go to college on the G.I. Bill, get involved professionally in reading, writing, and publishing after graduating, and become "among this new educated public," he adds a final, unblinking comment on what really killed off those days: "One thing I almost forgot about the rise and fall of the golden age described here. It began to falter not when the book publishers who loved books gave way to those who preferred profits to reading. It happened when the publishers and editors began cutting back on their drinking. If there is one national flower in book publishing, it is the martini."[26] That amusing comment on drinking is a sign of the times, a statement about the specific conditions in which American book people chatted and made decisions about books. But his main point—that publishers can love both good books and profits—is well worth remembering too today, during a time of supposed "disruption." In fact Silverman's clear-headed words challenging the supposed split between the author and the publisher resemble Johnson's own words on the subject. In writing of Johnson's literary activities in the spring of 1755, and specifically of his submission of the final sheets for the *Dictionary*, Boswell, always eager to get in a good word for his homeland, writes, "It is remarkable, that those with whom Johnson chiefly contracted for his literary labours were Scotchmen, Mr. Millar and Mr. Strahan. . . . Johnson said of him, 'I respect Millar, Sir; he has raised the price of literature'" (*Life*, 1:287–288).

Now that AMS Press is no more, gone are Gabe's direct benefactions to eighteenth-century scholars and their readers. Gone are those tasty, high-caloric, after-hours spreads at conferences, which were especially welcome to younger scholars on tight travel budgets. (And gone, too, are the old-style lunches that a few of the editors of his publishers shared with him!) But the memory of Gabe's benefactions will live on in part because this Festschrift on Gabe's work bears the entirely fitting imprint of Bucknell University Press, another longtime benefactor of eighteenth-century scholars and their readers. Under the twenty-two-year stewardship of Greg Clingham, Bucknell University Press raised the quality and profile of eighteenth-century scholarship in general, and notably during a time when the job market in the humanities broke down. For many younger scholars, AMS Press and Bucknell University Press provided much-longed-for good news—and thousands and thousands of pages of good reading in elegantly published volumes. Along with Strahan and Johnson, and along with Cerf and his Random House authors, Gabe Hornstein, Greg Clingham, and the healthy stable of AMS and Bucknell authors have reminded us, and perhaps even proved to us by example, that such powerful and uncompromising writers as Swift, Pope, Martin Amis, and the journalists at *The Nation* may not have written the final word on the state of our own cultural moment after all.

NOTES

1. John Richetti, introduction to *The Cambridge Companion to the Eighteenth-Century Novel*, ed. Richetti (Cambridge: Cambridge University Press, 1996), 2.

2. Jonathan Swift, "Verses on the Death of Dr. Swift, D.S.P.D.," in *The Poems of Jonathan Swift*, ed. Harold Williams, 3 vols. (Oxford: Clarendon Press, 1958), vol. 2, ll. 254–268.

3. Alexander Pope, "The Dunciad Variorum," in *The Poems of Alexander Pope: A One-Volume Edition of the Twickenham Text with Selected Annotations*, ed. John Butt (1963; repr., London: Routledge, 1989), book 2, ll. 13–14, 21.

4. Martin Amis, *Money: A Suicide Note* (London: Penguin, 1985), 71.

5. Colin Robinson, "The Trouble with Amazon," *The Nation*, 15 July 2010, https://www.thenation.com/artile/trouble-amazon/.

6. Steve Wasserman, "The Amazon Effect," *The Nation*, 29 May 2012, https://www.thenation.com/article/amazon-effect/.

7. See Robert DeMaria Jr., *The Life of Samuel Johnson* (Oxford: Blackwell, 1993).

8. Samuel Johnson, preface to *A Dictionary of the English Language*, ed. Gwin J. Kolb and Robert DeMaria Jr., vol. 18 of *The Yale Edition of the Works of Samuel Johnson*, Robert DeMaria Jr. et al., gen. eds. (New Haven: Yale University Press, 2005), 112.

9. See Arthur Murphy, *An Essay on the Life and Genius of Samuel Johnson, LL.D.*, in *Johnsonian Miscellanies*, ed. G. Birbeck Hill, 2 vols. (New York: Harper and Brothers, 1897): "He had lodged with his wife in courts and alleys about the Strand; but now, for the purpose of carrying on his arduous undertaking, and to be near his printer and friend Mr. Strahan, he ventured to take a house in Gough-square, Fleet-street" (1:382).

10. Samuel Johnson, *Rambler* 106, from *The Rambler*, ed. W. J. Bate and Albrecht B. Strauss, vol. 4 of *The Yale Edition of the Works of Samuel Johnson*, Robert DeMaria Jr. et al., gen eds. (New Haven: Yale University Press), 1969), 200–201.

11. J. A. Cochrane, *Dr Johnson's Printer: The Life of William Strahan* (Cambridge: Harvard University Press, 1964), 7, 8.

12. Samuel Johnson, *The Letters of Samuel Johnson*, ed. Bruce Redford, 5 vols. (Princeton: Princeton University Press, 1982), 1:69 (henceforth *Letters*).

13. James Boswell, *Boswell's Life of Johnson*, ed. George Birbeck Hill, rev. and enl. L. F. Powell, 6 vols. (Oxford: Clarendon Press, 1934–1964), 1:241–243 (henceforth *Life*).

14. Johnson wrote in a letter to Millar on 11 July 1753, "When I sent back your books I returned by mistake to you a *Young upon Opium*, which I had from Mrs. Strahan; please to let me have it back" (*Letters*, 1:72).

15. For a more extensive commentary on Johnson's financial predicament and its relation to the death of his mother and the emergence of *Rasselas*, see Gwin J. Kolb, "Introduction," in Samuel Johnson, *Rasselas and Other Tales*, ed. Gwin J. Kolb, vol. 16 of *The Yale Edition of the Works of Samuel Johnson*, Robert DeMaria Jr. et al., gen. eds. (New Haven: Yale University Press, 1990), xix–xxvi.

16. See Cochrane, *Dr. Johnson's Printer*, esp. 156–157, for more on Johnson's relation to Strahan's son George.

17. J. D. Fleeman, review of Cochrane, *Review of English Studies* 16 (1965): 432–434, quotation from 432.

18. This postwar, somewhat euphemistic phrase was applied to Cerf by my mother, Mae Scanlan, who knew Cerf somewhat, and who talked with me about his desire for the limelight.

19. Columbia Center for Oral History Research, "Bennett Cerf," in *Notable New Yorkers*, transcript 734.

20. Bennett Cerf, *At Random: The Reminiscences of Bennett Cerf* (New York: Random House, 1977), 54.

21. Bennett Cerf and Donald Klopfer, *Dear Donald, Dear Bennett: The Wartime Correspondence of Bennett Cerf and Donald Klopfer* (New York: Random House, 2002).

22. In his correspondence to Klopfer, Cerf did not indent the first line of each paragraph; he used the "block style."

23. See the National Archives website on the Servicemen's Readjustment Act, signed into law by President Franklin D. Roosevelt on 22 June 1944, shortly after the American invasion of Europe (http://www.ourdocuments.gov/doc.php?doc=76). For a broader view of the influence of the G.I. Bill, see Susan Mettler's authoritative and deeply moving book on the subject, *Soldiers to Citizens: The G.I. Bill and the Making of the Greatest Generation* (New York: Oxford University Press, 2005).

24. Mortimer Adler, *How to Read a Book* (New York: Simon and Schuster, 1940).

25. I should confess that when I was about to head off to college, my father, Tom Scanlan, who had written a master's thesis on Shakespeare in the early 1950s, took me to a bookshop to help me pick out a complete Shakespeare. Every college kid needed one, he asserted. He was devoted to his own complete Shakespeare, edited by the legendary George Lyman Kittredge of Harvard. Dad explained that if I were to study Shakespeare seriously in college, my professors would help me choose the best scholarly edition, but for general reading, he bought me the Random House Shakespeare, illustrated by Rockwell Kent.

26. Al Silverman, *The Time of Their Lives: The Golden Age of Great American Publishers, Their Editors and Authors* (New York: St. Martin's Press, 2008), 13.

CHAPTER 2

Eighteenth-Century Publishers and the Creation of a Fiction Canon

Leah Orr

Scholarship on eighteenth-century fiction has mainly located the creation of the canon in academic approaches: the Defoe-Richardson-Fielding triumvirate of Ian Watt, or the broader range of "popular fiction" described by John Richetti, among others.[1] The creation of a poetry canon, however, is said to begin in the late eighteenth century with publishers like John Bell, who capitalized on the long English poetic tradition, the growing reading public, and the legal and economic circumstances that ended the established trade's monopoly on older English books.[2] An examination of reprint publishing shows that fiction also has a history of ambitious publishers seeking to establish a canon of texts that would continue to sell as reprints, beginning as early as the late seventeenth century. This chapter looks at several key early collections of book-length, previously published works of fiction in order to argue that publishers sought to create a fiction canon much earlier than has been acknowledged. In so doing, they included works that were more diverse than those found in later versions of the early fiction canon.

EARLY COLLECTIONS OF FICTION IN ENGLISH

The first collections of fiction in English were designed not to establish a canon, but to sell unsold sheets of books already printed. Building on the copyrights he purchased from Richard Bentley and James Magnes, Richard Wellington had cornered the market on fiction in English in the 1690s.[3] By the 1720s, there was far more fiction available—but no established set of genre norms or criteria that might help establish a canon of recent classics, leaving the field open for innovative publishers like John Watts to attempt to carve out a market for fiction reprints. As we might expect, these collections featured publishers reprinting their own works; Wellington and Watts did not step on the toes of other booksellers by publishing works whose copyrights were claimed by others. Both Wellington and Watts featured works translated from French and Spanish as prominently as those originally written in English—perhaps even more so. These collections show that early publishers saw English fiction as a cosmopolitan, polyglot genre that crossed national boundaries. That would change over the course of the eighteenth century.

The earliest attempt at a fiction collection was not so much a collection as a repackaging. Richard Bentley was the leading publisher of English fiction in the late seventeenth century and, to judge from his advertisements listing multiple titles of various sorts, had evidently recognized that readers of short works of fiction would happily buy several at once of whatever he had available.[4] In 1692, he put this concept into book form with *Modern Novels: in XII Volumes*, a series that bundled together his fiction publications into a nonce collection.[5] *Modern Novels* consists of unsold sheets of previous publications, going back to 1676, and the works included have their original title pages. Bentley did not add any editorial material or otherwise present it as a cohesive collection; he seems simply to have printed a new title page for each volume and bound it with the older works, aiming it for the reader looking for the convenience of several works in one volume.

The first true collection of fiction, marketed as a selection with an editorial apparatus that differed from the separately published editions, was published a few years later by Richard Wellington, who succeeded Bentley as fiction publisher par excellence. Wellington's *Collection of Novels* (1699) would be almost unrecognizable to a modern scholar looking for English predecessors to the realist novel. Rather than the English fiction canon we might expect—Sir Philip Sidney's *Arcadia* or Aphra Behn's *Oroonoko*, perhaps—the *Collection* features one English work and three translations from French. Only one of the works has an author named on the title page, and that attribution (to Cardinal Richelieu) is false. Wellington's introduction to the volume is worth quoting in full, as it is one of the earliest and most complete statements about collecting fiction:

> The Following Histories and Novels have already found so kind a Reception in the World, that it would be needless to Commend them. The frequent Demands for them upon the Account of their Scarcity, encouraged the Reprinting them. In the former Editions they were Published singly, whereas now they are compiled into a Volume, which is portable and cheap: And if this Volume meets with a quick Sale, I will oblige the Ladies with a Second, which shall contain the Subscribed Novels. In the mean time I wish them much Diversion in the Perusal of this, and remain their Humble Servant.[6]

There are several important points in this preface that remained influential on later collections of fiction. First, the criteria for selecting a work of fiction for reprinting would be its past success in the print market. Wellington emphasizes the salability of the works, not their aesthetic, literary, or historical importance. The reason for reprinting them in a collection is continued customer demand, not the desire of a bookseller to reintroduce older works to an unknowing public. Customers have the upper hand here in shaping the selection of texts to be reprinted. Second, Wellington presents the collection as being more convenient for the reader than the original, separately published works. The two qualities emphasized here—"portable and cheap"—recur in promotional material for collections of fiction (and poetry) throughout the eighteenth century. This marks a fundamental difference between fiction collections of this sort and collected works editions of individual authors, which were often in folio or quarto size or sold as multivolume sets, and, consequently, marketed to wealthier clientele.[7] Third, and perhaps most important for literary scholars, Wellington explicitly identifies his target audience as "Ladies" and suggests that the fiction is meant for "Diversion," not moral or intellectual edification. This association of fiction with women readers and entertainment would also continue throughout the eighteenth century, and would become a problem for publishers who sought to market fiction to other audiences or to serve other purposes.

The selection of fiction in this volume supports what Wellington says about its past popularity—and, of course, draws on the successes of Wellington's own backlist (mostly from Bentley). *The Secret History of the Earl of Essex and Queen Elizabeth* had been in print since 1680, and was the first item in volume 1 of Bentley's *Modern Novels*. This work is a pseudo-history, imagining a romance between Elizabeth and Essex, the queen's subsequent distress at his betrayal, and her decision to have him executed. The other works in the volume are translations from French texts: *The Art of Pleasing in Conversation* (by Pierre Ortigue), *The Happy Slave* (Sébastien Brémond), and *The Double Cuckold* (also Brémond). While these are from different linguistic traditions and are apparently from the earlier printings of these works, complete with old title pages, they do make sense together. All feature noble characters and love plots, and the Brémond fictions are historical, like *The Secret History of the Earl of Essex*. One might reasonably think that a reader interested in one of these would also appreciate the others. The first volume of Wellington's *Collection of Novels* evidently did sell quickly, for the second volume appeared as promised the following year. Like the first volume, the second contains a mix of original and translated fiction without distinction, comprising *The Heroine Musqueteer* (Jean de Préchac), *Incognita* (William Congreve), and *The Pilgrim* (Brémond).[8] These have individual title pages, all dated 1700 and apparently newly printed for this collection, so the works could be sold separately.[9] Wellington took Bentley's idea of a fiction collection as a way to sell unsold sheets, and made a more cohesive collection, with works selected to make sense together, an address from "The Bookseller to the Reader" at the beginning of the first volume, and newly printed title pages for the second volume.

The efforts of Bentley and Wellington in carving out a market for fiction reprints were succeeded by the more ambitious project of John Watts, whose *Select Collection of Novels in Four Volumes* (1720) was expanded to six volumes in 1722 and printed in a second edition in 1729. Although he has received less attention from literary scholars than Jacob Tonson, with whom he often worked, Watts ran what Henry Robert Plomer calls "one of the most important printing houses in London in the first half of the eighteenth century," and produced high-quality editions of literary and classical works.[10] The young Benjamin Franklin worked for Watts as a pressman and compositor, having moved from the smaller printing house of Samuel Palmer in the hopes of more money and better work.[11] Like those of his predecessors, Watts's collection also featured fiction from the seventeenth century rather than the newer publications that had so drastically changed the genre in England in the previous two decades. In contrast to Wellington's brief introduction, Watts's collection includes a more detailed preface, a dedication to Princess Anne, and a translation of Pierre-Daniel Huet's "Traitté de l'origine des Romans."

Watts's *Select Collection* attempted to raise the prestige of fiction by repackaging it in the kind of elegant collection previously done for poetry. The dedication to the princess begins by declaring, "Entertainments of this Nature being made up of the most moving Circumstances of Life, and generally supposed to be acted by Persons of an Eminent and Conspicuous Condition, should be adjusted with all the Propriety, and embellish'd with all the Ornament, that Wit, Language, and Good Breeding can exert."[12] Such a claim was not commonplace for fiction in the early eighteenth century; more than seventy years later, Jane Austen would far more famously mount a similar defense of fiction as a genre "in which the most thorough knowledge of human nature, the happiest delineation of its varieties, the liveliest effusions of wit and humour are conveyed to the world in the best chosen language."[13] For Watts to raise fiction to such a height of psychological depth, social respectability, and verbal artistry in 1720 was highly unusual.

The preface adopts a more defensive attitude than the dedication, drawing upon Huet's position as a Catholic bishop to support the respectability of studying and reading fiction. There is an explicit moral basis to the selections. Not only must they provide "Instruction and Entertainment," as Huet recommends, but also "the utmost Care has been taken, that no Novel shou'd have a Place, which cou'd possibly offend the Gravity of the Aged, or the Modesty of the Young" (*SCN*, 1:sig.A7v). The preface makes clear that Watts planned the collection carefully:

> The Publisher being fully appris'd of the Nature of his Undertaking, and observing how wretchedly some of these Novels have been formerly translated

into *English*, did not only get them done over again by complete Masters both of the Subject and the two Languages; but likewise took Care to have the others, which had never been attempted, to be translated by as able Hands, all of 'em being Men of Letters. (*SCN*, 1:sig.A8r)

Watts's efforts paid off, and in the sixth and final volume, the dedication (by "S. C.") says without much exaggeration that the collection is "the most choice and best collected of any that has been hitherto publish'd" (*SCN*, 6:sig.A3r).[14]

The selection of works does not bear much relation to Wellington's collections, except that they are nearly all translations from French or Spanish. Just one work, Brémond's *The Happy Slave*, appears in both collections (in different translations). Watts changed the selection in his 1729 second edition, which he explains has "considerable *Additions and Improvements*."[15] Among the new pieces were several very English works: *The History and Fall of the Lady Jane Grey*; *The History of Jane Shore*; *Memoirs of the Unhappy Favourite; Or, the Fall of Robert, Earl of Essex*; and *Memoirs of the Imprisonment and Death of Mary, Queen of Scots*. This represents an intentional program of anglicizing the collection by inserting works that were not only newly written in English (as the preface claims), but were also about famous incidents and people from English history. Watts also commissioned a new engraved frontispiece for each individual fiction title, "that no Embellishment suitable to a Work of this kind might be wanting" (*SCN*, 2nd ed., 1:sig.A9r). He was trying to craft a deluxe edition, suitable for an upper-class market.

These early fiction collections proved (1) there was a market for fiction in a collection, (2) fiction could be presented as a respectable genre, and (3) older fiction could be reprinted and resold successfully. This provides an important counterpoint to critical thinking about early eighteenth-century fiction as being of low status and appealing to readers largely because of its newness or "novelty."[16] The selection of works in these collections, however, may be surprising to a modern scholar—for with a few exceptions (*Incognita*, *The Princess of Cleves*), most of these are seldom mentioned in scholarship on the early novel in England. For Wellington and Watts, the fiction worth collecting was mainly foreign and from the late seventeenth century. As Watts's changes to the second edition of his collection suggest, however, the market was inclining toward more original English fiction, and there was more available for possible collection. Watts's additions foreshadow the anglicizing of the fiction canon in England that would occur over the next few decades.

Consolidation of the Canon: The 1770s

Few publishers attempted to replicate Watts's success with a project of comparable scope. There were a number of collections of novels in the mid-eighteenth century, but for the most part these were anthologies of short tales that had never been published before, not collections of previously published long works attempting to establish a canon of classics.[17] In the 1770s, however, several important publishing efforts again tried to reprint longer fictions for a new audience. John French's four-volume *British Novelist: Or, Virtue and Vice in Miniature* (1774) included abridged versions of works by Miguel de Cervantes and Alain René Le Sage, as well as midcentury English writers like Henry Fielding, Samuel Richardson, and Tobias Smollett, evidently meant for those readers who had not read them in full. George Kearsley's three-volume *Collection of Novels* (1777), "selected and revised" by the novelist Elizabeth Griffith, was marketed to a higher-class readership and included seventeenth- and early eighteenth-century steady sellers like Marie-Madeleine de La Fayette's *The Princess of Cleves*, Penelope Aubin's *The Noble Slaves*, and Eliza Haywood's *The Fruitless Enquiry*. Like Wellington and Watts, French and Kearsley saw a need for a collected canon of fiction classics—but unlike their predecessors, their canons were distinctly British.

In contrast to Wellington and Watts, John French was a minor-league publisher whose name appears in the imprints of a few dozen works in the 1770s and 1780s, mainly books about music or reprints of established poets like Pope, Thomson, and Young. His ambitious collection of abridgments of previously published works of fiction, titled *The British Novelist*, is an outlier in his list. The title page of *The British Novelist* declares that the works are "faithfully abridged, so as to contain all the SPIRIT of the ORIGINALS. The Whole forming a Complete LIBRARY of NOVELS." French was evidently attempting to appeal to the segment of the population that was able to build book collections of their own instead of just buying the occasional work of interest.[18] *The British Novelist* was also a marked departure from its predecessors in its emphasis on authors rather than titles: whereas Wellington and Watts did not identify the authors of the works they reprinted, let alone promote them, *The British Novelist* not only made the "novelist" the focus of its title, but also, on the title page, listed thirteen authors by name (eleven of whom were British). While not all of these are represented in the four volumes French actually published, he may have planned to include them in later volumes.

French's preface explains his purpose in selecting and abridging the works he included, focusing on their appeal to the busy and frugal reader. Like Huet and others, he emphasizes the dual instructional and entertaining value of fiction, but French regrets its length:

> These, however, with the many episodes, digressions, and remarks, have swelled to such a number of volumes, that few ordinary readers can either find money to purchase, or time to read them. But a still greater disadvantage attending them, is, that the abstract parts are too heavy and unentertaining

to youth, so that, being disgusted with one part, they give up the whole, and lose the most rational instruction.[19]

French makes the "youth" his target audience, but the books might appeal to any readers. Some of the works are prefaced by very brief introductions that emphasize their popularity and moral importance. The abridgements are rewritten into the third person, with a focus on plot, motive, and action rather than character. These various constraints sometimes result in nearly unrecognizable revisions: the ninety-four-page version of *Clarissa*, for example, makes Lovelace unsuccessful in his attempts to seduce or rape Clarissa (French, *BN*, 4:66).

The selection of texts in *The British Novelist* is interesting considering French's explicit program of moral instruction, as some of them would seem to be more entertaining than moral. Although Aphra Behn is named on the title page, none of her works appears in the four published volumes, and the earliest work is *Gil Blas* by Le Sage (first published in English in 1716). This is also one of only two works by an author from outside Britain (the other is a translation of Charles de Fieux de Mouhy's *La Paysanne Parvenue* under the title *The Fortunate Country Maid*). With the exception of *Gil Blas*, all the works were first published in England in the 1740s and 1750s, making them old enough to have established their popularity, but not so old as to be forgotten. All of the works in *The British Novelist* were published in at least one full-length version in the previous decade, and the choice of *Gil Blas* as the one early text may have been on account of Smollett's highly successful 1749 translation. For John French, the novels that form a "Complete Library" were English works from the mid-eighteenth century.

French's collection of abridgments was evidently not reprinted, and perhaps not completed (based on those authors named on the title page whose works were not included). A very different approach to the fiction canon was posited by George Kearsley in his *Collection of Novels*, a three-volume duodecimo set with engraved frontispieces. Kearsley had begun his career with some notoriety as publisher of the radical newspaper *North Briton*, for which he was arrested briefly in 1763; by the 1770s, he had a less controversial business publishing reprints of established texts in the English literary canon (Shakespeare, Milton, Gay, Johnson).[20] *Collection of Novels* makes sense as part of this venture, for it reprints several works that were popular in the late seventeenth and early eighteenth centuries, newly "selected and revised" by Elizabeth Griffith. While Griffith had not previously published with Kearsley, this project also makes sense with her career: in the early 1770s, she had published three novels of her own as well as *The Morality of Shakespeare's Drama Illustrated*, a book of essays explaining the moral basis of Shakespeare's plays (and establishing her as a writer of unimpeachable morals).[21] In her preface to *Collection of Novels*, Griffith explains her view of the origin of fiction after the Restoration, when "the stately romance resigned its station in the female library, to the gross effusions of amorous nonsense; which was, at that era, first introduced into these kingdoms, under the more modern title of *Novels*."[22] To allay any objections, Griffith reassures her more prudish readers that "as the sole purpose of this Compilation is to unite the *utile dulci*, by selecting some of the best Novels now extant, and framing them into a Collection, in which no writing tending towards immorality or indecency shall obtain a place, she flatters herself that the publication of these Pieces will be favourably received by the Public" (Griffith, *CN*, 1:sig.A3v). Echoing French, Griffith's preface hopes "that these volumes may be thought worthy of a place in the most select libraries," pointing to the newer book buyers who would not already have copies of these older works in their family collections (Griffith, *CN*, 1:sig.A4v).

The choice of works in Kearsley and Griffith's *Collection of Novels* reflects the preface's claims of resurrecting older texts that had not been reprinted recently. Along with a number of shorter pieces, the collection includes *Zayde*, *The Princess of Cleves*, *The History of Count Belfor and Leonora de Cespedes*, *Oroonoko*, *The Fruitless Enquiry*, *The History of Agnes de Castro*, and *The Noble Slaves*. The first three of these were in Watts's collection of 1720–1722, but the others were not. All but *The Fruitless Enquiry* (1727) and *The Noble Slaves* (1722) were first published in the seventeenth century, and only *The Fruitless Enquiry* had had a London edition in the previous two decades. There is also a decided preference for works by women writers, and Griffith's short introductions identify and briefly discuss Behn, Haywood, and Aubin (1:199, 2:161, and 3:47).[23] Griffith's editing tends to minimize the sexual content of the fictions, appealing to a different set of sensibilities than they did in the late seventeenth century. In *Oroonoko*, for example, she excises Behn's direct statement of Oroonoko and Imoinda's consummation ("having Opportunity, Night and Silence, Youth, Love and Desire, he soon prevail'd; and ravish'd in a Moment, what his old Grand-father had been endeavouring for so many Months").[24] Griffith's version simply picks up Behn's text a few sentences later, implying that they only had a conversation (Griffith, *CN*, 1:223). Griffith presents a subtly sanitized version of these older texts that might appeal to Kearsley's more modest readers.[25]

Like their predecessors Wellington and Watts, French and Kearsley recognized the potential market for fiction reprints to a readership that had not collected the works when they were originally published. Because the market for fiction had changed by the 1770s, both French and Kearsley mediated the works they reprinted—by abridgment or editing—to appeal to a readership with less patience for long works and less interest in sexual content. Both presented their collections as intended for readers seeking to build a collection of classic, well-known works, but they chose very different titles for inclusion. To French, the more immediate fiction context of the mid-eighteenth century was worthy of reprinting; for Kearsley, the nearly forgotten works of the late seventeenth and early eighteenth centuries were better for the collector interested in the origins of the novel form in English. Both saw moral instruction, particularly of the young, as a key purpose of fiction, and they imposed this onto texts that were not explicitly moral in their original versions. Whether they were correct or not, we may never know—but neither collection was reprinted.[26]

AN ENGLISH CANON, BY PARTS: *THE NOVELIST'S MAGAZINE* (1780–1788)

The collection that most closely resembles what modern scholars might describe as the canon of English fiction is James Harrison's *The Novelist's Magazine*, published serially from 1780 to 1788 and eventually reaching twenty-three bound volumes. Unlike the collections by French or Kearsley, *The Novelist's Magazine* was not explicitly attempting to market to the nouveau riche collector aspiring to build a home library, but rather aimed at an audience that had less money to spend and would rather buy fiction by sixpenny parts than a several-shilling volume. This is not to say that *The Novelist's Magazine* was a hasty production, for it was not: each volume includes engraved plates and was produced to a high standard, with clear text and wide margins. Richard C. Taylor, in his extensive discussion of the series, argues that "Harrison's effort recognized the slowly improving social status of the novel and attempted to contribute to its prestige; further, it was an opportunity to reissue works whose copyrights had expired and a means of encouraging and controlling the survival of what he felt were the 'best' novels of the century."[27] Taylor overstates the uniqueness of Harrison's venture—as we have seen, he was preceded by other collections of fiction reprints—but he is right in pointing out Harrison's vision in producing a high-quality publication in inexpensive parts.

What exactly constituted a "part"? Most surviving copies are bound into volumes, with the engravings inserted at appropriate places and a specially printed title page. There are a few examples of individual parts that have remained unbound, which show how the work originally appeared. Number 184 contains the beginning of *The Life and Adventures of Peter Wilkins*, a work by Robert Paltock originally published in two duodecimo volumes in 1751.[28] The title page to Number 184 of *The Novelist's Magazine* states its "Price SIX-PENCE only" and says that it is "Embellished with a beautiful descriptive PLATE; representing an interesting Scene from PETER WILKINS, designed by STOTHARD, and engraved by the ingenious Mr. WALKER." This part ends mid-sentence on page 38; the next part, 185, picks up with the sentence and page 39 as though there were no break between them. The last page of Number 184 contains descriptive advertisements for other serial publications by Harrison.

The 189 pages of *Peter Wilkins* are divided into four parts, but the fact that parts break between pages without regard to complete sentences or chapter endings suggests that readers were not actually expected to read them serially, but instead to collect and bind them. *Peter Wilkins* was part of volume 12, which also included *The Female Quixote* (by Charlotte Lennox), *A Journey from This World to the Next* (Henry Fielding), and *Joe Thompson* (Edward Kimber), for a total of 704 pages. If each part averaged 50 pages, volume 12 would comprise 14 parts, and at 6d. each, would cost 7s.—which was still less expensive than buying new copies of the books separately. A page at the end of *Peter Wilkins* has "Directions for placing the Cuts," specifying which illustration should go with which page, thereby confirming that the work was specifically designed for binding. The directions note,

> The BINDER is desired, for the Credit of this Work, as well as of himself, not to bind up any of the Sheets while they are in the least damp, to take Care that the Whole is folded as even as possible; to plough off but little of the Margin; to attend carefully to the placing of the CUTS as above directed, which he must not suffer to remain in the Book while it is beating, as they will in that Case be damaged by the Letter-Press; and to bind them up with the *Tissue Paper* before them.

The final product was not at all something that could be purchased by what Taylor calls "a mass audience," at least in terms of numbers: an "elegantly bound" copy of the whole set was advertised in James Lackington's catalog in 1793 at the high price of £9 18s. 6d., and single volumes for 6s. 6d.[29] While it certainly would have appealed to buyers who could afford such an expense only piecemeal, it was not a product for the lower class.

The choice of texts departs from Harrison's predecessors in several important ways. *The Novelist's Magazine* is subtitled "Gentleman and Lady's Entertaining Miscellany," and title pages of the individual parts claim it had "the scarcest and most approved Histories, Adventures, Anecdotes, Memoirs, Tales, Romances, &c. Which have at any Time appeared in the English Language. Together with Elegant and new Translations of all Foreign Novels worth Reading."[30] It includes all the works that were in French's *British Novelist*, and others from the eighteenth century. Many of these were famous already: *Robinson Crusoe*, *Gulliver's Travels*, *Tristram Shandy*, *Rasselas*, and *Tom Jones* were all included, as well as translations of *Don Quixote*, *The Devil upon Two Sticks*, *Arabian Nights Entertainments*, and *Telemachus*. There were also books that were good sellers in the eighteenth century but rarely read today, like *Pompey the Little* and *The History of Jemmy and Jenny Jessamy*. But some of the works included were more of a risk. *The History and Adventures of an Atom* might be thought worth reprinting, since it was by Smollett, even though it had not been reprinted since it first came out in 1769, and, indeed, a reprint from the 1790s suggests that Harrison was not the only publisher who thought it might still appeal.[31] The choice of *Henrietta, Countess Osenvor* proved to be less successful; the work had not been reprinted in English since its first appearance in 1770, and no further editions came out in the eighteenth century after Harrison's. Claudia L. Johnson says rather dismissively that *The Novelist's Magazine* "reprinted anything likely to sell," which is true as far as Harrison's explicitly commercial purpose—but some of the works he chose did not have a publication history in England that would indicate their success.[32]

The Novelist's Magazine seems to be reflecting popular taste as well as recuperating some works that had not been so popular, but that Harrison thought worth reprinting. Without introductions or other prefatory material besides the dedications and prefaces that originally accompanied the works, *The Novelist's Magazine* presents all its reprinted texts together without distinguishing between the famous and the obscure. It does not separate translations from original English texts, and it lists titles on the title pages without authors. The works are a good sampling of the subgenres of fiction popular in the mid-eighteenth century: collections of tales, books of adventure, epistolary fictions, humorous fiction, and fiction set in exotic or fantastical places.[33]

The Canon at Length: *The British Novelists* (1810)

Thirty years after Harrison began his *Novelist's Magazine*, a new collection of fiction would appear that demonstrated just how much tastes had changed in the late eighteenth century—and how fiction had changed. *The British Novelists*, a fifty-volume production by a group of major London publishers headed by F. C. and J. Rivington and edited by Anna Laetitia Barbauld, marked a sharp divergence in the novel canon from previous collections. As Claudia Johnson notes, *The British Novelists* prioritized the relatively recent over the early, with just seven (out of twenty-nine) works originally published before 1755 (167). Johnson argues that Barbauld's collection, with its selection of radical texts and books by women writers, was superseded by *Ballantyne's Novelist's Library*, edited by Walter Scott, where "The British novel becomes principally the complete works of a few men who by virtue of his selection become great authors" (174). Despite this, Barbauld's selections were not entirely marginalized: all but three of them remain in print in paperback to this day, suggesting that her project of canonization was more successful than Johnson seems to think. Barbauld's *British Novelists* does include more women writers than *Ballantyne's* did. A longer look at the previous collections of fiction, from Wellington and Watts to French, Kearsley, and Harrison, shows, however, that Barbauld's *British Novelists* rejects the international view of English fiction that prevailed up through the late eighteenth century in favor of a more nationalistic model that prefers authorial diversity over linguistic, generic, and chronological diversity.

The British Novelists was a creation of the publishers, led by Longman, who sent Barbauld copies of possible texts to review. William McCarthy details Barbauld's previous connection with the *Atheneum*, which Longman published, and it was that magazine which first advertised *The British Novelists*.[34] He also calls attention to the reduced canon compared to previous collections: "Their (or her) stripping out of works not British was part of a broader slimming of the previous canon of fictions. Barbauld's canon was smaller because it dropped many titles that look today, and must have looked to her as well, like the ephemera of their time" (426). Barbauld was responsible for selecting the texts that ultimately wound up in the collection, but Longman set the parameters within which she could choose.

Barbauld's preface to the collection provides a history "On the Origin and Progress of Novel-Writing," citing examples from various national traditions and languages. She traces the origins of fiction in "the earliest accounts of the literature of every age and country," including ancient works like *The Golden Ass* (from the second century A.D.).[35] She has little patience for the magic of traditional folklore or the ornate language of seventeenth-century romances, preferring instead the realist and moral novel, and citing as predecessors French works like *The Princess of Cleves* and *Telemachus*. From the English tradition, Barbauld mentions highlights of Renaissance prose fiction, like Sidney's *Arcadia* (1580) and Roger Boyle's *Parthenissa* (1651–1659), and, unusually, James Harrington's *Oceana* (1656), which was not discussed as a novel in previous histories of fiction (*BN*, ed. Barbauld, 1:34–36).[36] Her focus in the eighteenth century shifts to those works that were popular, especially those that had interesting formal characteristics, like *Tristram Shandy*, or moralistic feeling, like *Clarissa*. As Anne Toner points out, Barbauld's essay emphasizes the entertaining value of fiction and its ability to achieve narrative closure.[37] While she appreciates naturalism, Barbauld does not mistake fiction for reality, explaining that "the reader of a novel forms his expectations from what he supposes passes in the mind of the author, and guesses rightly at his intentions, but would often guess wrong if he were considering the real course of nature" (*BN*, ed. Barbauld, 1:56). Barbauld sees fiction as being entertaining and morally instructive, but not a representation of real life.

Unlike the *Collection of Novels* edited by Griffith, which was explicitly trying to represent the history of the genre in its selection, *The British Novelists* includes only those works that Barbauld finds to be "some of the most approved novels." She explains further several criteria for her selection: (1) "Variety in manner has been attended to"; (2) "A few of superior merit were chosen without difficulty"; (3) "Some regard it has been thought proper to pay to the taste and preference of the public"; and (4) "Copyright also was not to be intruded on, and the number of volumes was determined by the booksellers" (*BN*, ed. Barbauld, 1:61) How do these criteria explain the selection presented in *The British Novelists*?

As her introduction would suggest, Barbauld generally emphasizes the entertaining value of fiction and its moral qualities, but her other criteria for selection come up when she explains why she chose one work over others. The "variety" of a novel, for example, is an important quality in *Tom Jones*, of which she claims, "There is perhaps no novel in the English language so artfully conducted, or so rich in humour and character," but concedes that "with regard to its moral tendency we must content ourselves with more qualified praise" (*BN*, ed. Barbauld, 18:xix, 18:xxvii). It is, in fact, *Tom Jones*'s variety that warrants its inclusion in addition to *Joseph Andrews*, which she finds to be "the most unexceptionable in point of morals of any of Fielding's novels," and yet "There is little or nothing in it of story, compared with the elaborate plan of his subsequent work [*Tom Jones*]; nor so great a variety of characters: on which account the performance is inferior" (*BN*, ed. Barbauld, 18:xvi, 18:xiii). Barbauld justifies including *Joseph Andrews* for its morality and *Tom Jones* for its variety, but both are needed to show the range of Fielding's art.

Barbauld's choices in her view represent "superior merit," which are easy to identify, for she does not restrain her praise. Her preference for Richardson is predictable, based on her edition of his correspondence, and the first fifteen volumes of *The British Novelists* are taken up by *Clarissa* and *Sir Charles Grandison*. She singles out *The Vicar of Wakefield* as "one of the most pleasing novels of a modern cast" and declares of *A Simple Story* that "to readers of taste it would be superfluous to point out the beauties of Mrs. Inchbald's novels" (though she nevertheless proceeds to do so) (*BN*, ed. Barbauld, 23:i, 28:i). Her grandest praise is saved for Samuel Johnson, of whom she claims, "Hercules, it is said, once wielded the distaff; and the Hercules of literature, Dr. Johnson, has not disdained to be the author of a novel. To say the truth, nothing which he has written has more the touch of genius than *Rasselas, Prince of Abyssinia*" (*BN*, ed. Barbauld, 26:i). There can be no doubt why she selected these works.

More interesting for understanding Barbauld's conception of the fiction collection, however, are those books where her praise is more tempered by personal disapproval. Of *Robinson Crusoe*, for example, she has mixed praise and criticism, saying that "though it has no pretensions to the graces of style, nor aims at touching the tender passions, [it] yields to few in the truth of its description and its power of interesting the mind," and "It has been translated into most modern languages, has passed through numberless editions, and has always been found particularly agreeable to the taste of youth" (*BN*, ed. Barbauld, 16:I, 16:v). Popularity was clearly the main reason in favor of *Crusoe*'s inclusion, though its depiction of a personal religious experience surely did not hurt. Other cases are even more direct. Barbauld says outright that "*The Mysteries of Udolpho* is the most popular of this author's performances, and as such has been chosen for this Selection," though she personally prefers *The Italian* and *The Romance of the Forest* (the latter of which is also included) (*BN*, ed. Barbauld, 43:v). Barbauld's effort to balance the "taste and preference of the public" with her own is most tasked in her inclusion of Smollett, who, she believes, should be represented despite her personal dislike for his work. She calls him "one of the most prolific as well as popular of our novel-writers," but also warns "that vice may pollute the mind, and coarseness vitiate the taste, even when presented in the least attractive form;

and it is therefore to the praise of the present generation that this author's novels are much less read now than they were formerly. The least exceptionable of them is *Humphrey Clinker* [*sic*], which, that a name of so much celebrity might not be entirely passed over, makes a part of this Selection" (*BN*, ed. Barbauld, 30:i, 30:xvi). Such explanation shows us that ultimately *The British Novelists* was a commercial production, and Barbauld's choices depended on what the publishers thought would sell to the widest number of customers.

These publishers certainly knew what might be salable, as they were some of the most prominent and active publishers in the late eighteenth and early nineteenth centuries, particularly for fiction. The imprint is headed by F. C. and J. Rivington, the third generation of a publishing dynasty that lasted until the twentieth century. They were at the heart of the Stationers' Company; by 1810, Francis Rivington had served as master of the company and Charles as "stockkeeper of the English Stock," the collection of jointly held copyrights the company owned.[38] Although Longman organized the project, the Rivingtons may have been given first billing because they were close to Samuel Richardson and held the copyright to *Sir Charles Grandison*.[39] Among the forty other publishers and firms listed in the imprint, several others were notable for their literary publications and may also help to explain some of the selection of texts. The firm of George Robinson (often as "G. G. J. & J. Robinson") appeared on the imprints of eighty different new works of fiction in the last two decades of the eighteenth century, including *The Mysteries of Udolpho* and *A Simple Story*, both reprinted in *The British Novelists*. Thomas Cadell (with William Davies as "Cadell and Davies") was a second-generation publisher whose family name had appeared on more than fifty fiction imprints, including *The Man of Feeling* and *Cecilia*, both in the collection. The firm of John and James Richardson (along with William, who died in 1807) had published more than thirty works of fiction. John Murray is known more for his poetry publications and cultivation of the careers of Byron and others, but a few years after *The British Novelists* came out, he would publish Austen's *Emma*. In short, the publishers in the imprint for *The British Novelists* were at the center of literary fiction publication and presented themselves as more discriminating in their selections than the publishers who catered to the circulating library market. *The British Novelists* was a collection designed to appeal to a literary-minded reader, and it basically established the canon of eighteenth-century British fiction.

———

These early, ambitious publishing efforts also helped form the canon for the nineteenth century, and showed that fiction, like poetry, could appeal to readers in a collection of reprinted texts long after its initial novelty was gone. In the process, they created a canon of fiction that was English and eighteenth century, erasing the earlier works and translations from the French that had featured so prominently in earlier collections. To many later literary historians, the eighteenth-century origins of the English novel were taken for granted—but for a brief period in the early eighteenth century, fiction collections showed a very different list of English works. These efforts to reprint fiction in collections for the English reading public were organized and sponsored by publishers who saw that readers would be interested in reading older works even in a genre said to depend on its "novelty" for its appeal, and that entertaining reading material was worthy of collecting into an expensive set for discerning readers.

NOTES

1. Ian Watt, *The Rise of the Novel: Studies in Defoe, Richardson, and Fielding* (Berkeley: University of California Press, 1957); John J. Richetti, *Popular Fiction before Richardson: Narrative Patterns, 1700–1739* (Oxford: Clarendon Press, 1969).

2. Thomas F. Bonnell, *The Most Disreputable Trade: Publishing the Classics of English Poetry, 1765–1810* (Oxford: Oxford University Press, 2008).

3. Giles Mandelbrote, "Richard Bentley's Copies: The Ownership of Copyrights in the Late Seventeenth Century," in *The Book Trade and Its Customers, 1450–1900: Historical Essays for Robin Myers*, ed. Arnold Hunt, Giles Mandelbrote, and Alison Shell (New Castle: Oak Knoll, 1997), 55–94; Leah Orr, "Tactics of Publishing and Selling Fiction in the Long Eighteenth Century," *Huntington Library Quarterly* 81 (2018): 399–423, esp. 411–412.

4. Leah Orr, *Novel Ventures: Fiction and Print Culture in England, 1690–1730* (Charlottesville: University of Virginia Press, 2017), 43–48.

5. For a later example of a fiction nonce collection, see *A Collection of Six New Delightful Novels* (London: E. Tracy, 1710), which gathers three different works published separately by Tracy the previous year.

6. *A Collection of Novels*, vol. 1 (London: R. Wellington, 1699), sig.A2r–v.

7. For example, William Shakespeare, *Comedies, Histories, and Tragedies*, 4th ed. (London: H. Herringman, for Joseph Knight and Francis Saunders, 1685); James Harrington, *The Oceana and His Other Works* (London: John Darby, 1700); Jane Barker, *The Entertaining Novels*, 2nd ed., 2 vols. (London: A. Bettesworth and E. Curll, 1719).

8. *A Collection of Pleasant Modern Novels*, vol. 2 (London: Jacob Tonson, Richard Wellington, E. Rumbole, and J. Wild, 1700). This is the second volume of what was originally titled *A Collection of Novels* and originally published just by Wellington.

9. The English Short Title Catalogue (ESTC) does not indicate that any of these were sold as separate editions.

10. Henry Robert Plomer, *A Dictionary of the Printers and Booksellers Who Were at Work in England, Scotland, and Ireland from 1668 to 1725* (Oxford: Oxford University Press for the Bibliographical Society, 1922), 304.

11. Benjamin Franklin, *Autobiography*, pt. 5, from the digital edition of *The Papers of Benjamin Franklin*, American Philosophical Society and Yale University, franklinpapers.org. On Franklin's time with Watts, see Hazel Wilkinson, "Benjamin Franklin's London Printing, 1725–1726," *Papers of the Bibliographical Society of America* 110 (2016): 139–180.

12. *A Select Collection of Novels*, 6 vols. (London: John Watts, 1720–1722), 1:sig.A4r–v (henceforth *SCN*).

13. Jane Austen, *Northanger Abbey*, ed. Barbara M. Benedict and Deirdre Le Faye (Cambridge: Cambridge University Press, 2006), 31.

14. This may be Samuel Croxall, who wrote a sermon published by Watts during the 1720s and was known for his translation work.

15. *Select Collection of Novels and Histories*, 2nd ed., 6 vols. (London: John Watts, 1729), 1:sig.A7r (henceforth *SCN*, 2nd ed.).

16. Lennard J. Davis, *Factual Fictions: The Origins of the English Novel* (New York: Columbia University Press, 1983), 48–49; J. Paul Hunter, *Before Novels: The Cultural Contexts of Eighteenth-Century English Fiction* (New York: W. W. Norton, 1990), 3–58.

17. For example, see *A Curious Collection of Novels* (London: J. Billingsley, 1731); *The Pleasant Companion* (London: J. Brooks, 1734); *The Theatre of Love, a Collection of Novels* (London: W. Reeve, 1759).

18. Abigail Williams, *The Social Life of Books: Reading Together in the Eighteenth-Century Home* (New Haven: Yale University Press, 2017), 95–105.

19. *The British Novelist*, 4 vols. (London: J. French, 1774), 1:i–ii (henceforth French, *BN*).

20. Trevor Ross, "George Kearsley (ca. 1739–1790), bookseller," *Oxford Dictionary of National Biography* (Oxford: Oxford University Press, 2004) (henceforth ODNB), http://www.oxforddnb.com/view/10.1093/ref:odnb/9780198614128.001.0001/odnb-9780198614128-e-47159?rskey=CQU4oh&result=2ed.

21. Elizabeth Griffith and Richard Griffith, *Two Novels, in Letters*, 4 vols. (London: T. Becket and P. A. de Hondt, 1769); Elizabeth Griffith, *The History of Lady Barton*, 3 vols. (London: T. Davies and T. Cadell, 1771); Elizabeth Griffith, *The Story of Lady Juliana Harley*, 2 vols. (London: T. Cadell, 1776); Elizabeth Griffith, *The Morality of Shakespeare's Drama Illustrated* (London: T. Cadell, 1775).

22. Elizabeth Griffith, *Collection of Novels*, 3 vols. (London: G. Kearsley, 1777), 1:sig.A2v (henceforth Griffith, *CN*).

23. Griffith does not identify Marie-Madeleine de La Fayette as the author of *The Princess of Cleves*, but she indicates that it is by a French woman.

24. Aphra Behn, *Oroonoko: Or, The Royal Slave, a True History* (London: W. Canning, 1688), 63.

25. In 1785, a copy of all three volumes of Griffith's collection, "neat," was valued at 7s. 6d. in *Samuel Hayes's Catalogue*, no. 332 ([London: S. Hayes, 1785]), 99.

26. The ESTC notes that Griffith's version of *The Princess of Cleves* was reissued by William Lane with a new title page in 1780, which would suggest that the original print run of *Collection of Novels* did not sell out. [La Fayette], *The Princess of Cleves* (London: W. Lane, 1780), ESTC citation no. N20713.

27. Richard C. Taylor, "James Harrison, *The Novelist's Magazine*, and the Early Canonizing of the English Novel," *Studies in English Literature 1500–1900* 33 (1993): 629–643, quotation from 631.

28. *The Novelist's Magazine* (London: Harrison and Co., [1780–1788]), no. 184.

29. Taylor, "James Harrison," 631; *Second Volume of Lackington's Catalogue for 1793* (London: J. Lackington, 1793), 28–29, 236. Taylor seems to have confused the 6d. price per part with the price per volume, which may explain why he believed it was a cheap production. See Taylor, "James Harrison," 632.

30. Title page to no. 184.

31. Tobias Smollett, *The History and Adventures of an Atom*, 2 vols. (1769) (London: C. Cooke, [1795]).

32. Claudia Johnson, "'Let Me Make the Novels of a Country': Barbauld's *The British Novelists* (1810/1820)," *Novel: A Forum on Fiction* 34 (2001): 163–179, quotation from 168.

33. On the subgenres of fiction in the mid-eighteenth century, see Jerry C. Beasley, *Novels of the 1740s* (Athens: University of Georgia Press, 1982).

34. William McCarthy, *Anna Letitia Barbauld: Voice of the Enlightenment* (Baltimore: Johns Hopkins University Press, 2008), 423.

35. *The British Novelists*, ed. Anna Laetitia Barbauld, 50 vols. (London: F. C. and J. Rivington, and others, 1810), 1:3 (henceforth *BN*, ed. Barbauld).

36. *Oceana* is not mentioned in Clara Reeve, *The Progress of Romance*, 2 vols. (Colchester: W. Keymer and G. G. J. and J. Robinson, 1785).

37. Anne Toner, "Anna Barbauld on Fictional Form in *The British Novelists* (1810)," *Eighteenth-Century Fiction* 24 (2011): 171–193, esp. 173.

38. Barbara Laning Fitzpatrick, "Rivington Family (*per. ca.* 1710–*ca.* 1960)," ODNB, http://www.oxforddnb.com/view/10.1093/ref:odnb/9780198614128.001.0001/odnb-978019861 4128-e-70881?rskey=CS3nss&result=1.

39. McCarthy, *Anna Letitia Barbauld*, 652n43.

CHAPTER 3

Elizabeth Sadleir, Master Printer and Publisher in Dublin, 1715–1727

James E. May

THE DUBLIN PUBLISHING SCENE

Prior to Robert Munter's *Dictionary of the Print Trade in Ireland, 1550–1775* (1988) and, especially, Mary Pollard's *Dictionary of Members of the Dublin Book Trade, 1550–1800* (2000), the historical record on early eighteenth-century Dublin printers was full of gaps and inaccuracies.[1] Although Pollard has provided new details about Elizabeth Sadleir and her family, even she has inaccuracies regarding when they were active at particular addresses. In the past eighty years, the only early eighteenth-century Dublin printers receiving in-depth attention, besides George Faulkner, have been Jonathan Swift's previous printers, John and Sarah Harding.[2] Now aided by the English Short Title Catalogue (ESTC), OCLC's WorldCat, and text digitization projects, especially Eighteenth Century Collections Online (ECCO), one can flesh out Sadleir's printing and publishing career and those publishers with whom she collaborated, especially John Chantry.

As a caveat, one must admit that even with the new tools, the historical record remains very partial. Advertisements for books no longer extant, missing volumes in almanac and periodical series, and the small number of surviving Catholic devotional and educational books and chapbooks indicate that much that was certainly printed has not survived. For instance, the fragility of the bibliographical record is evident when no copy has survived of the first Dublin printing of James Anderson's *Constitutions of the Free-Masons*, which is repeatedly listed among books sold opposite the Watch-House by John Chantry (see the *Dublin Weekly Journal* of 3 April 1725). It is also evident in the weird disparity between the ESTC's total for records in adjacent years: 1723: 142, 1724: 255; 1725: 407. Of the roughly 138 extant items printed in Dublin in 1723 (newspapers excluded), 82 are recorded for three or fewer copies, 40 for only one, including a prayer book of 118 pages printed by King's Printer Andrew Crooke: *The Countess of Morton's Daily Exercise*. The disappearance of much that was printed prevents confident assertions about publishing in the period. We cannot be certain how many presses were operating in any given year, nor know whether some names and initials found in only one or two imprints are those of actual printers. Surviving productions leave one uncertain who owned particular cut ornaments, and, in some cases, whether the multiple uses of the same ornament the same year by different printers indicates a loan or two printers occupying the same shop.

In short, there are no reliable studies of any printers working in Sadleir's Dublin, let alone women printers. This chapter breaks new ground, not only by providing more information about Sadleir, but also by fleshing out what was happening in Dublin printing and publishing in those decades. During the years 1715–1727, when Elizabeth Sadleir was an independent printer, printshops nearly doubled in number, from thirteen to twenty-five, and there were over a dozen only publishing. In 1720, when the Irish Parliament was not in session, fifteen printers (including three women) produced 122 ESTC records; in 1723, with Parliament meeting, seventeen (including four women) produced roughly 140 records, with 76 printed by five presses (James Carson, Crooke, George Grierson, Thomas Hume, and Aaron Rhames), all printing largely for themselves (in 1723, only William Helme and Stephen Powell appear to have printed solely for others). During this period, though most of the production came from those belonging to the Guild of Saint Luke, half those printing were not guild members (some, like George Faulkner, entered only after establishing a trade). Some intruders, like John Harding and Nicholas Hussey, were poor printers, as were some guild members, like Cornelius Carter, all pulling down the quality of Dublin printing. Others, such as Samuel Fuller, James Watts, and the partners Pressick Rider and Thomas Harbin, were good printers, as was Elizabeth Sadleir, good enough to be included in big projects along with the best printers of the first third of the century—we also discover that she is the lone female in many collaborative projects with other good printers.

The brevity of many printers' careers (half a dozen active in 1723 were not in 1721 or would not be in 1725) did not allow the acquisition of much skill by a printer and his servants. Some died a few years after setting up: William Wilmot began publishing in 1724 and died in 1727; Mary Fuller began the same year she died, 1735; and Theophilius Jones set up in 1734 and died in 1736. Some were driven out by charges of libel and sedition (Daniel Tompson, Rider & Harbin, William Shaw Anburey, Watts, and the Catholic James Malone); even a loyal Whig could be arrested for printing a speech, or, as James Carson was, "for presuming to print the Archbishop of Dublin's Name among the Subscribers" for a 1719 book (Pollard, *Dictionary*, 91) Some who set up to run newspapers failed (such as

Anburey, Hussey, Thomas Toulmin), some blew in from London and back out (William Helme, 1721–1724, and Andrew Hinde, 1714). Many simply went broke: bankruptcy could happen to even a good printer, such as Thomas Hume (1715–1729). Catholics were handicapped by censorship and quarter-brother fees to the guild. Also, the small profits obtained from Dublin's low consumption of newspapers (which carried few advertisements) and other printed matter meant the continued use of degraded type and equipment, which led to shabby work by some like Carter, though he survived for decades. Yet Sadleir continued to print, even when that entailed a change of address, or a change of collaborators.

The dominance of printers over publishers in early eighteenth-century Dublin is apparent in the usual imprint formula, reading "Printed by," not "Printed for," as in London. Of 138 non-newspaper records for 1723, 115 contain the formula "Printed by" or the equivalent (such as "ex officina" or "Printed at the Rein Deer"), and only 15 read "Printed for." Printers more easily dominated the trade when so much that was printed was topical or chap literature less than a sheet in length and distributed by hawkers and the trade in general, which, accordingly, did not require or receive the imprint of a publisher. At this time, if we except government publications, like acts and votes of parliaments, the vast majority of works longer than a sheet reprinted a text from outside Ireland. These reprints are not piracies, for there was no law prohibiting such reprinting, and the trade tended not to compete with rival editions for more than a few to half a dozen texts a year. Books, that is, works of over a hundred octavo or fifty quarto pages, although they have survived in much greater rates than shorter works, account for about a seventh of the Dublin records in the ESTC for the period— in some years, they account for less than an eighth (for instance, only 23 of 194 records for 1721). Of 163 ESTC records for Dublin, 1713, only 9 are books (only 2 of which are original to Dublin, one being the *Votes* of Parliament), but book production increased—to 14 in 1718, 19 in 1720, 20 in 1722, and 31 in 1723—as the number and wealth of publishers increased, and as they turned to the public for subscriptions, and in several cases, set up their own presses.

Attending to the increasing importance of publishers allows attention to several men important in Sadleir's career, particularly the neglected figure John Chantry, who infused the Dublin trade with ambition and a collaborative approach. Chantry, after an apprenticeship and a successful career in London, arrived in Dublin by 1719. After joining the guild, he began selling used books and publishing for himself, usually as a silent partner with others' names in the imprint and relying for self-reference on only his address, which was opposite the Watch-House the North Side of College Green in 1720–1727, and on the corner of Sycamore Alley, Dame Street from 1727 to August 1732. He may have partnered with Hyde and Owen in publishing the three folio volumes of Edward Hyde, Earl of Clarendon's *History of the Rebellion*, always found in his booklists along with his editions of Clarendon's *History of the Rebellion . . . in Ireland* (for

Patrick Dugan, 1719–1720), and of *Lord Clarendon's History of the Grand Rebellion Compleated* (J[oseph]. Leathley and Dugan, 1720). Besides Dugan and Leathley, Chantry partnered with—and gave the imprints to—printer James Carson and the young publishers Richard Norris and William Smith, and, in 1729–1730, Stearne Brock, who took over Chantry's shop in September 1732. Assisted by the young booksellers, Chantry undertook subscription campaigns well advertised in the papers for lengthy folio editions, like Geoffrey Keating's *General History of Ireland* (by J. Carson, and sold by the Booksellers, 1723), the two folios *Thirty Six Sermons and Discourses* by Robert South (Dugan and Leathley, 1720), and Thomas Wood's *Institute of the Laws of England* (J. Watts, and sold opposite the Watch-House, 1724). In 1720, a two-volume subscription edition of a Dublin playwright, *The Works of Mr. Charles Shadwell*, was published by Dugan, Leathley, and George Risk, with Chantry as a silent partner (its sole advertisement is for Chantry, in a booklist at the end of the second volume), and he put his own address in the imprint of Thomas Lewis's *Origines Hebrææ* (by P. Rider and T. Harbin, and sold opposite the Watch House, 1725).

One of the things that kept publishers solvent was subscription publishing by many, including Chantry, which provided Sadleir important press work. Although he pressed the gas pedal, Chantry cannot be said to have begun the vogue for subscriptions in Dublin, for roughly the same number of subscriptions during 1715–1727 were undertaken by John Hyde, at times with partners Robert Owen and Richard Gunne, and by Grierson, usually acting alone. Hyde, Grierson, and Gunne published Richard Fiddes's *Theologica Speculativa* in 1718; in 1720 followed a second Fiddes folio with Rhames, its printer, replacing Grierson. Grierson's biggest subscription editions in the period are the three folios of Louis Ellies du Pin's *New History of Ecclesiastical Writers* (1722–1724), and his eight octavos of Shakespeare in 1726. After helping print subscription folios in 1720, Sadleir printed two editions over five hundred pages long that she could never have undertaken without the subscribers' subvention: *The Works of . . . Richard Hooker* in folio and Gilbert Burnet's *Exposition of the Thirty-Nine Articles* in octavo, the latter with 182 subscribers, some taking multiple copies. Authors besides Shadwell also stepped up to launch subscriptions, such as Matthew Concanen, first for *A Match at Foot-ball* (probably by Sadleir, for the author, 1720), and then *Poems, upon Several Occasions* (A. Rhames, for E. Dobson, 1722). Seasoned Dublin printers partnered with publishers and authors on occasion too, as Edward Waters with Luke Dowling and Cornelius Nary for the latter's folio *New History of the World* (1720), and with Charles Coffey for *Poems and Songs upon Several Occasions* (1724). Thus, subscriptions enabled the publication of original writing in Dublin, such as Murroghoh (Morgan) O'Connor's *Poems, Pastorals, and Dialogues* (S. Powell for J. Thompson, 1726). Perhaps before Chantry's arrival, the campaign had begun for *Lucan's Pharsalia* (James Carson for Leathley, 1719). But, while the ESTC records only several large subscription editions in Dublin for the dozen years before Chantry's arrival in 1719, it records over twenty-five for the dozen years following. Lengthy subscription editions led to contracts for parts of books with multiple printers, Sadleir among them.

Besides the use of subscriptions to cover costs, another development empowering several publishers was their setting up their own presses, which would have challenged Sadleir, since those presses took work away from her, as well as from her colleagues Hume, Powell, and Rhames. George Grierson, who in 1732 succeeded Andrew Crooke as king's printer, set up his own press in 1720, spending considerably to acquire a stock of newly cut ornaments, and John Hyde and Eliphal Dobson Jr. in 1725 set up a press in space rented from the guild, buying cut ornaments, and presumably type and other equipment, from Rhames, with which they printed books for themselves individually and jointly as well as for Richard Gunne and Robert Owen, with whom Hyde and Dobson often co-published. Social and economic developments, like increased wealth and literacy, spurred the printing of more books, and advertisements greatly increased. To mention another factor involving the trade directly, as in London, lengthy works began to be sold in serial editions with sale by sheets and then volumes. But since Dublin was not in a class with London for wealth or population, reprinting lengthy folios and even octavos involved considerable risks; sales might not cover expenses (in part because some subscribers would not make the final payment), as is suggested by many of the subscription editions mentioned here surviving at twelve or fewer locations, including one of Sadleir's books in 1721.

WOMEN PUBLISHERS IN IRELAND

As noted, women were active in the Dublin press trade, normally taking over a shop on the death of their parents, brothers, or husbands. The women running presses in 1715 besides Elizabeth Sadleir included the widows Ann Sandys, who used her late husband's imprint ("E." or "Edwin," d. 1708), and Elizabeth Dickson, the widow of Francis (d. 1713), who in 1714 married Gwyn Needham, whose name usually replaced hers on imprints, and in 1722, following the death of husbands, Catherine Hicks and Deborah Powell. The recently deceased Elizabeth Ray had helped her son John run the family's press briefly in 1709–1712, after her husband Joseph's death, and then in 1713 printed three imprints after her son's death. Sarah Hyde, Elizabeth Ray's daughter, would run her husband John's trade from late 1729 before removing from the printing side of the business in 1734. Unlike Sadleir, many women did not put their Christian names on imprints; even if they had, imprints would fail to reflect the numerous married women engaged in the trade, particularly in composing, binding, and retailing. While there are exceptions like Deborah Powell and Margaret Rhames, widows in Dublin as in London often failed to maintain their husbands' presses for more than four years, if only due to their own deaths; those from the first four decades of the century who did not keep their presses running for more than four years include Anne Crooke, Jane Dobson, Mary Fuller, Sarah Harding, Sarah Hyde, J. Jones, Elizabeth Ray, Mary Whalley, and Mary Wilmot.[3] Ann Sandys, as printer of the *Dublin Gazette* (1709–1724), may have worked more at the press than the ESTC records for her suggest (fifty-one for 1708–1723), but she printed only eight imprints after 1715. Sadleir printed more than any woman printing in Dublin in 1715–1727, excepting Deborah Powell, who was left a major business by her husband Stephen, with a large ornament stock as well as apprentices. By contrast, Sadleir did not own large or better stocks of woodcut or cast ornament, a challenge she often met, apparently, by borrowing ornaments.

Although other women operated printing and publishing Dublin businesses in 1715–1727, Elizabeth Sadleir is the most distinguished and knowable of those certain to have been personally engaged in printing books. Sadleir alone of Dublin woman printers during the period was a good printer who built up a publishing business with dozens of titles and was sought out by many publishers to print pamphlets and books, often acknowledged in imprints. Sadleir alone of the women mentioned greatly increased the number of editions printed and published after taking charge. Also, she alone of them co-printed with men major subscription volumes for Chantry, Dugan, and Hyde. To judge from the small number of editions by printshops, the shops' failure to use press figures, their general paucity of type and ornament, and the recurrent typographical idiosyncrasies of many printers, one can conclude that few shops had more than one press or employed more than a single crew. Sadleir had such a shop of modest means (for a time she had none of her own), unlike Grierson, Rhames, and Powell, who probably ran multiple presses at times before 1727. This is not to say that she had none assisting her, for she could not have personally composed and imposed all the sheets she printed around 1720–1721; the products of her press in those years display a range of typographical features, as in the number of leaves of gatherings signed. But she seems to have produced too little in both her early and late years to have employed more than family and a couple of servants. Also, her limited inventory of ornaments provides an ongoing, identifiable signature; for instance, one of her factotums appears in works dated 1719 and 1727, and the tailpieces discussed below of a flower bouquet and of a peacock each appear in over a dozen works by her between 1719 and 1724–1725, and then in Harding editions.

Elizabeth Sadleir

Elizabeth Sadleir was the most accomplished woman printing books in Dublin during the second and third decades of the eighteenth century. She printed both works that she published and works published by other Dublin publishers

(1717–1727). Being a woman printer-publisher was by no means singular: Sadleir should be understood in comparison with other women running presses during the first third of the eighteenth century in Dublin, such as Deborah Powell and Ann Sandy, who inherited the S. Powell and E. Sandys presses from their late husbands, and others who took their own imprint after the deaths of their husbands, such as Elizabeth Ray, Sarah Harding, Sarah Hyde, and Margaret Rhames. However, Sadleir's career is distinctive, first, because she was a good printer, probably working without any journeyman assisting her; besides building up a bookselling business with many titles of her own, she was also sought out by publishers to print substantial books, in whose imprints her work is often acknowledged. What I hope to do in this chapter is survey the range of her printing, showcase several of her best editions, and trace her many collaborations.

Elizabeth Sadleir was descended from Ralph Sadleir, a typefounder trained in England, who brought the family to Dublin before dying in 1703.[4] His typefoundry is the earliest identified in Ireland. Pollard notes that the Sadleir foundry must have supplied Francis Dickson with the old long primer, pica, and double pica fonts listed as cast in Ireland in Dickson's will of November 1713 (Pollard, *Dictionary*, 506). No record exists of Ralph Sadleir selling type or printing anything, but he was succeeded by two who did print: Francis and Sarah Sadleir (sometimes "Sadlier"). Francis may be supposed Ralph's son, and Sarah could have been Ralph's widow or Francis's wife or sister. As was not known to Pollard but revealed by the ESTC, the two were active from as early as 1706, when they shared an imprint, to at least 1711. Sixteen imprints are extant for work printed by Francis or Sarah Sadleir. Imprints dated 1707, 1709, and 1711 refer only to Francis, but most Sadleir imprints between 1706 and 1712 state only their Channel-Row address (now Brunswick North, northwest of central Dublin). From 1712 to 1714, Sarah prints without Francis in central Dublin on School-House-Lane, presumably the shop used by Edward Waters to 1711. Then, from late 1715 to 1723, Elizabeth Sadleir's name appears on imprints printed at School-House-Lane. Sadleir inherited the type cast and cut by her family, and she may have been a letter cutter, for on 17 January 1719 in Dickson's *Dublin Post-Man* and on 20 January 1719 in *Harding's Dublin Impartial News Letter*, she advertised type for sale, with Dickson's advertisement beginning "Mrs. Sadler, alias Fooks" and Harding's "Elizabeth Sadleir, alias Fooks, in School-House Lane." Both ads have nearly the same text; to quote from Harding's: she "will sell good Long Primer, in as good Mettle as ever was mixt in England or Ireland, for a British Shilling per pound, and other sorts of Letter preportionably [*sic*]; Printers . . . are desir'd to come and treat with Mrs. Sadlier in School-House Lane aforesaid, where they may see a Specimen of several sorts of Letters, and may if they please try the Mettle."[5] James W. Phillips discovered that a 1713 deed for a building "in Burr Court on the East Side of School-house-lane" states that the property was "now in possession of the Widow Fowlkes Printer."[6] The only imprint with a name resembling "Fowlkes" in the ESTC is the two-page folio of Benjamin Hoadly's *Remarks on the Present Conspiracy,* with the imprint "Printed, by Margaret Ffooks 1723." It has a framed headpiece of a seated man holding up a heart within a circlet, flanked by buxom angels and candles, 53 × 153 mm (cut in right framing rule), used by Sadleir repeatedly, as in volume 1 of South's *Thirty Six Sermons,* 1720 (where also occur factotums of cast pieces similar to that in this broadside) and in Richard Hooker's *Works* 1721.

While we do not know the exact relation of Francis and Sarah Sadleir, for Francis to have shared imprints with Sarah, it is much more likely that he was the heir of Ralph and son of Sarah than that Francis and Sarah were brother and sister or husband and wife. If so, the facts can be explained in two ways, the second being the better: (1) Elizabeth Sadleir was a daughter of Ralph and Sarah, and sister of Francis, who married a Fowkes but printed under her maiden name "Sadleir," the name of the printing house she commanded; or (2) Elizabeth was the wife of Francis and daughter of a Margaret Fowkes, who with her mother-in-law Sarah set up a press shop in 1712 on School-House-Lane, in property deeded in 1713 to Elizabeth's mother, perhaps to escape financial insecurities related to the Sadleirs, or because her mother provided the capital. Either hypothesis allows Elizabeth to use her mother's name on the 1723 broadside (printed concurrently by Rhames for Dobson). Elizabeth's widowed mother probably worked at the shop: given the tendency for people in the trades to marry one another, she probably brought skills to the business. Printer Francis Dickson, who owned Sadleir type, was married to an Elizabeth Fooks, who succeeded him (Pollard, *Dictionary,* 151). Having a family in the book trade would help explain why Sadleir in the 1719 advertisement is called "alias Fookes." The survey of Sadleir's career below will testify to her assisting printers John Harding and later his widow Sarah. The Catholic-hating, ardent Whig John Whalley, astrologer besides newsman, accused Harding's "mother-in-law" of printing an attack on him in December 1721.[7] (Whalley could have referred to no woman printer in Dublin other than Sadleir.) If Sarah was the daughter of Francis and Elizabeth Sadleir (or even Elizabeth's niece), not only would the Hardings have received the benefit of Sadleir's assistance and the family's woodcut inventory, but it is much more likely that she would have been named "Sarah" after her grandmother.

Sadleir was one of the more productive printers working from 1715 to 1727. To judge from ESTC records for those years, her output ranks eighth among the score of printers then active, with fifty-one editions (including four for "Sadlier"). ESTC misses all she printed in 1724–1725 and fails to gloss two with her initials dated 1726 and [1726?]. I identify about 81 works printed, co-printed, or published by Sadleir, plus about 12 more that she probably printed. Of these 81, 33 occurred in 1715–1719; 10 or more in 1720; 21 or more in 1721–1723, her last years on School-House-Lane; 6 and possibly 12 in 1724 to early 1725 when, without an address, she printed in part at and with John and Sarah Harding; and 10 or 11 on the Blind Key in 1725–1727. If we can identify 81 works, it is safe to assume Sadleir probably printed over 100, for some have disappeared and many extant are unrecognizable among productions with incomplete imprints. Many titles here attributed to Sadleir lack her name in the imprint but can be assigned to her largely because they have cut ornaments that we know she then controlled. Dublin printers progressively employed more cut ornaments after 1710, with Carson, Crooke, Hume, Powell, Rhames, and Waters leading the way. Sadleir was slow to acquire cut ornaments, using them rarely before 1719. Before 1718, only her edition of Pufendorf has a cut ornament, and that borrowed. Also, some publications, especially during the Wood coinage crisis, eschewed cut ornaments to prevent anybody from identifying the printer.

The first works with imprints naming Sadleir as printer were published by Grierson, but beginning in 1717, most of her imprints listed her as seller. She also began to print for a range of publishers, including Chantry, Dugan, Fuller, Hyde, Leathley, Owen, Risk, Smith, Matthew Gunne, and Jeremy Pepyat, and she printed for authors as well. She printed two almanacs over a number of years: Cork watchmaker John Knapp's *Almanack or Diary Astronomical* for 1717–1722, and Peter La Boissiere's *Starry-Interpreter* for at least 1721–1722, and for 1727. She probably printed La Boissiere's 1720 edition (Printed for J. Hyde, R. Gunne, R. Owen, and E. Dobson, 1720), a forty-eight-page octavo with red lettering in its first eight leaves, matching those of 1721 and 1722 that bear Sadleir's imprint. While later she also published Knapp's almanac (on consignment from Knapp), she was first hired by Grierson only to print it, presumably because she had experience with almanacs, for Andrew Cumpsty's *New Almanack for . . . 1714*, with red lettering, was "Printed by and for Sarah Sadleir, and sold by the Booksellers." She employed red lettering in the calendars when some did not, and, if she were working the Sadleir letter foundry, she could have produced the astrological symbols they employed. She may have overinvested in her own publications during the early 1720s, and her finances may have been taxed supporting the Hardings in 1719–1723, when John was repeatedly in jail or in hiding (Pollard, *Dictionary*, 274–275). In any case, Sadleir gave up the School-House-Lane shop by the end of 1723, printing very little in 1724, and those works without an address. She sold stock, including two lengthy works printed in 1721, the first apparently at her own considerable expense (on good paper), Burnet's *Exposition of the Thirty-Nine Articles* and *The Works of . . . Mr. Richard Hooker*, both reissued by Hyde and Dobson in 1724.

But unlike most who lost their printshops, Sadleir did not disappear, in part because she was hired to print for Chantry and his young associates like Dugan, and more especially for Fuller. During 1724, she probably printed at others' shops, particularly Harding's in Moleworth's Court. Certainly she had assisted Harding by giving or loaning cut ornaments to him since 1721 (most ornaments that

Sadleir and Harding shared were first used by Sadleir), and in 1721, John Harding printed a folio broadside, *The Last Farewell of Ebenezor Elliston*, for sale by Sadleir: it is the only instance of Sadleir's publishing anything printed by another or of Harding's printing anything for a publisher. Part of her motivation in leaving School-House-Lane may have been to assist the Hardings, who, after John was released in February 1724 following months in jail (Munter, *History*, 149n2), were printing and publishing two newspapers much related to the effort, spearheaded by Swift, to reject William Wood's half-pence coinage. Given the arrest of both Hardings on 7 November 1724, with John held for at least three weeks, possibly until dying there on 19 April, Sadleir must have been needed to print pamphlets by Swift and others with Harding's imprint.[8] After Harding's removal from the trade, Sadleir printed at her own shop on the Blind Key (or Quay) until mid- or late 1727, with Sarah Harding sharing the premises before she took a shop of her own in Copper-Alley in 1727–1729; however, Sarah moved back to the Blind Key in 1729, when she married Nicholas Hussey. While on the Blind Key, Sadleir and printer William Wilmot (d. 1727) exchanged cut ornaments and probably collaborated in other ways.

From the start of her acknowledged press work (1715), Sadleir printed lengthy books for Dublin publishers and contributed to the printing of others. The first was a challenging edition entrusted to her by George Grierson: Andrew Tooke's translation of Samuel Freiherr von Pufendorf's *Whole Duty of Man, According to the Law of Nature*, 4th ed. ("Re-printed by Elizabeth Sadleir, for George Grierson, 1715").[9] As in the regularity of signatures, the book is strikingly well printed, a demonstration piece proving that Sadleir had mastered printing after working the trade for years. With its single-ruled frame and spare use of black letter, the title page is handsomely laid out; solid rules are used on the title page and in the text, as to enclose the running titles. It has but one cut ornament, a framed headpiece of a flower basket on a draped platform (page 1), borrowed from Thomas Hume.[10] It is remarkable that Sadleir's earliest book is as learned and lengthy as this, undertaken for a burgeoning publisher. Grierson, who, freed in 1709, had a dozen publications in 1714, including several books on navigation and a collection of poems all printed by Powell. He had hired a number of other printers, such as Hume, Rhames, and Sandys, but not yet Sadleir. In 1716, the Pufendorf was reissued with an imprint "by" Sadleir and "for" Grierson with the addition of "Mr. Barbeyack's Annotations" and an index, added in a new series.[11] Grierson was Sadleir's foundational patron, also hiring her in 1716 to print a twenty-two-page pamphlet, the first extant edition of Knapp's *Almanack* (for 1717), and a substantial book: Matthew Henry's *Communicant's Companion*, 252 pages in duodecimo.

In 1717, Sadleir began printing for herself in earnest, publishing eight items for sale "in School-House-Lane near High Street": this was also her "house" as one of two 1722 imprints for Thomas Gordon's *Conspirators* indicates. Seven of these imprints, like some tracts Sadleir would print in 1718–1719, are reports, sermons, or tracts related to Bishop Benjamin Hoadly and the Bangorian controversy. They include Hoadly's *Nature of the Kingdom, Church, of Christ. A Sermon . . . March 31st 1717*, as well as tracts and sermons by Charles Collins, William Law, Andrew Snape (both a sermon and also *A Letter to the Bishop of Bangor*), and Joseph Trapp's *Real Nature of the Church or Kingdom of Christ: A Sermon*. Thomas Hume, who printed more titles from the controversy, also printed the *Report of the Committee of the Lower House of Convocation*, and two editions of Snape's *Letter*. Sadleir began her imprints for items by Law, Snape, and Trapp by naming the London publishers, a more common practice with her than with most printers; she does so on three 1718 imprints as well (none of the fifty-four editions for Hume in 1716–1719 recorded in the ESTC does). Her biggest production was *The Book of Common Prayer and Administration of the Sacraments . . . Together with the Psalter* ("by and for Elizabeth Sadleir, 1717"). Sadleir's edition competed with Rhames's quarto for Eliphal Dobson Sr. in 1712 and octavo for Jeremy Pepyat in 1716.[12] Grierson (or Knapp) again hired Sadleir to print Knapp's almanacs in fall 1717 and 1718 (for 1718 and 1719).

In 1718, Sadleir published four controversial tracts, one involving Whigs versus Tories, and she began to employ cut ornaments, allowing the better identification of her work. Also, she more liberally employed the Sadleir family's inventory of cast flowers and blocks (fleurons) for ornament, sometimes with sufficient individuality to distinguish her work from that of others using the same inventory. In both editions of Charles Owen's *Plain Reasons* (M. Gunne, 1718) and of Thomas Sherlock's *Vindication of the Corporation and Test Acts* (Sadleir, 1718), Sadleir employed an unframed headpiece with a central flower with a rounded bud from which erupts a stylus or tongue, flanked by a vine with sharp, white-tipped leaves like saw-teeth, 16 × 68 mm. She used the headpiece again in works with her imprint by Charles Gildon (1719) and Richard Bradley (1720), and in others without her imprint: George Sewell's *Tragedy of Sir Walter Raleigh* (G. Risk, 1719), Edward Welchman's *Dialogue betwixt a Protestant Minister and a Romish-Priest* (for John Hyde, 1719), Delariviere Manley's *Power of Love* (Patrick Dugan, 1720), and still others in 1723–1724; and she loaned the piece to Harding in 1721 and to Wilmot in 1724.

In 1719, Sadleir printed ten works, probably one or two more, both for herself and others. She now both printed and sold Knapp's *Almanack* for 1720, and, as claimed above, probably La Boissiere's *Starry-Interpreter* for 1720. There was good money in printing almanacs, what with their large print runs, and consumers interested in buying a new almanac every year, so they tended to be printed by major printers: Crook, Powell, Waters, and Sadleir more or less cornered the market. Sadleir also began in 1719 to print the first three of a half dozen plays she would print over the next several years, with two for herself: Charles Johnson's *Masquerade* and Nathaniel Lee's *Rival Queens*, and, to judge from a cut headpiece, she printed George Sewell's *Tragedy of Sir Walter Raleigh* (G. Risk). The *Tragedy* is also linked to Sadleir's press by its frequent use of "VV" for "W," also true of Sadleir's editions of Lee's *Rival Queens* (1718–1719) and John Sturmy's *Love and Duty: or, The Distress'd Bride* (1722). A search of Dublin editions dated from 1515 to 1722 in ECCO finds the "VV" for "W" most frequently in editions by Sadleir and Waters.

Sadleir's work for other publishers in 1719 includes two hundred pages of volume 3 of Clarendon's *History of Rebellion and Civil Wars in England* (John Hyde and Robert Owen, and perhaps Chantry, 1719), the most ambitious publication thus far in eighteenth-century Dublin, surpassing Rhames's folio editions of *The Holy Bible* in 1714. Sadleir joined the best Dublin printers for this work: volume 1 has the ornaments of Hume, Powell, and Rhames; volume 2 those of Waters and Carson; and volume 3, after the preliminary two sheets, those of Sadleir from Cc1/1 to Iii1v/206 (books 10–12), followed on Kkk1/213 (skipping page numbers) by those of Carson. For Sadleir, entering this company was an achievement: the other printers, all with long careers, were members of the guild with larger operations. A little detective work involving the use of ornaments reveals, more specifically, Sadleir's role in many other publications, including some where there is no specific allusion to Sadleir as printer. On C1/1, U1/69, and Tt2/155 she used a framed factotum with white-on-black image of a crown above and lion left and unicorn right of the opening, with black-and-white framing lines inside and out, the inside left rule with a gap 70 percent down, 36 × 35 mm (a variant has an outer frame of white dots). The ornament will appear four times in South's *Thirty Six Sermons* (1720) as well as in Burnet's *Exposition* (1721), and Longinus (Sadleir for Fuller, 1727). On the final page of Sadleir's sheets appears a tailpiece with five long-stemmed flowers above an eight-petal sunflower, below which are wide branches ending in two flowers, 32 × 49 mm, her most frequently used tailpiece (which could be considered her signature ornament). Sadleir used it in her edition of Richard Bradley's *Plague at Marseilles* (Sadleir, 1720), Manley's *Power of Love* (Patrick Dugan, 1720), Francis Quarles's *Argalus and Parthenia* (Sadleir, ca. 1720), and nine times in her volume of South's sermons. She also used it on A2v and 278 of one of several printings for Dugan in 1719, namely an unrecorded edition of Defoe's *Farther Adventures of Robinson Crusoe, Being the Second and Last Part of his Life* (Printed for Patrick Dugan, on Cork Hill, 1719), listed in January 2019 on Biblio.com and eBay by Stephen Whitehead of Tristan Books, Oakland.[13] *Farther Adventures* was also printed in 1719 for J. Gill, J. Hyde, et al., publishers of two editions of *The Life and Strange Surprising Adventures of Robinson Crusoe* (1719, printed by Waters to judge from the cut ornaments). On A3 of *Farther Adventures* is Sadleir's unframed floral headpiece with the stylus erupting from a bud described in Owen and Sherlock 1718. On A2 appears an unframed headpiece, incomplete on the left side, of a crown flanked by a triple-lined vine giving off a rose left and thistle right and flowers at the corners,

33 × 78 mm (illustrated in Woolley's edition of *The Intelligencer*). This ornament is later found more often in Harding's work than Sadleir's, such as in Richard Boulton's *Essay on the Plague* (1721), but Sadleir used it in William Philips's *Hibernia Freed* (Dugan, 1722). Also for Patrick Dugan, Sadleir printed Charles Gildon's *Life and Strange Surprizing Adventures of Mr. D——De F——* (Sadleir for Dugan, 1719), with the unframed floral headpiece in Owen and Sherlock in 1718. It also has two unframed white-on-black headpieces, one with a circular head of a rayflower, like the seed-globe of a dandelion, flanked by flowers with seven petals and further to the side by rose-like flowers, 20 × 81 mm, nicked 69–70 over, and the other with a rose-like flower head with two rings of eight petals and two leaves flared at top and bottom, flanked by a vine with streaked leaves placing flowers at the sides, 19.5–20 × 81 mm, with one corner chipped off. Sadleir used the two side by side as a folio-sized headpiece on page 23 in Hooker 1721, and both appear in Shadwell 1720, encouraging the suspicion that Sadleir contributed to the two-volume octavo.

While Chantry did not advertise the Defoe and Gildon works, he did silently co-publish with Dugan works that Sadleir printed in 1720. One is Clarendon's *History of the Rebellion and Civil Wars in Ireland* (Dugan, 1719–1720).[14] At the end of volume 2 of Shadwell's *Works* is a two-page list of eight books sold by the "Booksellers of Dublin And at Mr. John Chantry's opposite the Watch-House on College-Green," including the Clarendon folios, Richard Cumberland's *De Legibus Naturæ* (Carson for Leathley and Dugan, 1720), and Edward Ward's compilation *Lord Clarendon's History of the Grand Rebellion Compleated* (for Leathley and Dugan, 1720). The list also includes three printed by Sadleir: Clarendon's *History* of Ireland, 2s. 8d., and Manley's *Power of Love* (Dugan, 1720), 2s. 2d., and, among four "in the press," Robert South's "Seventy Two Sermons" in two volumes folio, each entitled *Thirty Six Sermons and Discourses* (Dugan and Leathley, 1720). The final item is the Shadwell itself, which, although it has some ornaments employed by Sadleir, has mostly Carson's ornaments scattered throughout, as well as his characteristic fleuron designs.

Sadleir's name is not on the imprints of the Clarendon, Manley, and the first South volumes, but their ornaments are hers. Clarendon's *History of the Rebellion . . . in Ireland* has three cut ornaments, all owned by Sadleir at this time: on B1/1 a white-on-black headpiece of a rayflower resembling a dandelion seed-globe, with the same nick found in Gildon 1719, and also an unframed ornamental "I" with five-petal flowers flanking at the top and below a cup flower, used by Harding in 1721–1722 and by Sadleir in 1723–1724, as in Thomas Skinner's *Life of General Monk*. Plus, on page 217 is a tailpiece of a peacock facing right, on a platform with a semicircular shield below etched horizontally in which—unlike a variant owned by Hume—is a white "U," 45 × 53 mm (illustrated in Woolley's edition of *The Intelligencer*). Sadleir used this peacock on seventeen pages from A2 to page 487 of the first volume of South's sermons and on C2v/xxx and six other pages in Burnet's *Exposition* (1721). Manley's *Power of Love*, a 240-page octavo, contains two cut ornaments already described, the signature tailpiece of a flower bouquet in the Clarendon folio and the unframed floral headpiece in Sherlock 1718.

Sadleir in the first volume of South's *Thirty Six Sermons* and Hume in the second used headpieces and factotums at the start of sermons (most are cut) and cut tailpieces at the end. The two volumes share some unifying typographical features, too, such as the signing of both leaves of the rectos. Lacking many cut ornaments of her own, Sadleir repeatedly used whatever she could get her hands on. For instance, on pages 28, 488, and on eighteen pages in between, she used an unframed factotum of a jeweled crown (with nine dashes in the band) held over the opening by two putti, whose wing feathers are at the outer edges. The right putto has a small mouth and his wing has six feathers, the third pointed down but not touching the fourth. The factotum had been used by Hume, who replaced it with another that he used in his South volume—the appearance of factotums with the same design helps unify the two volumes. Sadleir's signature tailpiece with a flower bouquet noted in Manley and the Clarendon folio appears in South on twelve pages from π2v to page 462. The black-on-white factotum with lion and unicorn in the Clarendon folio recurs here on four pages between 140 and 449. As for headpieces, Sadleir relies on a framed cut of a flower basket on a draped platform within an arched scroll frame, outside of which dogs leap outward toward birds at upper corners; it breaks into three pieces during the run, beginning on page 290, and is fully cracked on page 316, then replaced after page 392, with a headpiece used in the prelims, which depicted a seated man faced left holding a flaming heart within a circlet flanked by buxom angels, described above as appearing in Hoadly's *Remarks on the Present Conspiracy* (1723); it also appears in Sadleir's Hooker. Aside from the third sheet with the subscribers' list, Sadleir apparently printed the whole volume. While a couple of factotums make rare appearances early on (probably borrowed), those noted recur throughout the book as do certain fleuron designs; furthermore, there are no typographical disruptions.[15]

Sadleir may have contributed to several other volumes co-published by Chantry in 1720, such as gatherings L–Tt of Richard Cumberland's *De Legibus Naturæ* (Carson for Leathley and Dugan)—these gatherings are signed $1–2 unlike others signed $1 and do not share signing and running-title errors in sections with Carson's ornaments. She printed Matthew Concanen's *Match at Foot-Ball* ("for the Author"), an octavo paginated 42 [2], with her signature flower-bouquet tailpiece and the unframed headpiece of three castles plus a factotum borrowed from Hume, who had aided her in the past and co-printed the Clarendon and South folios with her that year. Although Harding also used the headpiece, he could never have borrowed an ornament from the Whig Hume, since Harding took government money to attack Hume (Munter, *History*, 149). Sadleir printed six

1720 editions for herself, including Richard Bradley's *Plague at Marseilles*, a twenty-four-page octavo with the floral headpiece in Sherlock 1718, Sadleir's signature flower-bouquet tailpiece, and the unframed factotum with two putti holding up a crown used in South. Another is Quarles *Argalus and Parthenia* (n.d., ca. 1720), a 156-page octavo noteworthy for having a woodcut frontispiece with a letterpress imprint. It also has a tailpiece of a flower basket with a ten-petal sunflower flanked at top corners by a flower resembling a tulip, 26 × 27 mm (illustrated in Woolley's edition of *The Intelligencer*). This cutting of a common design is distinguished by its having three rows of weaving at the base of the basket with shading ///// below \\\\\ below ////. Sadleir had used this in Welchman's *Dialogue* (1719); later it appears in works with Harding's imprint and others printed by Harding or Sadleir.

Eight items are extant from Sadleir's presswork in 1721 (four in only one copy). Sadleir published all herself except for a homiletic full-sheet broadside for Fuller: Ambrose Rigge's *Brief and Serious Warning to Such as Are Concerned in Commerce*. This is the first of ten or more works for Fuller, who had been headmaster of Dublin's Quaker school before setting up as a publisher in 1720 and adding a press in late 1727, after Wilmot's death and about the time Sadleir closed her shop, acquiring at least some cut ornaments from Wilmot. Sadleir's publications include a sixty-eight-page *Catalogue of Books* sold at Captain Edwards's on College Green, the Knapp and La Boissiere almanacs, *The Fatal Extravagance*, published as Joseph Mitchell's but credited to Aaron Hill, a sermon by Benjamin Hoadly, and a broadside elegy printed by Harding. The Burnet and Hooker, which demonstrated her mastery of printing, have understandably survived in over a dozen copies. Wrongly listed in the ESTC under the Church of England as author, is Burnet's *Exposition*.[16] It is faithfully signed on the first four leaves of gatherings, except for leaf F4, and only one leaf is missigned; there are only a couple of pagination errors, one usually corrected. This is a large octavo by Dublin standards, measuring about 200 × 120 mm when trimmed, with usually forty-five lines per page. It has relatively few variants from the London folios of 1705 and 1720, and was printed with admirable perfection of recto and verso page settings on two good white-paper stocks. There are only three cut ornaments, all found in the South volume: the factotum of crown flanked by lion and unicorn (A2, C3/1), the peacock tailpiece (on seven pages between pages xxx and 345), and the flower-bouquet tailpiece first used in Clarendon and Defoe 1719 (on pages 20, 137, 170). Not listed in Chantry's booklist, this seems to have been Sadleir's publication; however, Dugan and Chantry are not among the subscribers, though Dobson and Hyde are.

Some co-printing occurred in Sadleir's other big production in 1721: *The Works Of the Learned and Judicious Divine, Mr. Richard Hooker, in Eight Books of Ecclesiastical Polity*, which is probably a shared printing, as implied by the disruptions to paginations and signatures.[17] The six-page addition on Hooker's life by

John Strype is well integrated after leaf H1; however, disruptions occur at Rr1/135 where the pagination falls back eight places and the signing skips Qq and shifts from each leaf to just the first of a gathering. Other problems involve the integration of gatherings Nnn–4I (pp. 211–[290]), signed on each leaf, particularly at the end where, after blank 4I2v, 4K–4L are skipped in the signing and the pagination leaps ahead eight places. The cut ornaments joined with the signing practice indicate that Sadleir printed the gatherings signed on every leaf, A–Pp and Nnn–4I, and another printer or printers contributed Rr–Mmm and 4M–5T. The appendix (^{2}A–R) has one ornament, on its last page: a large tailpiece of two putti hanging from a scroll frame with a flaming urn above between them, 82 × 83 mm; it belonged to Powell, appearing on *P2/59 in part 2 of Peter Heylyn's *Cyprianus Anglicus: Or, The History of the Life and Death of the Most Reverend and Renowned Prelate William, . . . Lord Archbishop of Canterbury* (Dublin: James Carson, for John Hyde, and Robert Owen, 1719). It is also near the beginning and end of Powell's section of Clarendon's *History of the Rebellion* in 1719 (volume 1, xii and 164). Also, on pages 1, 59, and 96 of his section of Clarendon appears Powell's woodcut of the white-on-black framed factotum with crown above flanked by lion left and unicorn right; in this version, unlike Sadleir's, there are white dots around the outer frame (it is nicked 5–100 percent over on the bottom). Since Powell's factotum is the sole ornament present in the two sections of Hooker signed only on $1 (on Rr2/137) and again three times (from 4M1/297 to 5M2/391), Powell must have been Sadleir's co-printer for the Hooker volume. Sadleir probably printed less than half the pages (236 of 502), yet was given the imprint, perhaps for unacknowledged printing in other Chantry editions or for casting off copy and designing the edition. Despite the disruptions noted, the two printers produced a fairly uniform volume, employing the same typographical style in the running titles (and the pagination is continuous before and after Sadleir's second section).

Although the imprint reads "Printed by Elizabeth Sadleir in School-House-Lane, near High-Street," John Chantry was probably a co-publisher of Hooker's *Works*. This would explain a number of facts. For one thing, Sadleir's sharing the printing with Powell, who despite printing more pages, is not mentioned in the imprint. This fits Chantry's practice of contracting multiple printers for long folios and octavos. Just as Chantry editions might have another publisher in the imprint, some had the printer's name there, as in Keating's *General History of Ireland*: "Printed for James Carson, and sold by the Booksellers, 1723"—to which Rhames contributed twelve preliminary leaves and Sadleir the concluding seven with a genealogical appendix. Chantry's involvement in the volume explains how Sadleir came up with the money to pay for the paper. Chantry advertised the Hooker in his list of books "Sold opposite the Watch House" on the final page of Richard Allestree's *Works of the Learned and Pious Author of the Whole Duty of Man* (P. Dugan, 1723), as "Mr. Hooker's Ecclesiastical Polity, I Eight books Fol."

This folio of seven texts by Allestree, the first three printed by Carson and the last four by William Helme, was advertised as "Just published" in Carson's *Dublin Intelligencer* of 22 January 1723, which contained a long booklist for Chantry, pricing the Hooker 16s. Chantry included Hooker in many lists, such as those in *Harding's Weekly Impartial News Letter* of 18 February and 20 July 1723, and in Thomas Skinner's *Life of General Monk* (Patrick Dugan, [1724]). The involvement of Chantry, a former London publisher, also helps account for the presence of the engraved frontispiece portrait and title page originally cut for Richard Hooker's *Lawes of Ecclesiastical Politie* (A. Crooke, 1666; Wing H2637). The illustrated title page has different publishers and dates added and removed over time; in Sadleir's edition, unlike the London editions of *Works* in 1705 and 1720, it reads "R. Scott, J. Basset, J. Wright, & R. Chiswell, 1682." Sadleir's share in the project brought her copies, some of which, upon leaving School-House-Lane, she sold to Hyde and Eliphal Dobson Jr., whose 1724 reissue lacks the two-page subscription list and adds a four-page index based on the 1723 London edition. Hyde and Dobson in 1724 also bought and reissued Sadleir's edition of Burnet's *Exposition.*

In 1717–1722, Sadleir had printed mostly for her own sale, but that came to an end in 1723, her last year on School-House-Lane—more of her 1723 imprints give no address than give the address. Even though she was, for a time, without a venue, she kept producing. The 1722 imprints include pamphlets involving political and religious controversy. She published two editions of Thomas Gordon's *The Conspirators; or the Case of Catiline*, both forty-four-page octavos, one "by Elizabeth Sadleir; and Sold at her House in School-House-Lane," and the other "for Elizabeth Sadleir, in School-House-Lane" (respectively ESTC T165357 and N67632). Although the latter (only at McMaster University) has Sadleir's peacock on its title page, the imprint reads "for" Sadleir, which is not the way she often styled herself and could have been a reprint by Harding, who used her ornaments beginning in 1720 and was the more likely to use full capitals for a proper name in an imprint. Sadleir may have helped Harding print his only book-length publication, William Duncan's *History of the Lives and Reigns of the Kings of Scotland* ("by John Harding, for the Author, 1722"), for it is a long work with ornaments previously used by Sadleir, including the peacock tailpiece. It was reissued in London with the title *The History of the Kings of Scotland* (for the Author, and Sold by T. Saunders, at the Bell in Little Britain, 1723). ESTC T79534 and N17890 give different authors for the two issues, neither the likely author. Sadleir also printed for Fuller a pamphlet on a dispute in September 1722: *An Exact Narrative of the Most Material Passages in the Late Dispute in Skinner's-Alley: Between Oswald Edwards, Baptist, John Stoddart, Quaker*, transcribed by Andrew Harvey, a thirty-two-page octavo not in the ESTC (copy at the University of California at Santa Barbara). Of the broadsides she printed, one is extant: *A Letter from the Lord Bishop of London* by John Robinson. She again printed Knapp's

Almanack with red lettering as usual in its first eight leaves.[18] Although no copy is extant of La Boissiere's *Starry-Interpreter* for 1723–1726, it seems likely that there was an edition for 1723 that Sadleir printed (La Boissiere remained active, publishing on an eclipse in 1724), and the next extant are those for 1727 and 1728, printed fall 1726 and 1727 by Sadleir and Sarah Harding, respectively. Sadleir also printed at least two plays in 1722. Though the imprint only names Dugan, Sadleir probably printed William Philips, *Hibernia Freed: A Tragedy*, which has three cut ornaments used by Sadleir as well as by Harding, two of which were first used by Sadleir: the peacock tailpiece in Clarendon, 1719–1720, and the headpiece of a crown in Defoe, 1719. Sadleir had published repeatedly for Dugan, Harding never had, and the typography, such as headpiece designs of cast pieces, resembles that of Sturmy's *Love and Duty* (Sadleir, 1722). Both plays have blank final pages, and it is noteworthy that Sadleir never printed a booklist, though they were becoming more common.

In 1723, Sadleir's name appears in only four imprints of seven she printed, scant production considering none is longer than eighty-eight pages and two are broadsides. Besides a full-sheet broadside elegy on George Whitehead, she printed the half-sheet with the imprint of Margaret Ffooks, discussed above, Hoadly's *Remarks on the Present Conspiracy*. For Fuller she printed Joseph Gill's *Answer to a Pamphlet Sign'd by Oswald Edwards an Anabaptist*, and a collection of treaties: *Particulars of an Indian Treaty at Conestogoe*, octavos eighty-seven and forty-eight pages long. For Dominick Roach, she printed two short poetical works in octavo: Matthew Prior's *Turtle and the Sparrow* (Sadleir for Dominick Roach), twenty pages, and, with only Roach's name in the imprint, Jean Bonnefons's *Pancharis, Queen of Love: Or; The Art of Kissing*, twenty-seven pages. The Bonnefons has Sadleir's unframed floral headpiece used repeatedly since Sherlock in 1718 and the ornamental "I" in Clarendon, 1719–1720. Probably Sadleir printed the second Dublin edition of *Mendico-Hymen Seu, Tuphlo-perogamia. The Beggars Match* (with Tho. Hume, for Jer. and Sil. Pepyat, 1723), a sixteen-page octavo translation of William Thompson's Latin original. Both she and Harding had access to the tailpiece on the title page of a flower basket (illustrated in Woolley's edition of *The Intelligencer*), used by Sadleir in Welchman, 1719 and Quarles, 1720, and by Harding in Richard Boulton's *Essay on the Plague* (by John Harding, and sold by the Booksellers, 1721). However, Sadleir's better relations with the trade, especially publishers aligned with the Whig administration, makes her the more likely printer than the ardent Tory Harding, who printed almost exclusively for himself and authors, and whose works do not contain ornaments borrowed from diverse printers.

In late 1723 or 1724, just before and after leaving School-House-Lane (presumably working at the Hardings or with a colleague like Carson or Watts), Sadleir printed several short items related to the Wood's half-pence controversy without her imprint, twice for Chantry and Dugan. She printed the text of Thomas

Skinner's *Life of General Monk* (for Dugan, [1724]), an octavo paginated [*xii*], xlvi [2], 272 [4], wherein Carson's ornaments are in the preliminary 12 pages, Powell's in the editor's preface, and then Sadleir's in the final 276 pages. Her ornaments include the headpiece of a rayflower like a dandelion seed-globe in Gildon, 1719, and the ornamental "I" and the peacock tailpiece used by her as early as Clarendon, 1719–1720. There are two booklists for Chantry alone, after the preface and the main text. The other job for Chantry and partners was the preliminary half-sheet of William Pittis's *Dr. Radcliffe's Life, and Letters* (for Pat. Dugan and W. Smith, [1724]), a 144-page octavo ending with a booklist for Chantry; its contents page begins with that white-on-black headpiece of a rose flanked by round flowers (with corner chipped off) used by Sadleir since Gildon, 1719. (The main text was printed either by Helme, who used the cut ornaments present in 1722–1723, or by Watts, who used them beginning in 1724, when he began his turn as Chantry's main printer.) Sadleir may have contributed to a later Chantry publication: the two-volume folio *Dictionaire Oeconomique: or, The Family Dictionary* (by J. Watts, and sold opposite the Watch-House and by F. Davys, 1727), by Noel Chomel and revised by Richard Bradley. The sole ornament in volume 2, on its final page before Chantry's booklist, is a fountain tailpiece used by Wilmot, Sadleir's neighbor on the Blind Key, in 1726–1727, and then in 1727–1729 by Sarah Harding (illustrated in Woolley's edition of *The Intelligencer*). Sadleir shared ornaments with both, and neither of the two is known to have contributed to a Chantry production.

Fuller also repeatedly hired Sadleir in 1724 and in the years following. She printed for him John Sowter's *Way to be Wise and Wealthy* ("Printed for and sold by Sam. Fuller, 1724"), whose title page has Sadleir's signature tailpiece of flower bouquet over wide branches.[19] Also present (on page 31) is her unframed floral headpiece with stylus from a round bud, first used in Owen and in Sherlock 1718. Sadleir printed three or more times for Fuller in 1726–1727: Robert Barclay's *Anarchy of the Ranters* ("by Eliz. Sadleir on the Blind-Key, for Sam. Fuller, 1726"), Longinus's *Treatise on the Sublime . . . Translated . . . By Mr. Welsted* ("Printed for Sam. Fuller . . . by Eliz. Sadleir, and Sold by the Booksellers, 1727"), with a few of Sadleir's ornaments, such as the white-on-black factotum of crown flanked by lion and unicorn first used in Clarendon, 1719, but also with ornaments borrowed from Watts.[20] Also, she printed Nathaniel Crouch's *Surprizing Miracles Of Nature and Art,* by "R. B." [for Crouch's pseudonym "Robert Burton"] ("Printed for Sam. Fuller, . . . by Eliz. Sadleir, 1727").[21] *Surprizing Miracles* has many woodcuts integrated into the text (others occupy full pages). Its only cut ornament is a tailpiece of three flowers growing on a mound (page 177), later used repeatedly by Fuller. A likely fourth title, given Fuller's reliance on Sadleir, is *A Brief Apology for the People in Derision Call'd Quakers,* by W[illiam]. Chandler, et al. ("Printed for Sam. Fuller, 1727"), an octavo of eighty pages faithfully signed $1–4, lacking ornamentation. Sadleir printed enough Quaker literature for Fuller that she need be considered the possible printer of other Quaker titles from 1715 until Fuller began printing (with Knapp's *Almanack* for 1728), such as *A Sermon Preach'd by William Henderson* (Dublin: n.s., 1718), the only likely alternative in 1718 to Sadleir for such a work was Samuel Fairbrother.

On the Blind Key in 1725–1727, Sadleir prints works with her own imprint, but most were less than a sheet in length, often broadsides, requiring little investment. Among the broadsides was *A Poem To the whole People of Ireland Relating to M. B. Drapier* ("Printed on the Blind-Key, by Elizabeth Sadleir, 1726"), by "A. R. Hosier," in fact praising John Harding and calling for assistance to his widow. After 1727, Sadleir may have helped Sarah, particularly with two almanacs that she printed, La Boissiere's for 1728 and Isaac Butler's 1729 *Advice from the Stars*, printed along with William Wilmot, published by another widow, Mary Whalley. Sadleir may well have worked as a journeyman for various printers, such as Fuller, whose earliest editions have almost inexplicable correctness.

The career of Elizabeth Sadleir in many ways epitomizes, or at least illustrates, the vagaries and instabilities of the publishing business in Dublin in the first part of the eighteenth century. She sometimes worked alone, sometimes partnered, sometimes worked for others; sometimes worked from her own home, but sometimes free-floated; sometimes acquired cut ornaments, sometimes borrowed them, sometimes loaned them. She may be said to typify the Dublin printer, and as such, she gives us a glimpse of the fragility of the Dublin book trade in the early years of the century. Where she stands apart from her contemporaries, however, is in her resilience: despite frequent changes in business practice, and frequent changes of venue, despite the unpredictable shifts of market demand, she just kept on printing, and she achieved a consistently high level of quality.

NOTES

For assistance in the examination of copies, the author thanks An Bui, Andrew Carpenter, Sophie Evans, Mitch Fraas, Patricia C. O'Donnell, Eugene Roche, Rick Stapleton, and Stephen Whitehead.

1. Robert Munter, *A Dictionary of the Print Trade in Ireland, 1550–1775* (New York: Fordham University Press, 1988). Munter previously had written *The History of the Irish Newspaper, 1685–1760* (Cambridge: Cambridge University Press, 1967), with a helpful bibliography (henceforth Munter, *Dictionary*, and Munter, *History*). M[ary]. Pollard, *A Dictionary of Members of the Dublin Book Trade, 1550–1800, Based on the Records of the Guild of St Luke the Evangelist Dublin* (London: Bibliographical Society, 2000) (henceforth Pollard, *Dictionary*), which, unless corrected in the text, serves as the source for names, addresses, and dates of printers mentioned in this chapter.

2. On the Hardings, in addition to M. Pollard, see James Woolley, "Sarah Harding as Swift's Printer," in *Waking Naboth's Vinyard*, ed. Christopher Fox and Brenda Tooley (Notre Dame: University of Notre Dame Press, 1995), 164–177, with a checklist of Sarah's publications; Wooley, "Poor John Harding and Mad Tom: 'Harding's Resurrection' (1724)," in *That Woman! Studies in Irish Bibliography: A Festschrift for Mary "Paul" Pollard*, ed. Charles Benson and Siobhán Fitzpatrick (Dublin: Lilliput Press, for the Library Association of Ireland, 2005), 101–122; and Jonathan Swift and Thomas Sheridan, *The*

Intelligencer, ed. Woolley (Oxford: Clarendon Press, 1992), whose textual apparatus includes on pages 290–291 illustrations of nine cut ornaments, four of which were used by Sadleir before being passed on to the Hardings (a: tailpiece of a flower basket with ten-petal sunflower; c: peacock tailpiece; f: fountain tailpiece; and i: unframed headpiece of crown flanked by thistle on left and rose on right). These will be referred to here as "illustrated in Woolley's edition of *The Intelligencer*." In a forthcoming article in *Swift Studies*, I examine Sadleir's relations with the Hardings, attending to the ownership and shared use of cut ornaments.

3. On all the women discussed in the paragraph, see Pollard, *Dictionary*. Margaret Rhames ran her press for a dozen years after Aaron's death in 1734 and then remotely longer; she was the first Irish woman to print a Latin text, George Ruggle, *Ignoramus, Comœm dia coram Rege Jacobo* (Dublin: s.n., 1736), ESTC T139817, which I identify as her work from cut ornaments, such as the tailpiece of a lion over crossed clubs on page 29 of Wm. Melmoth's *The Great Importance of a Religious Life* (Dublin: M. Rhames, for S. Hyde et al., 1735).

4. As Munter, in *History*, reports, W. G. Strickland called attention in 1922 to a decree at the Irish Public Record Office (later destroyed) involving the estate of "Ralph Sadler, late of Dublin, Letter Founder, who died intestate" (44). Pollard, in *Dictionary*, discovered that Ralph was buried 4 May 1703 and had been apprenticed "in London to Robert Andrews, typefounder and Joseph Moxon's successor," from 1680 until freed in 1687 (506).

5. James W. Phillips, in *Printing and Bookselling in Dublin, 1670–1800: A Bibliographical Enquiry*, with foreword by M. Pollard (Dublin: Irish Academic Press, 1998), originally a PhD dissertation (University of Dublin, 1952), quotes the ad in Harding's paper (197). Munter quotes it from Dickson's.

6. Phillips, *Printing and Bookselling*, 198 and 198n3, citing the Registry of Deeds (Liber 11, 406).

7. Pollard, *Dictionary*, 275, referring to *Whalley's News-Letter* of 27 December 1721, where "Whalley anathematized Harding's mother-in-law as pr[inter] of a pseudo-Whalley prophecy." The work in question would have parodied such works as Whalley's *A Prophecy for the Year 1716*. The edition is not extant, but it may exist in a reprint: *Doctor John Whaley's Strange and Wonderful Prophecy . . . 1721* (Dublin printed, and Glasgow reprinted, 1721), ESTC T165598, an eight-page octavo.

8. Irvin Ehrenpreis, *Swift: The Man, His Works, and the Age*, vol. 3: *Dean Swift* (Cambridge: Harvard University Press, 1983), 277. Ehrenpreis noted that Harding died in jail in April 1725 (308), though Pollard thought he was released 28 November (*Dictionary*, 275), and Munter claims he was released in February 1724 (*Dictionary*, 127). In the letter to Harding dated 14 December prefacing *A Letter to the Right Honourable the Lord Viscount Molesworth* (J. Harding, n.d. [31 December 1724, Ehrenpreis, *Swift*, 286]), Swift writes of "your own and your wife's confinement" as if ongoing (iv, vii).

9. ESTC T180303, octodecimo, gathered in 12s and 6s, regularly signed $1–5 in 12s and $1–3 (–B3) in 6s; pages 24, 302.

10. The headpiece appears on A2 over the preface of Sir Richard Blackmore's *Essays upon Several Subjects* (Grierson, 1716), and again within this nonce collection in *An Essay upon the Laws of Nature* (Grierson, 1716), with Hume's monogram ornament on the title.

11. A^{12} B^6 C^{12} D^1 (+1 blank?) and paginated 303–340, [22].

12. Not in ESTC, a copy at University of Pennsylvania collates 8vo: π^1 A^4 B–Ii⁸ Kk⁴; pages [518].

13. The Defoe volume is octavo in 8s, 278 pages.

14. In 8vo: A^2 B–E⁸ F–N⁴ O–S⁸ T⁴ U^2 (–1, perhaps a final blank); pages [4], 217, [1].

15. The volume collates: π^2 A^2 B–6L² [faithfully signed $1–2]; pages [viii], 500.

16. This has the Articles on only pages xix–xxx in a volume collating octavo: A–Nn⁸ Oo²; pages [vi], xxx, 525, [20]. ESTC gives [18] missing blank Nn8 before the subscription list.

17. A–G^2 H^2 (H1 + 3 signed *, **, *) I–Pp^2 Rr–4I^2 4M–5T^2; [appendix:]^{2}A–R^2 [$1–2 in A–Pp Nnn–4I (–I2, K2) signed; "K1v" missigned "K2"; $1 only in Rr–Mmm 4M–5T and^{2}A–R]; pages [*viii*], 1–22 [*6*], 23–144 [=Pp2v] 135 [=Rr1]–289 [=4I2] [1], 297 [=4M1]–420; 1–68.

18. Octavo : A^8 B–E^4.

19. Sowter's volume is duodecimo: A^2 B–D^6 [$1–3 signed]; pages [2], 38.

20. The Barclay volume is octavo: A–G^8 H^4 [1/2 $signed]; pages viii, 111 [1]. Longinus is octavo: A–F^8 G^2 H–I^8 [1/2 $signed]; pages 135 [1],

21. Octodecimo: A–M$^{12/6}$ N^4 [$1–5 signed in 12s and $1–2 in 6s]; pages 223 [1, booklist for Fuller].

PART II

Neglected Authors

CHAPTER 4

Ihara Saikaku and the Cash Nexus in Edo-Era Osaka

Susan Spencer

Gabe Hornstein was an admirer of Japanese culture, and he frequently visited Japan (see figure 4.1). I found out that only after his passing, so he and I never had a chance to talk about it, but I'm quite certain that he would have shared my affection for the irreverent satirist Ihara Saikaku (1642–1693), the greatest professional prose writer of Japan's brief but brilliant Genroku era (1688–1704). I don't know if Gabe ever actually encountered Saikaku's work, but one thing I do know is that he had a special place in his heart for irreverent satirists. Since Saikaku's literary production was inextricably linked with the early development of commercial book publication in urban Japan, his work seems appropriate as a subject for a chapter in this volume, an East Asian analog to the development of relationships between publishing houses and authors so ably traced by J. T. Scanlan in chapter 1.

Furthermore, Saikaku's critical reputation is currently on the rise: in 2015, Katarzyna Sonnenberg's well-received monograph comparing technique in Daniel Defoe's *Moll Flanders* with Saikaku's 1686 masterwork *Kōshoku Ichidai Onna* (a title usually translated as *The Life of an Amorous Woman*) with Daniel Defoe's *Moll Flanders* introduced eighteenth-century scholars to one of Saikaku's longer works, and in 2017, David Gundry published his *Parody, Irony, and Ideology in the Fiction of Ihara Saikaku*, the first book-length study in English of Saikaku's style and recurring themes.[1]

Saikaku achieved modest success in his native city of Osaka for his theatrical compositions for both kabuki and puppet performers, and he was well respected among a wider audience throughout Japan as a prolific, if not always consistent, composer and critic of *haikai no renga* poetry. His unmistakably original genius, however, lay in the prose style that he virtually invented, or at least

Figure 4.1. The portrait frontispiece to *Saikaku Okimiyage* (Saikaku's parting gift), posthumously published in the winter of 1693 under the direction of Saikaku's disciple, Hōjō Dansui (1663–1711). The book was a Festschrift volume, featuring memorial verses from friends and colleagues as well as several hitherto-unpublished stories, allegedly all of them written by Saikaku himself. The prominent appearance of the author's name as an integral part of the book's title, at a time when it was common for works of fiction to appear anonymously, is evidence of his celebrity, and of the compiler's recognition that one last book by the master would be a best seller. The nature of Dansui's contribution to this volume is uncertain; he claimed merely to have assembled manuscripts that had been left behind, but the uneven nature of the style and the late appearance of the work may indicate that the text had been left unfinished or had at least been reworked, if not actually rewritten. The publisher's afterword seems to admit as much, stating, "We may rejoice in the fact that Books Three and Four [of *Saikaku Okimiyage*'s five-volume set] are in his own hand, and that we are able to publish them without revision." Courtesy of Waseda University Library.

perfected: the *chōnin-zōshi*, an anecdotal and usually satirical book of loosely connected stories and vignettes that exposed—yet at the same time covertly admired—the aspirational efforts of a brash new class of citizen emerging in the Genroku period: the profit-oriented *chōnin*, or townsmen.[2] The nature of his subject matter reflects an awareness of his *chōnin* audience and their desire, like their Western counterparts, to read about people with lives and problems resembling their own. As his writing moved away from self-consciously literary parody of earlier works with individual protagonists and more into anecdotal observations of the complex world of commercial exchange, the titles of his works began to reflect a business philosophy: 1688's series of vignettes about how fortunes can be made or lost, *Nippon Eitaigura* (translated as *The Eternal Storehouse of Japan*, or *The Japanese Family Storehouse*), or 1692's *Seken Munesan'yō* (*This Scheming World*, or *Reckonings that Carry Men through the World*), which recounts the strategies of the merchant class when outstanding debts came due at the turn of the new year, are squarely focused on concerns that would be wholly alien to the traditional agrarian society of the preceding century.

As it happens, Saikaku came along at a time of cultural change that shifted power away from the samurai and encouraged his satirical spirit, both by providing him with targets and by creating an audience for his work. We might pin down the turning point to May 1615, the fall of Osaka Castle, the final obstacle in the Tokugawa shoguns' march toward the domination of all Japan. While the fall of the castle confirmed Tokugawa success, it at the same time required immediate restoration, since Osaka's situation as a military and commercial powerhouse made the region a defense priority. The reconstruction of the city center was one of the most ambitious architectural projects in an age of intense building, since Osaka was still strategically located "at a vital military crossroads within the economic heartland."[3] In the midst of this haste to rebuild, the daimyō Hosokawa Tadatoshi made the crucial suggestion to hire wage laborers rather than extracting forced laborers from the traditional feudal corvée, since "the latter, after all, had to engage in rice production, the ultimate source of wealth in early-modern Japan."[4]

The decision to follow the daimyō's advice was the beginning of the end for the traditional economy. Samurai-class stipends in the Tokugawa period were paid out in *koku*—that is, in measures of rice. One *koku* was roughly the amount of rice needed to feed a man for a year. Rice was still thought of as the standard currency among the upper classes, though gold and silver coinage had increasingly found its way into everyday exchanges, especially among townsmen and commoners. Originally minted for the purpose of foreign trade, since seagoing foreigners were less than enthusiastic about taking payment in rice, the standard gold *koban* issued by the shogunate was supposedly worth the equivalent of one *koku*. However, over the course of the seventeenth century, the cost of rice dropped dramatically relative to the value of gold. As a result, the samurai, who relied on stipends paid in *koku*, lost purchasing power when compared with members of the *chōnin* class who earned their incomes in gold and silver. By the time of the Genroku period, the samurai aristocrats frequently found themselves less wealthy than, and sometimes even indebted to, their social inferiors. To engage in trade had long been considered the lowest of professions, valued far below the peasant farmer, or the artisan who actually created something tangible. Then suddenly, beginning in the final decades of the seventeenth century, the most disdained members of the population found themselves at the forefront of prosperity and often on the cutting edge of fashion.

While the *chōnin* merchant class can't exactly be described in terms of a nascent middle class, since social mobility wasn't a factor and trade was still limited to a guild system, political stability created an opportunity to stay put in the cities and to amass considerable fortunes without fear of a sudden outbreak of warfare or the forced conscription required to carry it out. Increased wealth, leisure, and security enabled the *chōnin* for the first time to acquire stylish possessions and enjoy the same amusements as their samurai compatriots, albeit within limits.[5] Enclosed licensed quarters—a walled-in combination of red-light district, theater district, and restaurant row, mandated by laws governing public morality—sprang up in major metropolises. When local booksellers were added to the mix, drawn by the easy flow of currency as pleasure-goers moved from one venue to another in search of amusement, a geographically restricted region within the city was created in which the literate and spending classes could mingle to consume or produce—or, in Saikaku's case, produce works describing consumption. The situation has been likened to London's coffeehouse culture that arose, coincidentally, at about the same time.[6] Edo's Yoshiwara licensed quarter (still a popular shopping destination today) was founded in 1617, Osaka's Shinmachi in 1620, and Kyōto's Shimabara in 1641:

> It was the mercenary basis of value in the gay quarters that especially suited them for enjoyment by the affluent townsman. In this world, where gold and silver ruled, the well-to-do merchant could assert himself and escape from the frustrations of outside society. For money, as Saikaku once pointed out, was the merchant's only pedigree. In the gay quarters class distinctions counted for little next to wealth, and the *samurai* who depended on his modest rice stipend, with its constantly fluctuating money value, or on loans of gold obtained from usurious merchants cut a poor figure next to the opulent and free-spending townsman. In the words of an eighteenth-century verse,

> *In the Yoshiwara*
> *The way of the warrior* [Bushidō]
> *Cannot conquer.* (Morris, 10)

Not only did the wealthy *chōnin* provide "much of the material support and creative spirit that resulted in the remarkable artistic revival of the Genroku period," but "this was the first time in Japanese history that the cultural leaders of the country belonged to a ruled, rather than the ruling, class, and it may well have been the very fact that the ascendant townsmen were frustrated in so many other ways by the rigid patterns of the Tokugawa regime that led them to direct their energies to the creation and support of a new culture" (Morris, 11).

One might argue that an even more significant change in the economy, and the role of hard currency within it, occurred somewhat further down the economic ladder when the restoration of the ruins of Osaka and its insatiable requirements for day laborers resulted in a massive distribution of coin wages. By the time Saikaku was writing, Osaka had nearly four hundred thousand inhabitants, larger than any European city other than London or Paris.[7] According to James McClain, by the time the Shinmachi licensed quarter was established in 1620, as many as two hundred thousand of those in residence could have been supported by the financial outlay for the castle project alone, causing a population explosion of workers, some permanent and others itinerant unskilled laborers who were paid on a daily basis as opposed to the traditional annual salary system ("Space," 52). Michael Hoffman, in an overview of "Japan's First Pop Culture," pins the ushering in of bourgeois and working-class entertainments to the year 1636, when low-denomination bronze coins known as *zeni* were first minted to pay workers for hire: "This was pocket money, small change. Pop culture is impossible without it."[8]

Although Hoffman relies on the reader to make the connection, we can easily infer that the availability of "pocket money" that made pop culture possible also resulted in the spreading popularity of affordable printed books and periodicals "to read and sell" as well as increased audiences for theatrical entertainments within the licensed quarters (see figure 4.2). Along with a larger audience came an important shift in printing technology. Until the 1590s, even classical works of literature were painstakingly written out and illustrated by hand, and printed texts had been solely the province of Buddhist monasteries. As the idea of publishing for profit caught on and booksellers began to set up shop over the course of the seventeenth century in the three great cities of Kyōto, Osaka, and Edo, copying by hand became prohibitively expensive. Initial experiments with movable type, of the sort popular in the West, were rejected by consumers as aesthetically unpleasing. The solution was to concentrate on the efficient production of high-quality woodblock prints of the type that even today we associate with Japanese aesthetics. Since a book's impact on the enjoyment of the reader depended on a combination of content, calligraphy, and illustration—a book without pictures would fail to sell to discriminating customers—the ability to integrate illustrations and ligatured text smoothly by designing the entire page as a single object made the woodblock an ideal medium for Japanese customers. Getting in on the ground floor of a new trend opened up a potential market where, as yet, competition was still quite limited.

Figure 4.2. The *yomiuri* newssheet, one of the first clay tile-block handbills ever printed in the Edo era, announcing the fall of Osaka Castle in May 1615. "Yomiuri" literally means "to read and sell," reflecting the ephemeral nature of this new style of affordable reading material. The necessity of hiring day laborers to rebuild the castle after the successful Tokugawa siege led directly to the invention of small-denomination coins in order to pay the workers, creating an economy where cash could easily change hands, and a ready market for mass-produced publications for recreational reading. Courtesy of the National Archives of Japan.

As woodblock print technology improved, so did literacy—the concentration of population in the cities fostered schools for children of all levels of society, and the ability to read was becoming a job requirement for any youngster who aspired to a job in a shop as opposed to the back-breaking labor associated with castle-building. Demand for materials to amuse this new class of leisure readers led to cheap, illustrated *kana-zōshi*, which Hoffman considers the predecessors to today's popular *manga* graphic novels. They were certainly the predecessors to the *chōnin-zōshi* that would become Saikaku's claim to fame.

Osaka especially emerged as the Tokugawas' commercial capital and an ideal market for aspiring authors and booksellers; as a lifelong resident, Saikaku found himself in the ideal position to observe his mercantile neighbors' propensities. Commonly referred to as "the nation's kitchen" due to its immense productivity and dizzying array of goods for sale, Japan's second-largest city was an innovative, bustling place where the rags-to-riches dream was an inextricable part of the culture.[9] Far enough from the political center in Edo and the traditional cultural center in Kyōto to operate without overly close scrutiny, Osaka fostered an independent entrepreneurial spirit that extended to all of its inhabitants regardless of profession; people had to figure out how to take best advantage of an economic system that hadn't yet established its new ground rules. The business of trade itself required a complete revision in the wake of the shoguns' controls on international commerce. Whereas China's market was global, embracing commodities from other Asian countries and from the West, Japan's market was severely restricted, thanks to the Tokugawa Act of Seclusion. This curb on international trade encouraged a national turning inward.[10] Although goods flowed freely back and forth, the portals through which they came were strictly limited, giving native craftsmen the advantage over their foreign competitors of direct access to local merchants. Through one-upmanship, they engaged in cut-throat competition to get advantage over one another as well.

The literary landscape, too, was fundamentally changed at the same time, since most books that made it past the gatekeepers—especially Western books, which might contain subversive references to illicit Christianity and other disruptive philosophies—were technical in nature, such as medical or scientific texts. Thus isolated from the literary movements that were circulating throughout the rest of East Asia and Europe, Japan's aspiring authors fell back on their own initiative to develop inherited genres into distinctly Japanese forms of literature in a marketplace that continually looked to its own resources for inspiration.

One such source was the eight-hundred-year-old tradition of *renga*, or linked verse, which had merged with *haikai*, vulgar or "earthy" verse, to create an elaborate framework that connected a sequence of 5-7-5 syllable verses through the mandatory use of seasonal words, "pillow" epithets, and "cut words" that juxtapose complementary or contrasting images. Complicated restrictions determined which images could be used in which combinations, how frequently the same or similar ideas could occur, and many additional requirements—sufficient guidelines to provide the young Saikaku at the beginning of his literary career with a clearly laid-out path to his future career as a respected critic of *haikai no renga* poetry.

Fascinated by the construction of *haikai* from childhood, Saikaku composed his first single-handed sequence of linked *haikai* in 1675, at the age of thirty-three, upon the unexpected death of his beloved twenty-four-year-old wife. The usual manner was to work in pairs or groups, where one participant would throw out an opening *hokku* verse to start the chain. As he writes in the preface to his *Haikai dokugin ichinichi senku* (*Haikai Solo Single-Day Thousand Verses*), however, as he sat near the deathbed, Saikaku's grief found outlet in poetic isolation: "I heard a nightingale's tear-thick call, and a hokku came. Alone, between dawn and sunset today, I made a thousand haikai for you, while a single calligrapher recorded them."[11] Christopher Drake, who published an extensive commentary and translation of the first hundred verses in two separate numbers of the *Harvard Journal of Asiatic Studies*, notes that Saikaku's account of this traumatic event corroborates a biographical account in Itō Baiu's *Kenmon dansō* miscellany of 1738, which describes his conversion from businessman to poet, literally overnight:

> Around the time of the Jōkyō and Genroku periods there was a *chōnin* named Hirayama Togo in the port of Osaka in Settsu province. He had wealth, but his wife died young. . . . He left the family business to his head assistant, and, without actually becoming a monk, he lived a life as free as that of a Buddhist mendicant, spending half of every year roaming wherever he pleased. He was possessed by *haikai*.[12]

Thousand-verse *haikai* sequences were nothing new, but if we can believe the poet's own account, this one was completed with astonishing speed. Most such sequences took three or four days to complete. In this case, Saikaku claims to have spun out the verses between dawn and sunset, which Drake has calculated to have been thirteen and a half hours on the 27 April date recorded in Saikaku's preface (the third day of the fourth lunar month of 1675), thus establishing a rate of one 5-7-5 linked verse every fifty seconds. The Haikai Requiem was printed privately, presumably for distribution to family members and attendees at his wife's memorial service. Only one copy is extant today, and even that one was thought lost until it surfaced at a bookseller's in 1947 ("Collision of Traditions," 6). But this initial feat became the genesis of what the poet would later refer to as the *yakazu*, or "myriad arrows," a newly invented performance art that would launch him as a public figure. These marathon verse-spinning sessions were a celebration of physical stamina combined with mental agility that turned out to be a real crowd-pleaser. He decided to take the show on the road, composing *hai-*

kai verses on the fly before an audience, while a group of scribes and judges jotted down the results and critiqued them.

It was at this point in his life that Hirayama Togo took on the pen name by which he would be known for posterity: "Saikaku," a pun on ingenuity, wit, or cleverness, a remarkably prescient choice that suits the scheming merchants of the author's prose tales as neatly as it fits the Master of Twenty Thousand Verses, an epithet by which he was known even years after he had largely abandoned poetic composition in favor of recording the vicissitudes of the "floating world" and *chōnin* life.

The "Twenty Thousand Verses" reference is to an incident where Saikaku's own success became the harbinger of doom for his ability to attract large audiences who were eager to embrace his novelty value as a verbal arrow slinger. He had established a reputation for continually topping himself: in 1677, he composed another single-day challenge, this time for public consumption, a solo speed sequence of sixteen hundred *haikai* in hundred-linked units that was published and sold as *Ōku kazu* ("many verses"). On that occasion, if one allows two hours for eating and other bio-breaks (sleeping would not be an option), the average time he took to compose a verse was approximately fifty-two seconds. His agility started a fad, with adept versifiers across Japan gunning for the master. He set a new single-day record of four thousand *haikai* in 1680. When his rival Ōyodo Michikaze managed to break it, he pulled off the incredible feat of a staged *yakazu* marathon in front of Osaka's Sumiyoshi shrine four years later, where he is said to have composed a mind-boggling 23,500 linked *haiku* verses in a twenty-four-hour period, an average rate of sixteen verses per minute—a record that, unsurprisingly, no one has ever attempted to touch. The Sumiyoshi triumph "proved Saikaku's complete dominance in the genre of *yakazu haikai* and effectively ended the 'Arrow Counting' fad."[13] Whether the results of that session were any good as poetry is open to question: despite the number of observers, the verses came so quickly they could do no more than tally the number.[14]

How could he top that? Although he never entirely gave up on *haikai* poetry and later edited five published volumes of other poets' work, Saikaku's own poems appeared only occasionally in collections. The subject matter of his poems in the 1680s became increasingly colloquial, with elaborate language and classical allusions giving way to familiar imagery taken from contemporary realities: "In one example from *Haikai sanga no tsu* (1682), Saikaku's verse expresses the harsh realities of life for merchants, who must settle all of their accounts by the end of the year or risk insolvency: *Ōmisoka sadame naki yo no sadame kana* ('New Year's Eve; a certainty in an uncertain world')" (Schalow, 417).

The subject of this poem seems prescient when one looks ahead to 1692, when Saikaku would publish an entire *chōnin-zōshi* collection of stories centered around the very same topic of settling debts at the turn of the new year. One might argue that the seeds of his fame were always present in his personality in one form or another. Haruo Shirane views Saikaku's prolific career as a discernable continuum rather than a series of stops and starts, with his distinctive form of composition spilling over into his first book-length narrative:

> He was able to write these sequences so quickly because a particular topic could be developed over a number of links, thus creating a kind of panoramic prose poem, in 5-7-5 and 7-7 alternative verse. It was a short step from this kind of speed *haikai* to vernacular *haikai* fiction, to which Saikaku turned next, in his *Life of a Sensuous Man* [which is] characterized by its elliptical quality, use of colloquial language, rapid descriptive movement, and interest in everyday commoner life.[15]

Perhaps Donald H. Shively's description of Saikaku's style best captures the entire body of his work:

> Excelling in unexpected twists and turns within his sentences, Saikaku substituted word associations or pivots on a pun for logical progression. He could not resist the ironic turnabout—things were not as they seemed—and he often changed direction before he could complete a serious thought. But this irreverent style effectively reflected the brash confidence of the new Osaka *chōnin*. (762)

Pivot words and word associations were an integral component of *haikai no renga*—and also of Saikaku's earliest prose. If we didn't know that *Kōshoku Ichidai Otoko* (*The Life of a Sensuous/Amorous Man*) was Saikaku's first break from his identity as a poet, we might very well be able to extrapolate that from the style. The book is considered virtually impossible to translate into English (or, for that matter, any other language), though a few half-hearted attempts have been made to do so because of its importance as a breakthrough text and the irresistible fact that parts of it are very, very funny (see figure 4.3).[16] Set initially among the brothels and licensed quarters of the Kamigata region near Saikaku's native Osaka, the story expands to cover most of Japan as it follows the sexual adventures of a peripatetic protagonist, Yonosuke, from his first experiments with a maidservant as a precocious seven-year-old to his eventual burnout as a gray-haired roué.[17] Having experienced every pleasure his country has to offer, Yonosuke fills a boat with like-minded cronies and a motley collection of good books, good food, stimulants, pornography, and sex toys, and embarks on a voyage in search of a mythical island inhabited entirely by women. Presumably, he's still searching.

As a literary oddity, *Kōshoku Ichidai Otoko* was never expected to be more than a novelty, and both Saikaku and his locally based publisher were entirely taken by surprise when the book, with Saikaku's own illustrations, was so warmly

Figure 4.3. A humorous illustration from the second volume of the first edition of *Kōshoku Ichidai Otoko*, printed in Osaka in eight slender volumes in 1682. Saikaku illustrated this edition himself. Frequent full-page pictures were expected in books designed for leisure reading, and books without them sold poorly. Howard Hibbett, in his classic study, *The Floating World in Japanese Fiction* (1959), remarked that a book published in the market for which Saikaku was writing "without illustrations, in some profusion, would seem as bare as a modern travel talk on the night the projector failed." Courtesy of Waseda University Library.

received by the reading public that it went into a third printing (Schalow, 417). When an established Osaka publishing house, the Akitaya, purchased the publishing rights and produced second and third editions for a crowd of purchasers that showed no signs of diminishing, Saikaku realized that he was onto something (Schalow, 148). When a pirated deluxe edition appeared in Edo in 1684, with all-new illustrations by Hishikawa Moronobu (see figures 4.4–4.6), the preeminent *ukiyo-e* artist of his day, he knew for certain that his fortune was made.[18] From that point he became a cosmopolitan author, moving between Japan's three great cities to do business and to pick up local color. The final book for which he designed his own illustrations, *Saikaku Shokoku Hanashi* (*Saikaku's Tales from Various Provinces*), published in 1685, recounts a number of anecdotes and stories that he picked up along the way. This first inclusion of his name as part of the title, especially in a society where the tradition for *kana-zoshi* had been to publish entirely anonymously, indicates his growing popularity even then.[19]

The 1685–1686 period was one of frenetic activity for Saikaku as a writer as he experimented with genres and themes to produce several books in quick succession, including *Unfilial Children* and two of his greatest masterpieces, *Kōshoku Gonin Onna* (*The Five Women Who Loved Love*) and *Kōshoku Ichidai Onna* (*The Life of an Amorous Woman*). *Five Women*'s focus on fleeting physical pleasure and abandonment of the Confucian duty-based ideology actively espoused by the Tokugawa administration, as well as its unusual focus on cash-wielding *chōnin* protagonists rather than the aristocratic characters who had hitherto dominated romantic fiction, is emphasized by William Theodore de Bary in his analysis of *Kōshoku Gonin Onna*; he remarks that "In Love We Trust might well have been the inscription on their coins, which were just coming into general circulation at that time."[20]

The most frequently anthologized of the five accounts in *Kōshoku Gonin Onna* was a ripped-from-the-headlines story of Osan, a young *chōnin* wife who, after a lifetime of model filial and marital obedience, abandoned family and reputation to follow her heart—or at least her own inclinations—by eloping with her husband's apprentice. Basing his story loosely on an actual scandal that occurred three years earlier in Kyōto, Saikaku capitalized on his contemporaries' love for gossip and the current popularity of a ballad circulating about the incident to recount Osan's descent from her status as an envied local belle to her public execution for adultery.[21]

The story first introduces its heroine at the age of twelve, the undisputed winner of an informal "beauty contest" in which idle townsmen including Osan's future husband assess the appearance of fashionable girls and women passing by on their way to view a particularly fine display of blooming wisteria. Saikaku caters to his audience, with its fascination for the latest trends; one wonders how much of Osan's much-vaunted attraction is based on her natural gifts, and how

Figure 4.4. The same illustration as figure 4.3 (but reversed) in the 1684 "pirated" edition printed in Edo, with illustrations by Hishikawa Moronobu. Moronobu has preserved the basic feel of Saikaku's original, but has created a simpler, more sophisticated composition: the architectural elements are more compact and the extraneous bystander has been replaced by a comical dog. Courtesy of Waseda University Library.

Figure 4.5. Another illustration by Saikaku from volume 2 of the 1682 Osaka
edition of *Kōshoku Ichidai Otoko*. Courtesy of Waseda University Library.

much is the result of her position on the crest of fashion—a quality that a careful reader of sufficient means might aspire to emulate. Much attention is devoted
to her elaborate coiffure, "held in place by five immaculate combs and a gold hair-
ribbon," and the "black, ink-slab pattern" on her chemise, the "peacock design
[that] could be perceived in the iridescent satin of her outer garment," her "lace
made from Chinese thread," and a "folded sash of twelve colors." Saikaku even
describes the clogs on her feet and the "stylish rainhat" carried on her behalf by

Figure 4.6. Moronobu's version of the same scene as figure 4.5. Courtesy of Waseda University Library.

one of her litter-bearers. As for the person of Osan herself, we get only the following description: "Her face was perfectly beautiful, and I shall not tire you with needless details" (*Five Women*, 126).[22]

Osan is an oddly calculating heroine whom we see, some years later, consciously making the decision to fall in love with Moémon, evidently out of sheer boredom. Before their flight, she prudently transfers five hundred gold *koban* from her husband's strongbox to her baggage. When the guilty couple stop to rest for tea at a modest wayside inn, they are surprised to encounter a display of trendy goods for sale, that, "reminiscent of Kyoto and therefore a tonic to the weary travelers, serves to lift their spirits." Overcome with nostalgia, they hand their host a *koban*, "But he scowled unappreciatively, like a cat that is shown an umbrella. 'Please pay me for the tea,' he demanded, and they were amused to think that less than fifteen miles from the capital there should be a village which had not yet heard of gold pieces" (146).[23]

While their assumption may be true, and secondary sources that mention this scene tend to take the statement at face value, the innkeeper may be cannier than he appears. One can imagine the awkward nature of a piece of currency as valuable as a gold *koban* in a remote location in a cash-poor economy, and the difficulty, perhaps outright impossibility, of changing it for lesser denominations that one might actually use. The gesture seems like offering a hundred-dollar bill at a curbside lemonade stand; it isn't that the recipient doesn't recognize it as legal tender and an object of value, but rather its utility is in question given the context. Unless one assumes that the entire *koban* was meant as a gift, or an astronomically high tip—which seems unlikely, in light of the fugitives' uncertain financial circumstances and their previous record of utter selfishness—the innkeeper might in fact have a very valid point, in which case the joke is turned on its head, and it is Osan and Moémon who are displaying naïveté. Saikaku, with his acute awareness of the value of money and his extensive travel experience, could not have been unaware of the difference between the cost of living in the country versus the city. The city-country dichotomy crops up in a number of Saikaku's writings, and not always entirely to the city's advantage: in the midst of the glowing account of "The Perennially Prosperous Shops of Edo" that concludes his 1692 collection *Seken Munesan'yō*, the omniscient narrator exclaims bathetically, "In the dry-goods shops of Temma the cotton goods remind one of the snow on Yoshino at dawn."[24]

Seken Munesan'yō (usually translated as *This Scheming World*, or *Reckonings That Carry Men through the World*) is perhaps the best example of the pivoting linked sketches to which Shirane refers in his examination of Saikaku's debt to his own previous career as a *haikai* artist. Although the brief anecdotes are unrelated on the surface in tone and content, with step-by-step instructional passages on how to one-up one's business rivals sharing the volume with elaborate illustrative stories that shift from poignancy to farce, for the most part all sections of the book are connected by the traditional New Year's Eve practice of paying off one's debts for the year and starting anew with a balanced account book. The characters are drawn from the super-rich to the poorest of the poor, and the stories range from a slapstick tale of a pair of gentlemen who disguise themselves as creditors and exchange houses every New Year, mingling with the rest of the debt collectors and loudly expressing surprise at the homeowner's absence, to a Decameron-style nested tale in which a handful of temple-goers confess the series of unfortunate events that led them to seek temporary sanctuary at the priest's annual ceremonial retelling of the story of Hirotaro. Not one of them is there for spiritual reasons, needless to say, and perhaps the most pathetic character is the fellow who admits he had come just for the purpose of stealing the others' shoes while they were at worship, but stayed for the sermon when he discovered that not enough people had shown up to make it worth his while. Or perhaps he is the least pathetic character, since he is the only one who isn't crushed by debt: he admits freely that his purpose in the shoe-stealing expedition was "to get drink money" (*This Scheming World*, 124).

One particularly elaborate story in *Seken Munesan'yō* incorporates a salutary lesson regarding the newly invented field of speculation and futures markets, and the importance of obtaining an Ise lobster for one's New Year's decorations.

> Now this particular year of which I write it happened that everyone in the city, vowing that his New Year decorations would be incomplete without an Ise lobster, determined to buy one even if it cost a thousand *kan*. . . . At a fishmonger's shop called the Era, located in the middle of Bingo Street of Osaka, there happened to be just one Ise lobster left. The bidding for it began at one and a half *momme* and eight. Even at that exorbitant price, however, the fishmonger refused to part with it, claiming that its like could not be found anywhere else. (31–32)

Unauthorized to offer such a large sum, the servant of a wealthy *chōnin* returns home and is quickly sent back with a carte blanche, but by that time the last lobster has been purchased and the household is left lobsterless. Though the master initially rejoices over saving money and rails against price gougers, his wife and son point out that it "just wouldn't do at all" to go without: "They could bear up under the thought of losing face publicly, but when the daughter's husband would make his first New Year's call on his wife's parents and would see no Ise lobster crowning the New Year's decorations—that scene was simply unthinkable" (32). The hapless father commissions an artisan "to fashion a lobster of crimson silk" for two and a half *momme*. "Look," he pointed out, "it will be useful as a toy for the baby even after the season is over. That's how a wise man does things. . . . And, what's more, it can be reused over and over again" (38).

The family remains skeptical, until eventually the ninety-two-year-old grandmother emerges from her quarters in the house's annex to see what all the fuss is about. After scolding her son for lack of forethought and delivering a long lecture on seasonal price fluctuations, she reveals that she has been keeping not one, but two Ise lobsters in a tank for the past couple of weeks, having purchased them before the rush: "Perfect specimens: even their feelers have never been joined together. And the price I paid for them? Just four *mon* apiece, you see" (34). As the family applauds, she explains that it has been her yearly practice to barter with a tradesman for five bundles of burdock (three, if the burdock is thick), and that it was her plan "to give him a lobster which cost me four *mon* in return for the burdock which ought to be worth around one *momme*" (34). Remarking upon their good luck that the tradesman hasn't shown up yet "with his usual year-end present," the grandmother drives a bargain to "let you have one of my lobsters, but remember that business is business even between mother and son. If you really want the lobster, then you'll have to send somebody to me with five bundles of burdock. I don't care who gets the lobster, as long as I get my burdock in exchange for it. And anyway, you can't celebrate the New Year without it" (34). Her hapless son has no choice but to capitulate, proving a point that Saikaku makes in several of his books that it is the canny first generation that manages to build up a fortune through clever dealings, the second generation that attempts to maintain the family's wealth through careful, if not always successful, attempts to cut corners and recycle when possible, while the third generation, here represented by the anxiety of the young *chōnin* son and his socially ambitious newlywed daughter, dissipates it through extravagant spending and conspicuous consumption.

"Why not try wearing a girdle of two pieces of silver wound around the waist?," Saikaku asks sarcastically elsewhere in the book, as he describes an expensive sash of "imported satin, twelve feet long and two feet wide" that is the current New Year's holiday fashion. "The hair comb may cost two *ryo* of gold, but wouldn't a woman balancing three *koku* of rice on top of her head attract more attention?" (20). At the same time, excessive corner-cutting can get in the way of eventual success. In the story "Blinds from Brushholders," Saikaku describes a boy who, during the four years he attended calligraphy school, saved every one of his discarded bamboo brush-holders. "Then in the spring that he became thirteen years old he made blinds of them and sold as many as three of them, at one and a half *momme* apiece, thus earning four and a half *momme* of silver." When his proud father boasts of this accomplishment to the monk in charge of the class, he is met with indifference. "During my life I have taught hundreds of boys," says the monk, "and not one of the smart ones like your son grew up to be a rich man" (117). The story continues, "On the other hand, the boy who had devoted himself wholeheartedly to calligraphy, though seemingly slow-witted, grew up to be broad-minded by nature" (119). Through his ability to concentrate and keep his eye on the end goal without distraction, the child finds success in adulthood as a famous inventor.

This is not to suggest that Saikaku is always consistent. Often, penny-pinching ways and small economies are described as good business. One of his most vivid characters is "the foremost lodger in the land," a self-made Kyōto millionaire named Fuji-ichi from *Nippon Eitaigura* (*The Japanese Family Store-*

house), whose thrifty ways are extreme. Fuji-ichi, who lives in a rented house some four yards wide, takes care not to walk rapidly along the main roads, lest he wear out his shoes too quickly; if he stumbles, he takes advantage of the opportunity to pick up stones for firelighters and store them in his sleeve. Or part of his sleeve, anyway: "It was he who first started the wearing of detachable cuffs," Saikaku reports, "a device which was both fashionable and economical."[25] He never wears more than a single layer of outer garments, stuffed with padding as necessary in cold weather, and only once in his life did he depart from his usual practice of wearing only plain dark blue silk, when he chose a dye of "a persistently undisguisable seaweed brown, but this was a youthful error of judgement, and he was to regret it for the next twenty years" (36).[26] Fuji-ichi, Saikaku's narrator insists unconvincingly, "was not a miser by nature. It was merely his ambition to serve as a model for others in the management of everyday affairs" (36).

The idea of serving as a model connects the various episodes in the chapter. We discover that Fuji-ichi gained his considerable fortune primarily from observing others: "As the clerks from the money-exchanges came by he noted down the market-ratio of copper and gold; he enquired about the current quotations of the rice-brokers; he sought information from druggists' and haberdashers' assistants on the state of the market at Nagasaki," the only port open to foreign exchange after the Tokugawas' 1635 Act of Seclusion. That he's questioning the *assistants* rather than the druggists and haberdashers themselves seems to suggest a whiff of industrial espionage.

At the end of the story, some local young men visit Fuji-ichi at his tiny house to request advice about how to follow in his footsteps and become millionaires themselves. As he answers their questions, they are distracted by the sound of a mortar grinding in the kitchen, a tantalizing promise of hospitality to come, and it becomes increasingly difficult to concentrate on his words. They speculate on what sort of delicacies their wealthy host might be about to serve them, an inheritance from their parents' generation's ideas about how noblesse oblige operates in a feudal economy. But Fuji-ichi is a modern *chōnin*, unbound by Bushidō codes of conduct. "As a general rule," he concludes, "give the closest attention to even the smallest details. Well now, you have kindly talked with me from early evening, and it is high time that refreshments were served. But not to provide refreshments is one way of becoming a millionaire. The noise of the mortar which you heard when you first arrived was the pounding of starch for the covers of the account-book" (39).

I would like to finish this chapter with a more comprehensive analysis of a single work, examining a few key episodes in Saikaku's *Kōshoku Ichidai Onna*, or *The Life of an Amorous Woman* (1686), which, with its less accessible 1682 counterpart *The Life of an Amorous Man*, is one of only two extended narratives in his prolific career that follows a single character for the length of an entire book. *Kōshoku Ichidai Onna* has been translated into English multiple times. Elements of its story and characterization have been analyzed in several academic articles and books, and significant excerpts are included in the influential *Longman Anthology of World Literature*.

The book follows the career of a self-proclaimed nymphomaniac as she moves up and down (mostly down) the social ladder, pursuing various means of making a living after a sexual indiscretion leads to exile from her prestigious position at an aristocratic court. *Kōshoku Ichidai Onna* differs significantly from the *chōnin-zōshi* genre with which the author is closely associated in its sweeping breadth of characters of various social ranks and locations, both urban and rural, though the picaresque structure of the narrative exhibits similarities with the punchy anecdotes that would become the hallmark of Saikaku's later style. The book also foreshadows its *chōnin-zōshi* successors in the manner in which prices, contracts, and means of exchange are explicitly described, as well as dodges that enable the canny trader to get *out* of the terms of a contract, similar to some of the clever means undertaken by the *Scheming World* characters outwitting their creditors on New Year's Eve.

The narrator, who never reveals her name, is an interesting parallel for the adaptive nature of Saikaku himself, who worked his way through multiple careers in his lifetime. On a larger scale, her story reflects how the ready transfer of cash exploded old distinctions of class and religious hierarchies, enabling individuals to represent themselves in their life stories and in their art in new ways that would have been utterly impossible in a society that up to this point had been caught in a feudal cultural stasis. Saikaku's decision to dispense with the wry, moralizing narrator who dominates *The Life of an Amorous Man* and instead cast the Amorous Woman's story as a first-person account provides today's reader with a window into how the introduction of currency as a primary means of exchange irrevocably changed the culture of Edo-era Japan ("account" seems an especially appropriate commercial term: both the author and his creation describe their lives as a series of debits and credits).

The frame narrative is established at the outset. We meet the protagonist as a very old lady in possession of an isolated hermitage, "The Cell of Love," where she lives well by receiving gifts in return for relating her history to handsome, fashionable young men. The hermitage is described initially in terms of a typical Buddhist retreat, with a "rough sloping roof" built into a rocky cave and a simple gate of bamboo grass (*Amorous Woman*, 122).[27] But as the description draws in closer, the detail gets more sensual: the "nun" is dressed in blue silk "splashed with a dappled crest of double chrysanthemums" and an "elegant" sash "knotted in front" (122).[28] Although her magnificent clothes are outdated, she is doing sufficiently well to burn a currently fashionable brand of incense and entertain her visitors with her virtuosity on some very expensive musical instruments (see figure 4.7). To receive the benefit of her experience and advice, however, a transaction must take place. The visiting gentlemen are aware that, for all the trappings of a social encounter, they are expected to bring their own saké and ply her with a generous portion before she stops prevaricating and gets down to spilling any details about her checkered biography.

The initial episode begins with the Amorous Woman—at that time, a mere Amorous Girl at the age of twelve—in service to a "most excellent lady" at the imperial court, where her competitive spirit is aroused by witnessing the amorous encounters of her patroness's fellow ladies in waiting (124).[29] She is already besieged on all sides by eager young men because of her distinct air of fashion; she is, at this stage of her life, the ultimate consumer and, at the same time, an influential creator of material culture: "I was no longer content to leave the styling of my hair to others," she proclaims, "but instead was guided by my own fastidious taste. . . . During this period I devoted myself assiduously to the practice of Court Dyeing and I may say that this art owes its later popularity to my efforts at the time" (124).[30] Confronted by such a multitude of love letters that "I was hard put to find a place to store them," when it comes to choosing a lover, she decides to bestow her favors on a type of man "that most women would regard askance," a low-ranking samurai, whom she accepts not because of his looks or airs, but because he writes the best love letters she's ever encountered (124, 125).[31] Their relationship, and her whimsical sentimentality, leads to their ruin: her lover's low rank and subsequent lack of backing lead to his execution and her expulsion. She will not make such a romantic mistake again.

Although she is prostrated with grief for a mourning period of several days, the enterprising heroine bounces back quickly, as she will throughout the rest of her life. After her parents try and fail to negotiate an advantageous marriage on her behalf (she is again thrown out of the house when she seduces her handsome would-be father-in-law), the heroine takes matters into her own capable hands and hires an employment agency to secure a contract as a rich man's official concubine. It's an expensive undertaking. For interviews, an applicant seeking such a position needs twenty silver pieces for daily rental of "a kimono of white silk or figured black satin, a wide sash of Nishjin brocade in the Chinese style, a petticoat of scarlet silk crepe, a cloak of the fashion worn at court; the fee even includes a quilt to spread inside the palanquin" she will ride in to travel to meet potential employers or their proxies, plus one silver coin as payment to her agent (133, see figure 4.8).[32] A hopeful candidate can purchase a substitute parent, "some townsman [chōnin] who at least has a small house to his name" if she hasn't got well-placed parents of her own: the parent-of-record will receive a regular gratuity from the girl's employer and, if she eventually provides her new master with an heir, the parents will also get part of her rice allowance (133). Her employment agency and chōnin "family" however, are paid in cash, suggesting the growing power of the merchants, as opposed to the members of the samurai class, who still dealt in rice.[33]

Figure 4.7. In the first illustration of *Kōshoku Ichidai Onna* (1686), Saikaku's elderly Amorous Woman welcomes male visitors to her remarkably plush "hermitage," where she entertains them by strumming love songs on the koto and recounting salacious details from her younger days, while the young men provide the saké and leave their shoes at the door. Courtesy of Waseda University Library.

Once she is posted to a position as concubine to a feudal lord, the Amorous Woman throws herself into her new job with such enthusiasm she overworks her employer and his life is endangered through sheer exhaustion, at which point his retainers arrange for her release. Without sufficient funds to hire another agent, she embarks on a new identity as temporary secret wife to a supposedly celibate Buddhist monk, a lucrative three-year arrangement for twenty-five pounds of silver—no rice—to be paid at the conclusion of her term of service. After some months, however, she wearies of the isolation and enforced secrecy. When she is threatened with violence by a luckless predecessor who resents the

Figure 4.8. In this illustration from volume 2 of *Kōshoku Ichidai Onna*, we see the expensive trappings and elaborate entourage necessary for a woman of fashion—or any woman who wishes to create an illusion of fashionable glamor. Courtesy of Waseda University Library.

loss of her job, the resourceful heroine falsely claims a pregnancy, whereupon the horrified priest hands over the proceeds of the collection box, along with bereaved parents' offerings of their infants' clothing, and suggests she disappear until after the birth. She takes the gifts and reneges on her contract. After all, she remarks pragmatically, "He could enter no action against me" (153).

Eventually, after trying numerous careers, the Amorous Woman finds steady employment as a first-class courtesan in an upscale brothel. As time goes by, she is demoted to second, then third class. Eventually she's kicked out to find a living as a streetwalker, which gets harder and harder as her age advances. At one point she exults in her ability to earn ten coppers from a naïve country youth on a dark night, convincing him they are "the same age" (199). He is sixteen. She is fifty-eight. On one particularly disheartening morning after spending an unlucrative night dodging street lights, the Amorous Woman resolves that this will be her "last effort in the Floating World at plying the lustful trade," whereupon she is

overcome by religious fervor as soon as she discovers that every one of the five
hundred statues of the Buddha in the shrine at Kyōto's Daiun Temple reminds her
of a former client (204). Inspired, she hangs out the shingle for her hermitage.

   Kōshoku Ichidai Onna is modeled upon a number of different popular genres,
as if Saikaku had been experimenting with other works that were doing well on
the market to determine what might sell. Dennis C. Washburn, in his study, *The
Dilemma of the Modern in Japanese Fiction,* describes it as a "parody of a confession" and suggests that "Saikaku played off numerous sources to create this parody, the subgenre of *kana-zōshi* known as *bikunimono* being one of the most
important."[34] *Bikuni* were Buddhist nuns who renounced the world, often taking to the road on outreach expeditions to teach passersby and elicit funds for
their home monasteries. Though the practice of these excursions was dying out
at the time Saikaku was writing due to Tokugawa disapproval of uncontrolled
women traveling freely through the countryside and performing impromptu sermons without official oversight, the term had recently been given new life by a
class of prostitutes who dressed as nuns while trolling for clients in the pleasure
districts—a development that must have been familiar to most of his contemporary readers, at least in the cities. Even the term "floating world," used by
the Amorous Woman in its colloquial sense to refer to the licensed quarters, was
adapted from a traditional Buddhist term for the ephemerality of life and its
pleasures.

   The *bikunimono* "were for the most part didactic tales in which a woman
unexpectedly loses the man she loves or depends on and then seeks religious solace from a nun. This nun then tells of her own past and attachments, leading
the woman to understand the true nature of the evanescence of the world and
to take vows" (Washburn, 67). The Amorous Woman seems to suggest a similar
aim when she concludes her narrative and we are returned to the frame tale. She
makes the ostensibly modest assertion that "for you young gentlemen, who came
here especially to visit me, I have tried to provide diversion befitting this spring
night." Yet she does manage to slip in a typical Buddhist warning about the
ephemeral nature of the floating world: "Today, having received unwonted visitors at this rude wooden door, and being bemused with saké, I have been led to
trouble you needlessly with a story far too long for this short life of ours" (208).

   On the other hand, the humble confessional stance might all just be window
dressing. Howard Hibbett suggests that the earnest manner in which the Amorous Woman chooses to deliver her story should be, and probably was, taken with
a hearty grain of salt by Saikaku's readers:

> The ending neatly frames the confession—and reminds us, adroitly, that
> pseudo-confession, pretending to open one's heart to another, was one of the
> wiles of the accomplished courtesan. She had used the same trick on other
> gentleman-guests to win their sympathy—and we remember that, when she

IHARA SAIKAKU AND THE CASH NEXUS 95

greeted the two young men who came to her hermitage, she smiled and exclaimed "Guests even now!" (69)[35]

"Guests even now!" might well be taken as a fitting epitaph for Saikaku himself. By inventing, virtually on his own, a genre designed by its nature to be ephemeral and disposable—if not exactly "to read and to sell," at most to serve as idle amusement in the midst of the more serious pursuit of business for people of a specific class, in a specific place and time—Saikaku changed the course of Japanese fiction forever, and carved out a permanent place for himself in Japan's literary history.

Gabe Hornstein's goal was, arguably, more modest. His aim was to produce beautiful, high-quality books that were a joy just to hold in one's hand, even more to read, and to provide a lively forum where like-minded individuals could share their interests and discuss the fruits of their research. In the process, he reshaped the field of eighteenth-century studies in his own genial image, in what one hopes will be a permanent impact, and impressed his personality on the road that each of us in this volume has been taking ever since we first encountered him and will continue to travel going forward.

Rest in peace, Gabe. We miss you.

NOTES

1. Katarzyna Sonnenberg, *At the Roots of the Modern Novel: A Comparative Reading of Ihara Saikaku's "The Life of an Amorous Woman" and Daniel Defoe's "Moll Flanders"* (Krakow: Jagiellonian University Press, 2015); David Gundry, *Parody, Irony, and Ideology in the Fiction of Ihara Saikaku* (Leiden: Brill, 2017).

2. The word *chōnin* literally means "people of the block," from the word *chō*, or city block. According to the official classification system of Tokugawa society, which was based on physical evidence of productivity, samurai ranked above peasant farmers, and peasant farmers above artisans. The *chōnin*, who produced nothing tangible, were the lowest stratum. As the century wore on, however, these categories became increasingly outdated as the liquid assets of the *chōnin* businessmen came to surpass even those of most samurai.

3. James L. McClain, "Space, Power, Wealth, and Status in Seventeenth-Century Osaka," in *Osaka: The Merchants' Capital of Early Modern Japan*, ed. James L. McClain and Wakita Osamu (Ithaca: Cornell University Press, 1999), 46. McClain's essay is an excellent resource about the cultural milieu that produced Saikaku and his neighbors, the ambitious Osaka *chōnin*. McClain and Osamu's book also includes several helpful maps that provide a visual feel for the areas of the city that are significant settings for the stories Saikaku tells about its inhabitants.

4. Gary P. Leupp, *Servants, Shophands, and Laborers in the Cities of Tokugawa Japan* (Princeton: Princeton University Press, 1992), 17.

5. Sumptuary laws designed to uphold visual distinctions between samurai and townsmen became increasingly strict over the course of the seventeenth and eighteenth centuries, though ingenious members of the *chōnin* class could always find a way to get around these and show off their wealth one way or another. For instance, a character in Saikaku's *Honchō Nijū Fukō* (*Twenty Cases of Unfilial Children in Japan*), the daughter of a wealthy silk wholesaler, carries with her a most impressive trousseau that includes "lacquerware of exquisite beauty decorated with raised patterns covered in gold dust; as for

her clothes, on the outside they conformed to the sumptuary laws, but they were lined with fabrics dyed in an array of dot patterns" (Gundry, *Parody, Irony, and Ideology*, 168). The hero of Saikaku's *Kōshoku Ichidai Otoko*, the profligate philanderer Yonosuke, impresses a famous courtesan by sporting a kimono made of paper, as a poor man might wear—only *his* paper is actually composed of calligraphic samples certified as authentic productions by centuries of famous poets, which draws condemnation even from the story's usually complacent narrator: "There was poetry by Teika written in his own hand, a sheet with three poems from the ink brush of Yorimasa, a long poem by the monk Sosei and other pieces of writing by poets down through the ages. It was all an outrageous waste and proof that the wearer did not know his place." *Excerpts from "Life of a Sensuous Man": An Episodic Festschrift for Howard Hibbett*, episode 25, trans. Christopher Drake (Hollywood: Highmoonoon, 2010), 172–173.

6. Perhaps the first direct comparison to London's coffeehouse culture was a remark by Ivan Morris, in his introduction to Ihara Saikaku, *The Life of an Amorous Woman and Other Writings by Ihara Saikaku*, trans. Morris (New York: UNESCO/New Directions, 1963) (henceforth Morris): "In some ways the gay quarters corresponded to the coffeehouses of eighteenth-century London as centres of elegance and wit; but in addition they were infused with an atmosphere of gallantry, glamour, and sensuality" (9). Earlier, Howard Hibbett, in "Saikaku and Burlesque Fiction," *Harvard Journal of Asiatic Studies* 20 (1957): 53–73, had commented on the marked similarity between the characters of Saikaku's irrepressible nameless *Amorous Woman* protagonist and Defoe's Moll Flanders, right down to the just-in-time religious conversion when the heroine is too old to be sexually attractive (69). Later critics picked up the analogy and ran with it. Peter Nosco, in the introduction to his translation of Saikaku, *Some Final Words of Advice*, trans. Nosco (Rutland: Charles E. Tuttle, 1980), a translation dedicated to Morris, develops the London coffeehouse idea over four pages, with a heavy emphasis on Defoe. Others have done the same, though Donald Keene, in *World within Walls: Japanese Literature of the Pre-modern Era, 1606–1867* (New York: Columbia University Press, 1999), has also noted a strong resemblance between the narrator of *Amorous Woman* and the narrator of *Tom Jones*. Most recently, Katarzyna Sonnenberg, in *Roots of the Modern Novel*, has devoted her entire study to drawing comparisons between the literary world of Saikaku and that of Defoe. Although the Tokugawas' 1635 Act of Seclusion ensured that there was no contact whatsoever between the two literary cultures, the parallels are so striking, it is almost irresistible to make connections.

7. The crisis over the fragmentation of arable land and shifting population statistics in the new peacetime economy is further documented by Nakai Nobuhiko and James L. McClain in their essay, "Commercial Change and Urban Growth in Early Modern Japan," in *The Cambridge History of Japan*, vol. 4: *Early Modern Japan*, ed. John Whitney Hall and McClain (Cambridge: Cambridge University Press, 1991), 591–595, where they point out that "by the 1670s the shogunate had become so concerned about the destabilizing aspects of the further subdivision of farmland that it issued a 'law restricting the division of farmland'" (593). Unable to inherit, younger sons and daughters were increasingly driven to the cities in search of employment as day laborers. So extreme was the migration that the Tokugawa administration had to backpedal and pass yet ever more restrictive rulings to protect their position, as Conrad Totman explains in *Japan before Perry* (Berkeley: University of California Press, 1981): "Fearful that the swelling urban population would impoverish society and wreck the regime, rulers . . . attempted by edict and action to force people back to the soil. And their efforts seemed to bear some fruit in that the rapid pace of urbanization slowed dramatically after the early 1700s" (191). Thus, at the time Saikaku was writing in the 1680s, the wave of cityward movement was near its crest.

8. Michael Hoffman, "Japan's First Pop Culture," *Japan Times*, 13 February 2011, https://www.japantimes.co.jp/news/2011/02/13/national/history/japans-first-pop-culture/.

9. It still is. A few years ago, a guest speaker at my university who spoke on the subject of "doing business in Japan" explained that all the rules one learns for dealing in Tokyo go out the window when one is dealing with colleagues in Osaka: while the former are interested in long-term relationships, building trust, and the culture of corporate cooperation, the latter just want to get to the bottom line. This can cause cultural misunderstandings with other Japanese as frequently as it does with foreigners. A fascinating study of the business climate in late seventeenth- and early eighteenth-century Osaka, including a year-by-year table of the market price for rice at Osaka's Dojima market, can be found in David Moss and Eugene Kintgen, *The Dojima Rice Market and the Origins of Futures Trading* (Cambridge: Harvard Business School, 2009). Despite its technical title, the essay is extremely readable, with humorous touches and a wealth of excerpts from primary texts, not just official documents, but also pithy popular maxims from contemporary road signs ("Know your station in life!") and proverbial expressions ("The offspring of a toad is a toad; the offspring of a merchant is a merchant"). See Donald H. Shively, "Popular Culture: The *Chōnin*," in Hall and McClain, *Early Modern Japan*, 706–770.

10. For further information about the effects of this policy in Europe and a fascinating theory about Swift's treatment of Japan as a subject, see Robert Markley, "Gulliver and the Japanese: The Limits of the Postcolonial Past," *Modern Language Quarterly* 65 (2004): 457–479. Markley further explores the idea in the final chapter of his book *The Far East and the English Imagination, 1600–1730* (Cambridge: Cambridge University Press, 2006), which deals entirely with attitudes toward Japan. More recently, Betty Joseph, in "Capitalism and Its Others: Intersecting and Competing Forms in Eighteenth-Century Fiction," *Studies in Eighteenth-Century Culture* 45 (2016): 157–173, esp. 159–163, has built upon Markley's observations to examine Daniel Defoe's attitude toward China as that of a comprehensible commercial rival, fundamentally different from Swift's description of Japan as a closed, mysterious, and unattainable market for English goods.

11. Translated by Christopher Drake, in "Saikaku's Haikai Requiem: *A Thousand Haikai Alone in a Single Day*: The First Hundred Verses," *Harvard Journal of Asiatic Studies* 52 (1992): 481–588, quotation from 503. Drake's translation and commentary, which is nearly one hundred pages long and covers just 10 percent of the entire composition, is an astonishingly detailed, in-depth study in English of Saikaku's wording and phraseology. See Drake's "The Collision of Traditions in Saikaku's *Haikai*," *Harvard Journal of Asiatic Studies* 53 (1992): 5–75, for the background story of the *Haikai* Requiem's composition and its effect on Saikaku studies after a single copy of the long-lost work was discovered when it was sold to a bookseller, and immediately resold to be preserved as a national treasure in the Tenri Library, in 1947.

12. Translated from Baiu by Drake in "Collision of Traditions," 6. The "calligrapher" who recorded Saikaku's requiem verses is known to have been Itō Dōsei, a close neighbor who lived near Saikaku on Uchi kajiyamachi, or Inner Smith's Block, a street of metalworkers and weaponsmiths. Drake suggests that "if Saikaku's relatives were in fact metalworkers, Saikaku's intense, energetic style of composition would have roots in the rhythmical work habits of smiths and metal casters, who had to work at high speed for two to three days on end when a furnace was started up and the metal molten" (19).

13. Paul Schalow, "Ihara Saikaku and Ejima Kiseki: The Literature of Urban Townspeople," in *The Cambridge History of Japanese Literature*, ed. Haruo Shirane and Tomi Suzuki, with David Lurie (Cambridge: Cambridge University Press, 2016), 415–423.

14. Keene, *World within Walls*, 47. Keene explains that the "myriad arrows" concept was drawn from archery matches "at which arrow after arrow is fired at a single target." He also claims that although the pace was impressive, Saikaku's verses "show no conspicuous talent, though some have been remembered," a damning with faint praise that might suggest why the master was so ready to give up his career as a practicing poet after he'd hit the ceiling of his ability to break his own speed records.

98   SUSAN SPENCER

15. Haruo Shirane, *Early Modern Japanese Literature: An Anthology, 1600–1900*, abridged ed. (New York: Columbia University Press, 2008), 22.

16. Charles E. Tuttle Publishing, which issued a flurry of several Saikaku translations from the late 1950s to the early 1980s, published a version of *Kōshoku ichidai otoko* under the title *The Life of an Amorous Man* in a translation by Kenji Hamada in 1963 (reissued in 2001), but with significant omissions of sections that were considered too racy or simply too difficult to convey because of their heavy reliance on allusion and wordplay. In 2010, the independent press Highmoonoon published a new translation by Christopher Drake of selected incidents from the book, heavily annotated, as part of a multivolume "episodic festschrift for Howard Hibbett."

17. Keene, in *World within Walls*, describes how the assertion of Saikaku's *haikai*-master nature makes the highly condensed text of *Kōshoku ichidai otoko* dauntingly difficult to read even for modern Japanese readers: "Necessary postpositions, indicating the subject of a sentence or the agent of the action, are cavalierly omitted, sometimes for euphonic reasons, sometimes because the meaning would be obvious in oral delivery. . . . The subjects of sentences are often left unexpressed, as if Saikaku assumed the reader could guess them; the first chapter of book 4 contains neither the name Yonosuke nor even a pronoun for him, though he is the subject throughout" (172).

18. *Ukiyo*, or "floating world," was originally a Buddhist term referring to the transient, unreliable nature of a soul's existence in the material world. It was appropriated by Saikaku's predecessor and rival Asai Ryōi, in *Ukiyo Monogatari* (*Tales of the Floating World*, 1666), who applied the same concept to the novelty and excitement—and the uncertain ebb and flow of fortunes in a cash-based economy—associated with the commercial world and especially with the licensed entertainment quarters among the brothels and theaters. Saikaku's earlier, sexier books are often referred to as *ukiyo-zōshi*. *Kōshoku Gonin Onna*, or *The Five Women Who Loved Love* (1686), seems to me to be a transition text from his erotic works to the *chōnin-zōshi* that were Saikaku's unique contribution to the history of Japanese literature. Although the focus is on amorous encounters, the *chōnin* characters are more obviously of the mercantile class than Yonosuke or his nameless female counterpart in *Koshoku Ichidai Onna* (*The Life of an Amorous Woman*). Schalow claims that "Saikaku finally turned to the subject of commerce" in his final three books, "far fewer than his books on love and the same number as his books on warriors," and that "here, for the first time, he could put on display his nuanced understanding for money-making" ("Ihara Saikaku and Ejima Kiseki," 419–420). Though this is true if one considers only a book's *central* theme, the idea of currency exchange runs through the entire body of Saikaku's work like the thread that holds together a stack of pierced *zeni* coins, which left a hole in the center for just that purpose.

19. Keene, in *World within Walls*, observes that "although [Saikaku] was preceded by Asai Ryōi as a popular writer, it is not much of an exaggeration to say that he reestablished prose fiction as an art after over four hundred years of anonymous writings" (211). A second book collecting anecdotes from multiple locations across Japan, *Futokoro Suzuri* (*The Pocket Inkstone*), was released two years after *Saikaku Shokoku Hanashi* (*Saikaku's Tales from Various Provinces*), in 1687. After that, however, Saikaku's focus—and his narrative voice—is emphatically that of a sophisticated city dweller.

20. William Theodore de Bary, in the introduction to his translation of *The Five Women Who Loved Love* (Rutland: Charles E. Tuttle, 1956), 15. This introduction, which is an excellent overview and analysis of *Kōshoku Gonin Onna*, was reprinted as the chapter "Saikaku's *Five Women Who Loved Love*," in the collection *Finding Wisdom in East Asian Classics*, ed. de Bary (New York: Columbia University Press, 2011), 310–320.

21. The popularity of Osan's story did not abate even after more than two decades had passed since her death. Saikaku's younger contemporary and erstwhile rival in Osaka's *joruri* puppet theater, Chikamatsu Monzaemon, revised the story again and released his

own version, *The Almanac of Love*, in 1715. Unlike Saikaku's cynical, earthy depictions, Chikamatsu's working men and women tend to be ennobled, with tortured consciences torn between passion and duty. His remorseful Osan, deeply embedded in a web of conflicting loyalties, bears little resemblance to the impulsive, self-indulgent character in Saikaku's version.

22. Appearing as it did in 1686, just three years after the first set of restrictive Tokugawa sumptuary laws governing *chōnin* attire, this extravagant description of the preteen Osan's gorgeous clothing must have seemed to the *chōnin* audience rather like a beautiful flashback to years past.

23. The phrase "showing an umbrella to a cat" was a proverb, equivalent to the idea of casting pearls before swine. Umbrellas are mentioned in other Saikaku stories as an exclusively urban novelty. A raunchy example from his *Tales from Various Provinces* (1685), "The Umbrella Oracle," describes an umbrella caught by the wind and blown into an isolated village in the mountains of Higo province, where it is declared by a local wise man as an incarnation of the sun god and lustily eyed by an amorous widow who offers to serve as a shaman at its shrine. Christopher Drake's translation of this story is available in Shirane's *Early Modern Japanese Literature*, 58–60. Saikaku's reference to a cat in this case may be an added bonus for today's followers of Japan's popular culture, since 310 years later, Nintendo decided to use the *koban* as a distinguishing feature on the forehead of the greedy Pokémon cat, Meowth.

24. Saikaku, *This Scheming World*, trans. Masanori Takatsuka and David C. Stubbs (Rutland: Charles E. Tuttle, 1965), 127.

25. Saikaku, *The Japanese Family Storehouse; Or the Millionaire's Gospel Modernised*, trans. G. W. Sargent (Cambridge: Cambridge University Press, 1969), 36.

26. Actually, this kind of mistake might not seem so entirely quirky to today's academic, if we just take a good look at some of our colleagues. But for Saikaku's fashion-conscious audience, that line must have seemed hilarious.

27. The translation of *Amorous Woman* referred to in this chapter is that of Ivan Morris (see note 6). Drake's newer translation (of *Koshoku Ichidai Onna*), which is excerpted in Shirani, *Early Modern Japanese Literature*, 35–66, is equally good and every bit as amusing; my choice of Morris is based on his book's easier availability for today's average book purchaser rather than on any inherent superiority. As an added bonus, Morris's compilation includes representative selections from *Five Women Who Loved Love*, *The Storehouse of Japan*, and *Reckonings That Carry Men through the World* (aka *This Scheming World*).

28. An *obi* sash knotted in the front, in a location where a client could easily get at it without interruption of his seductions, was an immediately recognizable indicator of a prostitute. Respectable women of all classes in seventeenth-century Japan tied their sashes at the back. Although the Amorous Woman is long past the age where such a style would have actual utility, it appears that old habits die hard.

29. It is made abundantly clear that if there is a root cause of the girl's discontent with the restrictions of her life at the palace, it isn't from any sense of mistreatment. Her lascivious nature is presented as the only possible impetus for her misbehavior.

30. At this point, the heroine is still acting within the bounds of old-style courtly practice. Genji himself, the ultimate Heian courtier, is described throughout Lady Murasaki's eleventh-century *Tale of Genji* as a trendsetter among his peers. Her outspoken eagerness to confess personal pride in this accomplishment, however, a quality Genji does *not* share, reads more like the competitive spirit of the mercantile *chōnin*.

31. For some reason, this admission about the fatal potency of those well-written love letters always seems to capture the attention of the male English majors in my classroom.

32. When describing the pitfalls and expenses of the life of a professional concubine in search of a permanent position, she takes care to warn against the crass behavior of "merchants from Osaka or Sakai" on sales trips to the capital, who are likely to take advantage

of the young girls' desperation by holding out the suggestion of a long-term arrangement, and then tricking them into accepting a hard bargain for a single night's encounter After all, they have already traveled to the site for an interview and otherwise the journey, and all that equipment rental, would be a total loss (134).

33. For details about this increasing income disparity and its causes, see Moss and Kintgen, *The Dojima Rice Market*.

34. Dennis C. Washburn, *The Dilemma of the Modern in Japanese Fiction* (New Haven: Yale University Press, 1995), 67 (henceforth Washburn). Gundry, in *Parody, Irony, and Ideology*, also emphasizes the parodic nature of Saikaku's early work, though his argument is that the use of parody is meant as a tribute to Saikaku's sources rather than an attempt to denigrate or satirize them. This too was a clever commercial decision, according to Gundry, as the ability to recognize such references flattered the *chōnins'* aspirations to educational sophistication and good taste.

35. Like Washburn, Hibbett mentions the probable influence of *bikunimono* confession narratives, and suggests that the Amorous Woman's occasional encounters with faded beauties who have come to grief seem to be implanted in the text as flags to warn about the unreliable nature of the material world. He points out, however, that if she is meant to have consciously included these as cautionary measures for the two young men who are her audience, she is remarkably inefficient at driving her point home, because she immediately moves on to more frivolous topics. Her awareness of her own mortality, despite her claims about her religious awakening, appears to be limited, at best. It is possible that Saikaku is creating a form of metanarrative in which the clueless heroine does not realize the lessons that she is, in fact, imparting.

CHAPTER 5

Frances Brooke's *Rosina*

SUBVERTING SENTIMENTALISM

Linda V. Troost

On 10 March 1997, Kevin Cope emailed me that Gabriel Hornstein of AMS Press was looking for someone to start a new journal. Might I be interested? Indeed, I was. An intimidating telephone conversation soon followed with Gabe, whom I had never met. He quizzed me about my editing experience, publication record, and critical slant, but his final question was unexpected. "How do you like your martinis?" "On the wet side," I confessed, aware that my unsophisticated answer would probably put paid to my chance of success. Nevertheless, I was brought on board and became the editor of *Eighteenth-Century Women: Studies in Their Lives, Work, and Culture*, and the appointment transformed my professional life. I learned a lot about women in the eighteenth century, and I learned boatloads about editing, book design, and desktop publishing, subjects that became part of my teaching repertoire. Gabe's vision of a journal that included all disciplines also connected me to scholars I might never have encountered otherwise, from graduate students to distinguished professors. I owe the successful trajectory of both my teaching and my scholarly career to Gabe's willingness to take a chance on me.

Gabe was generous in many other ways. He once sent my husband a case of burgundy as thanks for his indexing *Eighteenth-Century Women*. Remembering that my field was British theater history, Gabe shipped me a copy of the AMS facsimile of *Bell's British Theatre*—in sixteen volumes—as a gift. At annual meetings of the American Society for Eighteenth-Century Studies, Gabe sponsored lavish late-night receptions for conference attendees and treated his journal editors to meals at wonderful restaurants. Wit and extremely good wine flowed freely at these editorial dinners under Gabe's watchful eye. In memory of him, I offer a chapter that allows me to return to my initial field of specialization and examine a dramatic work by an eighteenth-century woman: *Rosina*, a comic opera by Frances Brooke. I like to think its multidisciplinary nature would have delighted Gabe, a man interested in many fields.

———

Frances Moore Brooke (1724–1789) wrote successfully in a variety of genres: the periodical essay, the novel, tragedy, and comedy. Although her works appear to exploit the sentimentality fashionable in the eighteenth century, they simultaneously criticize facets of sensibility and offer women alternatives to a passive life trapped by emotion. Her own life was an example of industry unhampered by sensibility. Originally from Lincolnshire, she moved to London in 1748, married the Reverend John Brooke, and quickly began associating with Samuel Johnson and theatrical circles.[1] Her first literary project, the periodical entitled *The Old Maid* (1755–1756), combined theatrical criticism from a woman's point of view with discussions of foreign affairs and social issues. Despite her literary connections, she could not interest managers in producing her dramatic work, so she turned to translating French novels and writing original fiction. She moved to Quebec in 1763, where her husband was serving as garrison chaplain, and returned to England with him in 1768. *The History of Emily Montague* (1769), the first novel set in Canada and the work for which she is best known today, drew on her experiences abroad.

Despite success as a novelist and translator, Brooke was determined to be a playwright. Around 1771, she started work on *Rosina*, an adaptation of a popular French comic opera by Charles Simon Favart (1710–1792), but she could find no one to produce it.[2] Brooke ended up shelving the work for a decade. She finally gained access to the stage, but through an unusual route. In 1773, her husband's brother, James Brooke, acquired a majority interest in the company of the King's Theatre in the Haymarket, and Frances Brooke and her husband, along with actors Richard and Mary Yates, joined him as co-grantees. The two women did much of the managing.[3] Frances Brooke had hoped to obtain a patent to perform spoken drama in English, thereby clearing the way to staging her own plays, but the lord chamberlain refused the requests, so the King's Theatre remained licensed to present only all-sung Italian opera and ballet.[4] Brooke and Yates made quite a success of it, and in 1778, Richard Brinsley Sheridan and Thomas Harris engineered "what might perhaps be termed a hostile takeover," buying them out for £22,000.[5]

Brooke's management experience proved valuable in teaching her the business of staging theatrical productions, and the 1780s finally brought Brooke the dramatic success she craved.[6] Her debut as a staged playwright occurred in January 1781, with a main-piece tragedy at Covent Garden, and two years later, she reworked her rejected comic opera into one of the great successes of the age. *Rosina*, with music by William Shield (1748–1829), began a long run at Covent Garden on 31 December 1782, becoming one of the most frequently staged pieces in the final quarter of the eighteenth century.[7] Brooke would have known Shield from her tenure at the King's Theatre, where he played second violin and, later, principal viola. He was now the house composer at Covent Garden, and *Rosina* was the first of his many major musical successes.[8] *Rosina* received 39 performances in its first season. By the end of century, it had seen 152 Covent Garden performances, plus 12 at Drury Lane, 34 at the Haymarket, and 3 in Hammersmith.[9] Eighteenth-century audiences also saw *Rosina* in major towns in England, Scotland, Ireland, the United States, and Jamaica. London performances continued steadily until 1837 and intermittently until 1861.[10] Newspaper advertisements indicate it also played widely in the British provinces throughout the century.

Eighteenth- and nineteenth-century editions of the text and music abound. Thomas Cadell printed fourteen editions of the libretto by 1796; more appeared in the next century.[11] Most major Victorian play anthologies include *Rosina*, marking its status as a "classic." Shield's music survives in over twenty editions of the keyboard-vocal score; a set of manuscript orchestral parts copied in 1832 exists in the British Library and was published in a scholarly edition in 1998.[12] About forty editions of individual songs from *Rosina* can be found in various libraries, half of them issued by American publishers, and many of its songs appear in Victorian music anthologies aimed at amateur singers. One reason for its popularity may be that the opera contains many short pieces for female voices, including duets and trios, and that the lyrics work well even outside their original context. In short, *Rosina* was well known through the nineteenth century, but its fame waned as musical tastes changed in the twentieth century.

Shield's music more than Brooke's libretto has been behind the comic opera's revival. Two notable Australians, in particular, are responsible. In 1964, Joan Sutherland recorded two coloratura arias, "Light as Thistle Down Moving" and "When William at Eve"; in 1966, Richard Bonynge recorded the entire comic opera.[13] In 1982, he conducted several performances of it at the Sydney Opera House as part of *Comedies of Three Centuries*.[14] Since then, *Rosina* has been performed either in concert or fully staged by small professional opera troupes, most recently in Gateshead as part of the 2017 William Shield Festival.[15]

Compared with its contemporaries, *Rosina* has survived the test of time, but it still enjoys only a small reputation today. Brooke's novels and her feud with David Garrick have attracted more attention from literary scholars than her blockbuster, and Shield's popular music is barely on the radar of music historians.[16] There are several reasons for such neglect. *Rosina* is a translation, and modern criticism privileges originality. Also, it looks slight, a pastoral not even two hours long, alternating song and dialogue, and spouting sentiments. As a comic opera, a popular genre that developed in the mid-eighteenth century, *Rosina* is neither all-sung opera, nor ballad opera, nor all-spoken drama, so it does not fit into a disciplinary box. Nevertheless, it deserves attention, and not just for its charming music. The comic opera addresses many of the issues Brooke and other women dealt with in fiction of the 1770s and 1780s, such as the loyalty and support of women for each other, and the dangers of excessive sensibility untempered by sense.

The plot is, admittedly, unoriginal. As Brooke notes in the advertisement to the published libretto, it derives substantially from two sources: Favart's 1768 Parisian comic opera *Les Moissoneurs* (*The Reapers*), with music by Egidio Duni, and the story of Palaemon and Lavinia in James Thomson's 1730 poem *The Seasons*.[17] Both look back ultimately to the Book of Ruth. Mr. Belville, a benevolent country squire, loves the charming gleaner Rosina, but "The timidity inseparable from real love has hitherto prevented his declaring himself" (42). Rosina returns his affection, but Belville believes she prefers his brother, Captain Belville, currently down from London for the shooting season. The rakish captain, alas, plans to bag more than partridge. First, he tries bribing Rosina with a purse of gold; when that fails, he arranges an abduction. Fortunately, two Irish laborers rescue Rosina, after which her foster mother reveals that Rosina is the orphaned daughter of genteel, though impoverished parents. Belville works up the courage to propose marriage to Rosina, and the wicked brother promises to reform his ways. Except for the pointedly British setting, the main plot closely follows that of Favart.

Brooke does make alterations. The benevolent country squire's amorous nephew becomes an amorous brother, and the squire becomes a bachelor instead of a widower. Brooke also shifts the emphasis of Favart's libretto to suit an English audience, or, as John Genest puts it, improves the French source "by judicious omissions."[18] Favart lingers on the nephew's attempt to seduce Rosina; Brooke focuses on the more wholesome romance between Rosina and Belville, downplaying her role as helpless victim.

Brooke's main innovation, though, lies in the secondary plot about two squabbling rustic lovers who serve as a foil to the sentimental Rosina and Belville. Rosina's foster sister, Phoebe, and a fellow rustic laborer, William, spend much of the play comically tormenting each other and themselves with jealousy. Brooke explains her reasons for the addition: "As we are not, however extraordinary it may appear, so easily satisfied with meer sentiment as our more sprightly neighbors the French, I found it necessary to diversify the story by adding the comic characters of William and Phoebe, which I hop'd might at once relieve, and heighten, the sentimental cast of the other personages of the drama" (v–vi). In fact, the travails of Phoebe and William at times almost overshadow the principal plot.

Much of the main plot's dialogue and a few of the song texts are translations of material in *Les Moissoneurs*, but Brooke did not rely on Duni's music. Instead, William Shield prepared a new pastiche score designed to appeal to a British audience by mixing original music with some borrowed music, the customary practice in English comic operas of the second half of the eighteenth century. Of the eighteen vocal numbers, ten are original pieces by Shield, three are Scots or Irish traditional tunes, two are French tunes, and three are contemporary borrowings from composers known to Shield.[19] Although popular in both Britain and Europe in the eighteenth century, pastiche scores lost prestige in the nineteenth century, which favored works by a single composer.

The musical selections help set the scene. Brooke locates the action of the comic opera "in the north" (12) of England, exploiting a shift in taste that Howard Weinbrot dates to 1770 (around the time Brooke was first drafting *Rosina*), when the English started to see Scotland, not as a barbaric land, but as one that embodied "physical, moral, environmental, intellectual and female virtue and beauty."[20] Although *Rosina* is not set in Scotland, its music nonetheless allies itself with Scotland's border regions. For example, Shield's overture concludes with a Northumbrian pipe tune played on the oboe; the score instructs the bassoons to "imitate the Bagpipe."[21] The tune used is the one we know today as "Auld Lang Syne."[22] Shield uses the tunes of two actual Scots songs and imitates the style in his own compositions. In two original songs—Belville's "Her mouth, Which a Smile" and Rosina's "Sweet Transports, Gentle Wishes Go"—Shield uses the melodic flavor of folk song and the "Scotch snap," a characteristic musical figure in Caledonian music.[23] Besides capitalizing on what was becoming a fashionable setting—the "north"—*Rosina* incorporated into the characters of Rosina and Belville the moral virtues associated with the rural landscape. Shield may have been the ideal composer for this comic opera, since he could orchestrate modal traditional songs successfully and imitate their idiom in more musically complex contexts.

The evocative setting, the balanced plots, and the showcasing of Covent Garden's vocal talent strengthen the potentially lightweight pastoral work. The genteel Rosina-Belville plot contrasts well with the rustic Phoebe-William plot, and both Brooke and Shield give the characters almost equal musical weight: Rosina and Belville each sing three solos to Phoebe's two and William's one, but the rustics sing two duets to Rosina and Belville's one, and sing in the opening trio with Rosina. In addition, all the characters sing both simple Celtic ballads (either real or imitation) and complex arias; there is no musical hierarchy. Finally, the comic opera showcases Covent Garden's female vocal talent. Brooke and Shield had three strong women singers to write for—Elizabeth Harper Bannister, Margaret Martyr, and Margaret Kennedy—and they made the most of their talents. *Rosina* has a preponderance of good parts for women. While there are two couples, William is played as a "trouser role," thereby putting three women into the top four roles.[24] The result is that the first fifteen or twenty minutes of each act is focused entirely on female singers: act 1 opens with a trio for Rosina, Phoebe, and William, followed by a solo apiece for Phoebe and Rosina. Had the song for Dorcas not been cut, there would have been four songs in a row performed by women opening the opera. The second act still has four in a row: solos for Rosina, Phoebe, and then William, followed by a duet for Phoebe and William. While Brooke's novels critiqued limited roles for women in life, Brooke did something about it by writing stage works with plentiful, meaty roles for women.

A comic opera also depends on its songs for impact, and the songs married text and music effectively. Brooke understood the importance of verbal sound and the challenge of singing in English. In a letter to Richard Gifford, who collaborated with her on a few of the songs, she commented, "I feel a line full of consonants just as I do discord in music."[25] Her experience at the opera house made her sensitive to issues such as the difficulty all singers have with clustered consonants (impossible to sustain musically) and certain English vowels. The singers in *Rosina* would have appreciated her care in providing open-vowel words, like "rose," "my," and "heart," on the final high notes that typically end rising musical lines. The songs trip off the tongue because the words play to a singer's needs.

Rosina's particular charm derives from both its songs and its story. On the surface, the comic opera appears a typical sentimental work containing the characteristic features of sentimental literature, as Janet M. Todd defines them: sudden plot reversals (Rosina's birth revealed), a prescribed vocabulary ("benevolence," "transports," "sweet"), and heightening devices (dashes, emotional breaks in the music).[26] It also exhibits the appropriate attitude on most of the eleven subjects Frank Hale Ellis isolates as characteristic of eighteenth-century sentimental comedy: the innate goodness of men (Belville), the moral superiority of women (Rosina), the wisdom of parents (old Dorcas), the goodness of the lower orders and foreigners (the rustics, the Irish day laborers), the benevolence of the natural world (rural delights), pity for animals (Rosina's for birds), the reliability of emotion as opposed to reason (William, Phoebe), the tendency of evil to shift toward good (Captain Belville), and the unimportance of money (the rejected purse).[27] Brooke sidesteps one pitfall in Favart's libretto—maudlin dialogue—by omitting lines and adding new passages. The opening scene of Brooke's opera comes dangerously close to saccharine sententiousness when Rosina praises poverty by remarking that a nightingale does not necessarily sing more sweetly in a gilded cage. Her wise foster mother Dorcas shrewdly replies that they sing "sweeter . . . than the poor little linnet which thou pick'st up half starv'd under the hedge yesterday" (7). Rosina's platitudes, then, characterize her own naïveté, not the playwright's.

Nonetheless, Brooke's *Rosina* also explores the limitations of sensibility and innocence, the exact opposite of one might expect from a pastoral village opera. Rosina's naïveté is her major difficulty. Despite her purity, goodness, and sweetness, she frequently misreads the intentions of others. Belville suffers from the same difficulty and, as a result, nearly ruins his own life. Ann Messenger notes that Brooke treats a similar idea in *The History of Emily Montague*: "Too much sensibility is a danger, especially to women."[28] In many sentimental plays or operas, the principals do not realize until late in the action that their secret passions are reciprocated: in Favart's libretto, Rosine and Candor discover their mutual love only during the third act. Brooke's Rosina, however, confesses after the opening chorus that she harbors "a hopeless passion" (9) for Belville. To demonstrate the sincerity of her feeling, she sings a melancholy song in a minor key, clearly expressing her hopelessness about the situation. Because of the financial reversals of her family, she cannot regard herself as Belville's equal.

Rosina's aria reveals her discomfort, and the scene that follows exposes how this unhappiness upsets her behavior as well. Brooke translates the scene verbatim from Favart, but, by having added Rosina's plaintive song before it, invests it with greater force by giving Rosina a motivation for her behavior. Startled by Belville's unexpected appearance to supervise the harvest, Rosina, still too uncomfortable to face the object of her affection, takes refuge in frantic gleaning, trying to appear nonchalant. Instead of waiting until the reapers leave the field, she gleans too close to the scythes and incurs the wrath of a rustic. Despite, or perhaps because of, Belville's defending her against the justly irate rustic— "Let fall some ears, that she may glean the more" (11)—Rosina flees in embarrassment, not to exchange dialogue with Belville again until the second act, thereby bringing the principal romantic plot to a halt. Her excess sensibility does her no good.

By the second act, however, she has regained her confidence. Her song, "Light as Thistle Down Moving," shows she recognizes other aspects of love, in this case, the love for her foster mother, Dorcas. Brooke uses the substance of Favart's song text but adds the striking rural simile that sets the tone for Shield's brisk and light setting. Returning from the fields with a basket of wheat gleanings on her head (the small family's source of income), Rosina puts aside self-pity to celebrate the unselfish love and help Dorcas has given her. The text of her song is as simple as her devotion to another woman:

> Light as thistle down moving which floats on the air,
> Sweet gratitude's debt to this cottage I bear:
> Of autumn's rich store I bring home my part,
> The weight on my head, but gay joy in my heart. (33)

From these four simple lines, however, Shield spins a showpiece. Trills, high notes, portamenti, extensive melodic development, and a rapid Alberti-bass accompaniment give the ninety-second song a fashionable sound for the 1780s. The lightness of the sixteenth notes in the bass line echoes the lightness of the text, and as her spirits rise through joy, the musical notes do, too. The song concludes with a number of high Cs. There is even a variant on word painting, popular in the century, when Shield sets the word "weight" on a high A, showing how unburdensome Rosina's labor is to her. Rosina may be a simple gleaner, but her song is sophisticated. Although Rosina began, in the first act, as a timid girl, overpowered by sensibility, she has by now gained strength, which shines through her music.

The song emphasizes Rosina's role in this world as an active agent, one who labors willingly and cheerfully to support her foster mother. She also can take a small step in her own romance. Immediately after her revitalizing song, Rosina sees Belville napping and indulges her passion: "What do I see? Mr. Belville asleep? I'll steal softly—at this moment I may gaze on him without blushing" (33). Like her songs, Rosina's love has developed dramatically. Instead of being passive and frightened, as in the first act, she now has the courage to do something for the object of her affection: "The sun points full on this spot; let me fasten these branches together with this ribbon, and shade him from its beams" (33). The friendship and love she feels for Dorcas remind her that proper love is active and benevolent, not passive and victimizing, and she extends her benevolence to Belville.

Of course, the plot demands additional delay before the denouement. Once Belville awakens, Rosina bolts into her cottage—courage extends only so far—but she finds Captain Belville lying in wait for her there. She dashes out and confronts Belville. Breathless, startled, and with nowhere to hide, Rosina cannot run off but must face him and his searching questions:

> BELVILLE But tell me, Rosina, for the question is to me of importance? have I not seen you wear this ribbon?
> ROSINA Forgive me, Sir; I did not mean to disturb you. I only meant to shade you from the too great heat of the sun.
> BELVILLE To what motive do I owe this tender attention?
> ROSINA Ah, Sir! Do not the whole village love you?
> BELVILLE At this moment, Rosina, think me a brother; or a friend a thousand times more affectionate than a brother. You tremble; why are you alarmed! (34–35)

Rosina evades his questions, unwilling to confess her love and missing the broad hints of a man in love. Belville, however, is equally unperceptive—he thinks Rosina trembles from fear, not from nervousness and love. Regrettably, both are too discreet to make the first move or read too much into the other's words and, as a result, accomplish nothing.

In the lyrical duet that follows, each misinterprets the other's words. The romantic implications should be clear, but they both miss them. Rosina thinks Belville offers himself only as a *guardian, protector, and guide* (35), his proper function as country squire, so she gives noncommittal answers to his queries. Belville is equally unperceptive and thinks Rosina fears something. He never realizes that her breathless, disjointed remarks might stem from love for him.

Figure 5.1. Excerpt from *Rosina: A Comic Opera*, keyboard vocal score (London: Napier, [1783]), 34. Public domain.

The audience cannot misread her feelings, though. Shield even writes breaks into her music to betray her romantic agitation and has the bass line's staccato eighth notes imitate her panting heart (figure 5.1). Favart's longer version of this scene has Rosine and Candor clearly realize the feelings of the other. Brooke, in contrast, renders this scene as indecisive in order to emphasize her point about the dangers of excess sensibility for both men and women. Both of the lovers are too delicate to make the first move or read into the other's words; left to themselves, the sentimental lovers talk and sing at cross purposes.

Belville manages to misunderstand everyone. He assumes from something Dorcas says that Rosina, who he has now learned was wellborn but orphaned, is in love with her brother. He also assumes that his brother's pursuit of Rosina is honorable, until he learns of the attempted abduction arranged by the captain and thwarted by some Irish day laborers. Even then, Belville is willing to let Rosina marry his brother if that is what she wishes. Rosina, however, has never regarded the captain with anything other than suspicion. Captain Belville's offer of marriage, made to appease his brother, forces Rosina into action, and she denounces the captain soundly: "This hope is a second insult. Whoever offends the object of his love is unworthy of obtaining her" (42). She would rather labor in the fields, earn her own income, and live in a cottage with Dorcas than marry the captain and gain riches. Brooke ensures that "the decision falls to Rosina" to choose, thereby empowering her.[29]

His brother rejected, Belville is inspired to try his own luck but cannot express himself. He phrases his offer so delicately that Rosina misses his intention: "I know another, Rosina, who loves you with as strong, though purer ardor: the timidity inseparable from real love has hitherto prevented him declaring himself—but if allowed to hope—" (42). Rosina assumes he is speaking of some other person and rejects this unknown party. Only when he speaks plainly at last—"Do you refuse me too then, Rosina? . . . Rosina, may I hope?"—does Rosina finally understand him. However, he does not understand *her*. She speaks of her confusion and blushes, and he automatically assumes, "'Tis enough; I see I am rejected." He has been diffident, but her behavior has been, in general, too discreet for her own good. It is now her turn to speak plainly and hasten matters to a happy conclusion: "'Tis the first time in your life, I believe, that you were ever mistaken."[30] Both Belville and Rosina nearly lose the ones they love through discretion, rather than the more usual indiscretion, but the result is, until the final moment, regrettably similar.

In this comic opera, as in her novels, Brooke warns us that some courtesy-book heroes and heroines can find sensibility paralyzing. Fortunately, there are alternatives to such a life. As Lorraine McMullen notes, Brooke generally pairs a lively and a sentimental heroine together in her novels to allow herself an opportunity "to endorse and to question the values of her age."[31] She uses the same method in *Rosina* to reveal the virtue of feminine action as well as show the risks of feminine passivity. *Rosina*'s sentimental characters triumph in traditional fashion, but only *despite* their emotional turmoil. They require a character like Captain Belville to act as a catalyst for their passive, undeclared emotions. In contrast, characters with common sense, like Phoebe and William, eventually triumph because they can activate their own lives and romances.

The rustic lovers Brooke invents for the secondary plot parallel Rosina and Belville because they, too, misunderstand each other. As often happens in English double-plotted drama, the two love stories comment inversely upon each other. One plot is serious, and the other comic. One couple barely speaks; the other argues constantly. One couple needs outside forces to move the romance to a point of crisis; the other manages its business on its own.

Phoebe and William, devoid initially of sensibility, nearly come to blows in the first act. When Harry talks privately to Phoebe, William becomes outraged and accuses her of abandoning him for the wealthier rustic. On Belville's orders, Harry is trying to get biographical information from Phoebe about Rosina, her foster sister, but William jumps to conclusions and ends up insulting Phoebe. The lies escalate into a rapid hate duet in 6/8 time, as William declares a devotion to Kate, the maid of the mill, and Phoebe sings, "*Young Harry's the lad for me!*" (15). Neither Phoebe nor William realizes that the other's pretense is designed to provoke jealousy.

By the second act, each lover has gained a modicum of sensibility, but within reason. Brooke develops Phoebe and William's second-act reconciliation into a major scene (two songs and a duet), carefully positioning it before Rosina and Belville's hesitant duet under the shady tree. At the start of the scene, Phoebe, who knows that William is secretly listening, reveals through song that she really has no interest in Harry. As Katharine M. Rogers notes about sentimentalism, "It gave women confidence to express themselves and to claim emotional fulfillment."[32] Phoebe can sing her heart to William instead of playing games with him, as she might have done in a Restoration comedy (and did throughout the first act). Admittedly, the song still veils her feelings a little, but it makes her heart more visible than it was. She can employ sensibility positively.

William also finds freedom in sensibility, but he keeps the game going longer. He knows perfectly well that "the slut likes [him] still" (27) when he sees

Phoebe throw away some flowers Harry had given her, but he teases her anyway by singing snatches of their first-act hate duet to provoke her into uttering complete truth. Phoebe becomes angry at his callousness, not realizing he is only pretending to misinterpret her feelings: "I'm ready to choak *wi'* madness but I'll not speak first an I die for't" (28). She starts to revert to her first-act game, but then—abruptly—she abandons it. Instead, she turns the conversation to themselves:

> PHOEBE My grandmother leads me the life of a dog; and it's all along of you.
> WILL Well, then she'll be better temper'd now.
> PHOEBE I did not value her scolding of a brass farthing, when I thought as how you were true to me.
> WILL Wasn't I true to you? Look in my face, and say that. (28)

Her confession of how much he means to her prompts William to abandon his game, too. He sincerely asks her to look him in the face directly, without pretense, quite a change from the beginning of the scene when neither even acknowledged the presence of the other. William has been hurt, though, and he reveals it by singing a ballad that is a thinly disguised narrative of their broken romance. The melody, a modal Scots tune, supplies enough melancholy to soften the hardest heart.[33] Because Phoebe is already lovelorn (and perhaps because she recognizes the justice of his complaints), the song reduces her to tears, a mark of sensibility. Once music has pulled all feeling into the open, nothing can stop the two from finally reconciling and expressing their delight in another duet. Despite their shaky grammar, the rustic lovers come to an understanding without the help of a third party, because, spared the paralyzing sensibility of the more genteel lovers, they eventually recognize the game each is playing. Sensibility does liberate their romance, but only because they are not in thrall to it.

Rosina and Belville, on the other hand, cannot recognize the motivation of each other, let alone manipulate the beloved into a confession of love. Therefore, they require someone who can rescue them from emotional entrapment. Kevin Berland notes that in *The History of Emily Montague*, Brooke "shared the increasingly widespread belief that feeling is somehow a means of attaining moral truth; the more intense the feeling, the more direct and reliable the emotionally perceived link between aesthetic and moral beauty."[34] Such depth of emotion, however, must be assisted by reason. In *Rosina*, sincere feeling leads to satisfaction for both sexes, but Brooke's comic opera stresses the importance of an open and active treatment of one's sensibility. Intense emotion divorced from properly directed action leads nowhere, as both Rosina and Captain Belville demonstrate in different ways. Emotion united with proper action, as experienced by Phoebe and William, in contrast, need fear no misunderstandings or require any rescuing.

The tight, complementary plots and the clever handling of songs make *Rosina* a successful dramatic piece, pleasing to both the admirers of sentimental drama and those who see the criticism underneath the sentiment. Despite writing in the traditional discourse of pastoral, Brooke subverts the traditions of the cruel pastoral maiden whose major function is to cause the shepherd-poet grief and allow him opportunities to lament his fate. Both the men (Belville and William) and the women (Rosina and Phoebe) suffer visibly. Brooke also shows us that Rosina can manage to maintain her dignity and independence because she is employed. Gleaning wheat from the fields may be all a woman can manage in this society, but it is more than most female literary characters get as a vocation. As Rosina demonstrates (as does Brooke's own life), a woman need not depend on a man; she can always pick up and use what he allows to drop. Her integrity is her strength. In fact, Rosina's virtuous example makes Captain Belville wish to reform. She may have little financial power, but she does have an active moral power over men. In the sentimental world, that talent is highly valued.

The editors of the *Biographia Dramatica* saw *Rosina* as a work that "corrects the mind, while it pleases the senses," but one does not know exactly what misconceptions they thought needed correcting.[35] They may have seen Rosina's gentle sentimentality as a model for submissive women to follow. Or they may have seen the warning Brooke conveyed about the perils that result from neglecting to temper sentimental behavior with sense. Either way, the comic opera *Rosina* touched hearts, delighted ears, and pleased audiences for decades.

NOTES

1. Lorraine McMullen's *An Odd Attempt in a Woman: The Literary Life of Frances Brooke* (Vancouver: University of British Columbia Press, 1983) is the standard biography of Brooke.

2. Brooke discusses the comic opera in her correspondence with the Rev. Richard Gifford, who assisted her with translating some of Favart's lyrics into English verse. See McMullen, *An Odd Attempt in a Woman*, 195–196.

3. McMullen, *An Odd Attempt in a Woman*, 151; Curtis Price, Judith Milhous, and Robert Hume, *Italian Opera in Late-Eighteenth-Century London*, 2 vols. (Oxford: Clarendon Press, 1995), 1:5, 56.

4. *The London Stage, 1660–1800: A Calendar of Plays, Entertainments, & Afterpieces, Together with Casts, Box-Receipts, and Contemporary Comment, Compiled from the Playbills, Newspapers, and Theatrical Diaries of the Period*, ed. William Van Lennep, Emmett L. Avery, Arthur H. Scouten, George Winchester Stone Jr., and Charles Beecher Hogan, 11 vols. (Carbondale: Southern Illinois University Press, 1960–1968), pt. 4, vol. 3, 1743.

5. Ian Woodfield, *Opera and Drama in Eighteenth-Century England* (Cambridge: Cambridge University Press, 2001), 6. Woodfield thoroughly and perceptively discusses Brooke's successful career as comanager of the King's Theatre.

6. Paula R. Backscheider, "Frances Brooke: Becoming a Playwright," *Women's Writing* 23 (2016): 328–335.

7. Only two main pieces, *The School for Scandal* and *The Beggar's Opera*, and one afterpiece, *Comus*, received more London stage presentations than *Rosina*. See Van Lennep et al., *The London Stage, 1660–1800*, pt. 5, vol. 1, clxxi–clxxii.

8. According to the Covent Garden ledgers, Shield received £100 for the score on 30 June 1784 (Egerton 2285), not £40, as W. T. Parke claims in his *Musical Memoirs*, 2 vols. (London: Colburn, 1833), 1:325.

9. Van Lennep et al., *The London Stage, 1660–1800*, pt. 5, vol. 1.

10. The last advertisement I could find was for performances at the Royal Surrey Theatre in the final week of September 1861. See *Sporting Life*, 25 September 1861.

11. Many of these "editions" are reprints with new title pages. The second Cadell edition is the first to include Brooke's name; the third adds her authorial preface. Cast lists do not change: the fourteenth edition of 1796 still gives the 1783 cast. Nineteenth-century editions update the performers' names.

12. *Musica Britannica*, ed. John Drummond (London: Stainer and Bell, 1998). Any original parts or full scores would have perished in the Covent Garden fire of 1808, so it is not certain if these surviving parts are faithful transcriptions of Shield's original scoring. They include the names of singers that match the cast of the 10 August 1832 production by the English Opera Company at the Royal Olympic Theatre, London (*Morning Post*). Until the publication of this score, the only available scores were from the eighteenth century, the edited score by John Oxenford and J. L. Hatton in their volume *English Ballad Operas* (London: Boosey & Hawkes, [1874]), which also includes *The Beggar's Opera, Love in a Village*, and *No Song No Supper*, and the Kalmus Vocal Series facsimile of the 1783 keyboard-vocal score, reprinted by Belwin-Mills around 1977.

13. Originally released on vinyl (Decca, 1966), the recording has been available digitally since 2001 under a variety of labels. It features Margreta Elkins (Rosina), Elizabeth Harwood (Phoebe), Monica Sinclair (William), Robert Tear (Belville), and Kenneth MacDonald (Captain Belville/Rustic), with Richard Bonynge conducting the Ambrosian Singers and the London Symphony Orchestra.

14. "Opera Guide: NSW," *Theatre Australia* 6, no. 4 (December 1981): 65, https://issuu .com/libuow/docs/theatreaustralia1981dec1982jan.

15. *Rocket Opera: Past Performances*, https://rocketopera.weebly.com/performances .html.

16. For Brooke's difficult relationship with Garrick, see Woodfield, *Opera and Drama*, 166–181; Kevin J. H. Berland, "Frances Brooke and David Garrick," *Studies in Eighteenth-Century Culture* 20 (1990): 222–227; and Katherine G. Charles, "Staging Sociability in *The Excursion*: Frances Brooke, David Garrick, and the King's Theatre Coterie," *Eighteenth-Century Fiction* 27 (2014–2015): 280–284. Shield's biography by Peter Smith, *From Tyneside Village to Westminster Abbey: The Life, Times, and Music of William Shield, 1748–1829* (Gateshead: Gateshead Schools' Music Service, 2005), was published by a regional organization for a local market.

17. Frances Brooke, *Rosina: A Comic Opera in Two Acts*, 3rd ed. (London: T. Cadell, 1783), v–vi. All quotations in the text are from this edition of the libretto and are cited parenthetically. The Palaemon and Lavinia story is from James Thomson's *Autumn*, from *The Seasons: A Hymn, a Poem* (London, 1730), ll. 189–312.

18. John Genest, *Some Account of the English Stage from the Restoration in 1660 to 1830*, 10 vols. (Bath: Carrington, 1832), 6:267.

19. Roger Fiske, *English Theatre Music in the Eighteenth Century*, 2nd ed. (Oxford: Oxford University Press, 1986), 612.

20. Howard D. Weinbrot, *Britannia's Issue: The Rise of British Literature from Dryden to Ossian* (Cambridge: Cambridge University Press, 1993), 513.

21. William Shield, *Rosina: A Comic Opera*, vocal score (London: Napier, [1783]), 5.

22. This Scots tune has a complex history that has provoked debate since at least the 1880s. One variant published in 1765 supplied Robert Burns with the melody for his 1796 poem "Coming through the Rye." Fiske, in *English Theatre Music*, suggests that the variant popularized in *Rosina*, and that survives nowhere else, was probably a Northumbrian pipe tune from Shield's youth. Burns wrote "I Fee'd a Man at Martinmass" (1792) to fit a combination of the two variant tunes. After Burns's death in 1796, George Thompson set Burns's "very free revision" of Allan Ramsay's song text "Should Auld Acquaintance Be Forgot" to

the combination tune and made a few musical changes. The Thompson version is the melody we recognize today (457–458).

23. The word "coming" in the song "Coming through the Rye" illustrates the syncopated rhythm of a Scotch snap.

24. After Mrs. Kennedy's retirement, the role of William was taken by a man. Modern productions, however, observe Brooke's original plan and cast the role with a mezzo-soprano.

25. Frances Brooke to Richard Gifford, ca. 1771, quoted in McMullen, *An Odd Attempt in a Woman*, 195.

26. Janet M. Todd, *Sensibility: An Introduction* (London: Methuen, 1986), 4–6.

27. Frank Hale Ellis, *Sentimental Comedy: Theory and Practice* (Cambridge: Cambridge University Press, 1991), 10–11.

28. Ann Messenger, *His and Hers: Essays in Restoration and Eighteenth-Century Literature* (Lexington: University Press of Kentucky, 1986), 170.

29. John Drummond, "Frances Brooke's *Rosina*: A Lesson in Morality," in *New Windows on a Woman's World: Essays for Jocelyn Harris*, ed. Colin Gibson and Lisa Marr, 2 vols. (Otago: University of Otago Department of English, 2005), 1:148.

30. These two lines are marked in the libretto as among the few omitted in performance. Brooke indicated in the advertisement that she kept such passages "to mark the characters with more precision" (vi). As this exchange gives Rosina a witty comeback, Brooke wants to show her growth.

31. Lorraine McMullen, "Double Image: Frances Brooke's Women Characters," *World Literature Written in English* 21 (1982): 356–363, quotation from 357.

32. Katharine M. Rogers, *Feminism in Eighteenth-Century England* (Urbana: University of Illinois Press, 1982), 143.

33. Fiske, in *English Theatre Music*, identifies the "Scots Tune" as "My Nannie O" (612).

34. K.J.H. Berland, "The True Pleasurable Philosopher: Some Influences on Frances Brooke's *History of Emily Montague*," *Dalhousie Review* 66 (1986): 286–300, quotation from 286.

35. *Biographia Dramatica; or a Companion to the Playhouse*, ed. David Erskine Baker, Isaac Reed, and Stephen Jones, 3 vols. (1812; repr., New York: AMS Press, 1966), 3:225.

CHAPTER 6

Pope's *An Epistle to Dr. Arbuthnot* and Justius Lipsius

SOURCES AND IMAGES OF THE WRITER

Manuel Schonhorn

An Epistle from Mr. Pope to Dr. Arbuthnot is one of the most admired and even the most anthologized of Pope's major poems. Its opening paragraphs, sixty-eight lines refashioned and improved from early drafts and fragments first composed in 1732, with their polished civility and controlled contempt for his unannounced visitors, have also been justly praised.[1] John Butt, the general editor of the Twickenham edition of Pope's poetry, has written that the poem is "the most Horatian of Pope's original works."[2] Butt's notes, attempting to elucidate the rich extent and range of Pope's autobiography/self-portrait, overwhelm the reader with allusions, sources, comparisons, and seemingly close echoes. Previous editors also tried to help the reader understand the poem's literary background. Edmond Malone offered a "perhaps"; Mark Pattison noted "a similarity"; John Wilson Croker "suggests."[3] Almost all of Butt's four-hundred-plus notes are generally contemporary, merging Milton, Restoration dramatists, the early century's poets, and Pope's friends and enemies. A few critics cited Ovid, Suetonius, and Persius, as well as Boileau—and, of course, Horace.[4] But their undue concern for particular "sources" has led them to neglect a grander, mythic pattern that structures much of classical and modern literature. For what has been completely overlooked is the classical topos of Pope's opening, "the portrait of the busy literary man constantly interrupted by those who want his help."[5] Pope, projecting his persona for posterity, was embracing an image of the writer recognized for his genius that is as frequent in elaborated autobiography as those fictions of heroism and miraculous escapes from danger that were the staple of the lives of the classical poets and tragedians. It is a chapter in the stories that are told about artists in all ages and climes that "reflect a universal human response to the mysterious magic of image-making."[6] Ernst Kris and Otto Kurz, in their groundbreaking and illuminating study *Legend, Myth, and Magic in the Image of the Artist*, called these episodes "anecdotes," attempting to invigorate a Greek word that is now narrowly and singularly defined in the *Oxford English Dictionary*, in Johnson's *Dictionary*, and in modern dictionaries. Anecdotes, as Kris and Kurz explains, are "the recurrence of certain preconceptions about artists in all their biographies. These preconceptions have a common root, and can be traced back to the beginnings of historiography. Despite all modifications and transformations, they have retained some of their meanings right up to the most recent past" (3). In fact, the reader suddenly encounters this besieged culture hero without his classical provenance in the midst of Hilary Mantel's justly applauded historical novel, *Wolf Hall*.[7]

Pliny attributes a remark to Eupompos, a fourth-century-B.C. sculptor, repudiating tradition and adhering to nature alone. It is later reported in the lives of other Greek artists of antiquity and, Kris and Kurz write, preserved in the later lives of Caravaggio, Guido Reni, and the famous Chinese painter of horses of the eighth century, Han Kan (16–17). An anecdote more familiar to us is the autobiographical and biographical theme of the premonitory signs of the artist's talent. Told by Vasari about Giotto, it is retold of Goya, and I have commented on it in the autobiographies of Sterne, Tristram Shandy, and Picasso.[8] Thus, "From the moment when the artist made his appearance in historical records, certain stereotyped notions [anecdotes] were linked with his work and person— preconceptions that have never entirely lost their significance and still influence our view of what an artist is" (Kris and Kurz, 4). Many of them, as we recognize today from our readings of Otto Ranke and Joseph Campbell, resemble those of the mythological hero.[9]

To Kris and Kurz's list of topics, formulistic phrases, and anecdotes, I can add the topos of the acclaimed man of letters sought by his contemporaries in his studio, but usually in his garden, to assist them in correcting or improving their literary productions. These unexpected intrusions we can read in Seneca and Suetonius, as they were importuned by visitors or interrupted by friends.[10] The French humanist and scholar Marcus Antonius Muretus (Marc-Anoine de Muret, 1526–1585) saw himself, and was seen by others, in this way. Ernst Curtius wrote that the Emperor Theodosius I asked Ausonius (d. 393) "to send him his works and cites the precedent of Octavian, to whom the foremost writers had brought their works."[11] And, of course, there is Horace's *Satire II*, vi, which, the Loeb editor remarked, "has been happily imitated by Pope." Except that it wasn't; it was imitated by Swift. Swift writes of Horace passing his day in the city of Rome, away from his loved rural villa,

> Twenty Fools I never saw
> Come with Petitions fairly pen'd,
> Desiring I would stand their Friend.
> This, humbly offers me his Case—
> That, begs my Interest for a Place—
> A hundred other Men's Affairs
> Like Bees, are humming in my Ears.
> "Tomorrow my Appeal comes on,
> "Without your Help the Cause is gone—
> The Duke expects my Lord and you,
> About some great Affair, at Two—
> "Put my Lord *Bolingbroke* in Mind,
> "To get my Warrant quickly signed:
> "Consider, 'tis my first Request.—
> Be satisfy'd, I'll do my best:—
> Then presently he falls to teize,
> "You may for certain, if you please;
> "I doubt not, if his Lordship knew—
> "And Mr. *Dean*, one Word from you—[12]

But the most graceful, charming, and self-deprecating "complaint" that I have read, which has been much commented on by others, is Justus Lipsius's self-portrait with which he introduced his study of Stoic philosophy (see the appendix at the end of this chapter). In many ways, as the notes detail, the "Alexander Pope" of *Arbuthnot* is a persona adapted from various literary models. But, given the obvious similarities and echoes, its trajectory, structure, and theme, I would like to suggest that Lipsius's autobiographical anecdote should be recognized as a source for the brilliant opening of Pope's *Epistle to Dr. Arbuthnot*.[13]

Lipsius's anecdote introduced his *Physiologiae Stoicorum, Libri Tres*, one of his major examinations of the Stoic philosophy.[14] An astute critic judged it "a scholarly, detailed, and sometimes pained Christianization of Stoic physics."[15] It was first published in Antwerp in 1604 and was reprinted in 1610 and 1644. Multiple print runs of 1,250 indicate its popularity. All the major libraries of Europe and the United Kingdom possess copies.[16] The *Physiologiae* became more accessible in his *Opera Omnia*, published in 1637 (Antwerp), and reprinted in 1675 (Wesel). The 1637 Antwerp *Omnia* edition was listed in the manuscript catalog of Shaftesbury's library (1708).[17] Rev. Thomas Sheridan, an intimate friend of Pope and Swift, owned the 1644 *Physiologiae*.[18] But for Pope's contemporaries, the 1675 *Opera Omnia* appears to have been the text of record. Fielding's library auction catalog (1755) lists an *Opera* in six volumes but dated 1605; his editors note that it is more a collection of separately published individual works.[19] While

Sterne's auction catalog lists a 1675 Wesel edition, his editors have cautioned us to be skeptical about the books offered since many owned by others were mingled with his personal collection.[20] Of greater significance, as early as 1715 and until his death in 1745, Swift owned the 1637 *Opera Omnia*.[21]

Of Pope's contemporaries who did not own and read Lipsius, many no doubt learned of his works, inconsistencies, and plagiarisms (even his terrible handwriting) in the double columns of Bayle's *Historical and Critical Dictionary*. He does not appear to have been much admired by Bayle, who quoted overwhelmingly from his adversaries, enemies, and major controversialists.[22] Addison jocularly notes Lipsius's pedantry in a *Spectator* essay on the novelty of Augustan clubs, and Fielding provides a nonsense note, seemingly by Justus Lipsius, over the provenance of Tom Thumb.[23] For Swift, too, Lipsius is a pedant, though not as ridiculous as his proverbial "fiddlers and dancing masters."[24] A nasty truth behind Swift's weak praise is that his many quotations from Tacitus may very well have been derived from his reading of Lipsius's eminently admired text— two are listed in his library catalog—judged "one of the most remarkable philological works of the sixteenth century."[25] Every educated neoclassicist knew and even read Lipsius, in addition to the classical Stoic writers, but neither Charles Cotton's *Moral Philosophy of the Stoicks* (1664, 1667, 1671), nor the inestimable Thomas Stanley's thoughtful sections in his *History of Philosophy* (1655, 1656), mention him. Moreri's *Great Historical Dictionary* (1694) has just a short inconsequential paragraph on Lipsius.[26]

Pope's library contained no edition of Lipsius, nor is it likely that any of his editions were among the many books he bequeathed to friends upon his death.[27] We can only speculate where he might have picked up and read the *Physiologiae Stoicorum*; we do not yet know the full library holdings of Pope's aristocratic friends, which could have provided him with access to Lipsius.[28] Pope's *Correspondence* records that he borrowed books from the library of Charles Montagu, Earl of Halifax, in 1714, when he was translating Homer.[29] He visited often and spent long hours at the Chiswick home of Robert Boyle, the third Earl of Burlington—Pope's fourth *Moral Essay* is dedicated to him—and whose rich library, now at Chatsworth, contained the volume of Lipsius that I will call attention to below.[30] And Pope had been reading at Edward Harley, the second Earl of Oxford's new library at Wimpole House, in Cambridgeshire.[31] (This is the almost unimaginable collection of more than fifty thousand items, of which the manuscripts, bought by Parliament, went to the British Museum, while the books and pamphlets were offered for public sale; Johnson and William Oldys wrote the indispensable catalog.)[32] Oxford's library held twenty-eight Lipsius titles, multiple *Opera Omniae*, in addition to the collected works of 1637 and 1675.

Pope, like many of us, commented in the margins of many of the books. Maynard Mack has transcribed his comments on Homer, Horace, and Virgil, among a host of classical writers. Pope also owned Charles Cotton's translation of Montaigne's *Essays*, acquired in 1706, "when he was eighteen," Mack writes, "and read in it, I suspect, many times before he died, but at any rate all the way through, at least once, with the greatest thoroughness."[33] "This is (in my Opinion)," Pope writes, "the very best Book for Information of Manners, that has been writ."[34] But if Pope thought highly of Montaigne, Montaigne thought even more highly of Lipsius. This is what Pope would have read in his copy: in volume 1, Montaigne, in writing about men of wit, singles out Lipsius "for the learned and laborious Contexture of his Politicks" (1:25, 240—by "laborious," Cotton means "diligent in work, assiduous"). Montaigne is more expansive when he writes about the character of Lipsius:

> How much do I wish, that whilst I live, either some or other, or *Justus Lipsius*, the most learned Man now living, of a most polite and judicious Understanding, and truly resembling my *Turnebus* [French scholar, 1512–1565] had both the Will, and Health and Leisure sufficient . . . to collect . . . the Opinions of the ancient Philosophers, about the subject of our Being and Manners. . . . What a beautiful and useful Work that would be! (2:12, 388)

In 2:2, 225, Montaigne continues his argument for the rationality, the conscious intelligence, of animals, denying that their considered actions are only the result of instinct. Reason dictates, he writes, those remarkable and observed actions of dogs and birds, especially magpies. To clinch his argument, Montaigne provides numerous examples of elephant intelligence, and exuberantly concludes, "But this Animal [the elephant] in several other Effects comes so near to human Capacity, that should I particularly relate all that Experience hath deliver'd to us, I should easily have, what I usually maintain, granted, namely, that there is more difference betwixt such and such a Man, than betwixt such a Man and such a Beast." In the margin of Montaigne's text, Pope had written "Vide Justi/Lipsii Epist./50 cent. l."[35] He had read Lipsius. Pope's citation, a refutation of Montaigne, directs the reader to Lipsius's epistle 50, to Jan van Hout (n.d.). It was included in Lipsius's first of five collections of celebrated letters, *Epistolarum Selectarum Centuriae Miscellaneae* (Antwerp and Leiden, 1586), and reprinted in the second volume of *Opera Omnia* (1637, 1675). Lipsius's letter, which is in praise of elephants, is in fact a burlesque encomium, satiric and ironic, perhaps the sort of ironic praise that Pope would have comfortably responded to, given his predilection for burlesque.[36] Citing Lipsius, Pope challenged Montaigne's belief in *animale rationale* with classic Stoic doctrine, for whom "animals have no rational faculty whatever. They are radically distinct from man, and there is no basis for any kind of moral community between the two."[37]

One swallow does not make a summer. To be honest, I admit that Lipsius's letter 50 is not the autobiographical anecdote of the *Physiologiae*. But, given Pope's range of interests, his scrupulous acquisition of information that is evident in the many marginal notes in his library books, and the distinct possibility that he may have had access to the voluminous library holdings of his aristocratic friends, I do not think it unreasonable to believe that Lipsius's charming and sympathetic portrait of the Stoic sage interrupted in his rich and varied pursuits, read by Pope, provided him with the formal trajectory and particular exemplifications, though brilliantly inverted, of the memorable figure of "the revered literary lion bedeviled by his own success totally caught up in a passing show that goads him into angry postures and tart replies."[38] Some literary studies, more than others, ask for the assent of the reader. This applies, I think, to source studies. I have presented the rich, extraliterary evidence that Lipsius's anecdote should be considered a source, as least, for Pope's introductory lines to his concentrated apologia.

Similarities are obvious. The diurnal moment, never mentioned by Horace. A servant calls. The lengthy list of needy dependents. Dialogue in a garden, direct or implied. Clearly, too, differences are obvious. Lipsius's ironic exasperation is reversed by Pope's assertive and dismissive frustration and anger. Lipsius's garden is a symbol of friendship and peace, Pope's, a repository of threats to his well-being. Lipsius's centrifugal tendencies are opposed by Pope's centripetal trajectory. Let me conclude with three symmetries of interest that could have led Pope to a greater intimacy with the writings of Lipsius, beyond his reading of the elephants in epistle 50.

1. *Dogs.* Dogs were one of Lipsius's known passions. His characteristic pose can be seen in the oft-reprinted Goltzius engraving, a book in one hand, the other on the head of Mopsius, his favorite dog. It is the frontispiece to many of the separate printings of his works. The most famous Lipsius portrait, by Rubens, includes three figures who give the picture its full meaning: Rubens, a bust of Seneca, and in the foreground, Mopsius. Lipsius's epigram on Mopsius, written in 1605, was reprinted in all of his collected works.[39]

Pope's Bounce, his much-loved bitch, we also know about because of his epigrams. He gave her whelps as gifts to his royal friends. His last couplet was written to his Great Dane:

Ah Bounce, oh gentle Beast; why wouldst thou die
When thou hast Meat enough, and Orrery?[40]

2. *Gardens.* For both, gardens were memorials of friendship and virtue. Lipsius's visitors were welcomed, in print and in life, to his garden. In fact, to induce him to remain the foremost lecturer at the University of Leiden, the authorities gave him the attractive present of a spacious garden for his private use and pleasure.[41] Pope's proudest lines, in his first translation of a Horatian satire, exult in the distinguished friends who invest his garden and grotto. Mack's intimate study of the mature Pope, *The Garden and the City*, revealed the essential place

of the garden in Pope's life and art. Mack's insights were reinforced by later, more intense studies of the gardening world in Pope.[42]

3. *Friendship*. All of us who have taught Pope and Swift, especially their correspondence, have been moved by the friendship shared, the love developed, and its fervor sustained, by gentle indignities and ironic insults. A glance at the *Concordance* to Pope's poems overwhelms us with its eight extra-large folio columns of "friend" and its cognates. They number 761, the highest of any entry listed. God comes in second, at 689. For Reuben Brower, Pope is "the poet of friendship." For David Fairer, one of the most insightful of Pope's readers, "*Arbuthnot* itself is unified by the theme of friendship."[43] Friendship is also the unifying theme of the Rubens portrait of Lipsius. It is the bond between teacher and student. It is a theme frequently commented on by all who wrote about him. Friendship shored up the Stoics' involvement with all humanity. Lipsius, like Pope, never seems to have overlooked an occasion where he could picture himself surrounded in his garden by men of virtue, learning, and honor. His friendships were long-lasting, "and he throve on the approval of his friends."[44]

I will end with the words of Lipsius's "beloved Seneca":

> Much still remains to be done, and much will always remain, in this domain, and he who shall be born a thousand years hence will not be barred from his opportunity of adding something further.[45]

APPENDIX

Justi Lipsiues, Physiologiae Stoicorum, "Libri Tertii, Dissertatio Prima," from *Justus Lipsius, The Philosophy of Renaissance Stoicism*, trans. Jason Lewis Saunders (New York: Liberal Arts Press, 1955), 62–63.[46]

AUD Hail, my dear doctor.

LIPS The same to you. But why so early? The sun has scarcely touched the fourth hour [come up].

AUD But your admonition yesterday stirred me up and sent me here. Don't you remember? You were saying Time should be made use of: it runs on and flows; and once gone can never be called back. I am ready, therefore, and I think about making good use of [time] and bringing things to fruition, and consecrate the mind on the Good from the earliest hour of the day. How should I know whether tomorrow or another midday will be granted? Since this speed of time overturns the spirit, since this mortality is insidious and uncertain: why should I not make haste? I accept what is to be the plunder of time. *While life is being analyzed and organized, it runs away* (Seneca, epistle 1).

LIP Yes, indeed, moreover while it is being snatched away, isn't life also
running away? So it happens with us, letters, satires, other cares, even
actions are constantly occupying us. And there is scarcely any time given
for leisure, unless something is left over after everything else has been covered. *Of all workers,* says Annaeus (*De brevitate vitae* 19), *misery is the
condition; but of those the most miserable are ones who do not labor on their
own affairs.* I think he has written about me, or certainly agrees with me:
I could almost exclaim, with Livus Drusus [famed Roman lawyer] that "to
me alone no holiday has fallen from boyhood up." I get up in the morning.
"Here are the letters, answer them." Having done that, I turn to other
things. My servant comes to say that some nobleman has called, or a youth
from France, Germany, or Sarmatia [Iran] wishes to pay his respects [to
attend my levee]. All of them want a token of my friendship to be inscribed
in their albums. I have hardly recovered my breath when one of my Bel-
gian friends appears. "Hello there! I've just written a poem—or pamphlet—
and I want you to read it." "Anything more?" "Criticize it and correct it."
"What else?" "Just write some preliminary verses or a recommendation."
Then I think I'm really free, but someone else comes in and wants an epitaph, either for himself or for his brother or his father or a friend, or else
an inscription for a house or an arch or an altar. Then what about my students, those like yourself? You know how valuable I am to them, and how
I listen to them, answer them, direct them, and set them in what I believe
to be the right way of study. This is the one sort of work I least regret
amongst all others; there is little difference whether I help them by talking
or writing. In the first case, perhaps more hear me, while in the other,
although fewer receive what I say, perhaps the result is more effective and
fruitful. So my life is spent, and I am resolved to put up with it; but *what it
is out of our power to amend, becomes more supportable by patience.* [Hor-
ace, *Odes,* I, xxiv, 20]. . . . Still, from time to time I return to myself, and I
turn over in my mind something beneficial and profitable to myself.

NOTES

I thank Raymond Waddington for his steady encouragement and scholarly advice, Pat
Rogers for his careful reading and corrections, Jim May and Kenneth Newell for their
helpful comments on an earlier draft, and Ruth Maher for all her technical support and
patience.
     1. Alexander Pope, *Imitations of Horace,* vol. 4 of *The Twickenham Edition of the Poems of
Alexander Pope,* ed. John Butt (1939; repr., London: Methuen, 1969), 96–100, ll. 1–68. All
further Pope quotations are from *The Twickenham Edition* and are cited parenthetically in
the text by volume, page, and sometimes line numbers. See also John Butt, *Pope's Poetical
Manuscripts: Warton Lecture of English Poetry, 1954* (London: The British Academy, 1954).
For Maynard Mack's masterful commentary on Pope's manuscripts, see his *The Last and
Greatest Art: Some Unpublished Poetical Manuscripts of Alexander Pope* (Newark: University of Delaware Press, 1954), 419–423.

2. Pope, *Imitations of Horace*, 94. But see Reuben A. Brower, *Alexander Pope: The Poetry of Allusion* (Oxford: Oxford University Press, 1959), 175.

3. For Edmond Malone, see Pope, *Imitations of Horace*, 113n248; for Mark Pattison, see 104n127; for John Wilson Croker, see 122n363. Some others are "resembles" (96n4); "modeled on" (123n368); "recollections" (96n11).

4. Two formidable essays that examine the paramount influences on *Arbuthnot* need to be considered: Niall Rudd's "Variation and Inversion in Pope's *Epistle to Dr. Arbuthnot*," *Essays in Criticism* 34 (1984): 216–228, and Elias F. Mengel's "Pope's Imitation of Boileau in *Arbuthnot*," *Essays in Criticism* 38 (1988): 295–307. For Rudd, "Horace is the dominant influence" (227), although, besides identifying six new references to Horace, Rudd also identifies allusions to Statius, Juvenal, Persius, and Lucilius. Mengel proposes twelve allusions to Boileau, besides the eight allusions recorded in *The Twickenham Edition*. For Mengel, "These twenty echoes of Boileau establish him as the major influence in Pope's poem" (295). I cannot see any value in replacing Horace with Boileau, nor in pinning Pope's *Arbuthnot* to any dominant sources. His rich and allusive memory signals multiple echoes for him and for his readers.

5. Mark Morford, *Stoics and Neostoics: Rubens and the Circle of Lipsius* (Princeton: Princeton University Press, 1992), 54. Horace recurs often to this scene for proof of his literary eminence; see Horace, *Satire II, vi*, ll. 32–39, and *Epistle II, ii*, ll. 65–70, in *Satires, Epistles, and Ars Poetica*, trans. H. Rushton Fairclough, Loeb Classical Library (Cambridge: Harvard University Press, 1961). For Pope's more "anecdotal" imitation of *Epistle, II, ii*, see Pope, *Imitations of Horace*, 171, ll. 88–126. While translating Horace in 1718, Pope complained of having "no peace from visitants, and appointments of continual parties of pleasure." See *The Correspondence of Alexander Pope*, ed. George Sherburn, 5 vols. (Oxford: Clarendon Press, 1956), 1:484, 352 (henceforth Pope, *Correspondence*).

6. See Ernst Kris and Otto Kurz, *Legend, Myth, and Magic in the Image of the Artist* (New Haven: Yale University Press, 1974), 6, a brilliant study. For anecdotes of miraculous dreams and miraculous escapes from danger, a recurring anecdote in the lives of artists, and told in Lipsius's autobiography, see Morford, *Stoics and Neostoics*, 98. Kris and Kurz's study of painters, sculptors, and architects was finely complemented and supplemented by the insightful studies of Mary R. Lefkowitz; see her "Fictions in Literary Biography: The New Poem and the Archilochus Legend," *Arethusa* 9 (1976): 181–189; "The Poet as Hero: Fifth-Century Autobiography and Subsequent Biographical Fiction," *Classical Quarterly* 28 (1978): 459–469; "Autobiographical Fiction in Pindar," *Harvard Studies in Classical Philology* 84 (1980): 29–49; and *The Lives of the Greek Poets* (Baltimore: Johns Hopkins University Press, 1981). But see Maarit Kivilo, *Early Greek Poets' Lives: The Shaping of a Tradition* (Leiden: Brill, 2010), who questions Lefkowitz's "radical approach" (4), yet concludes that the story of Hesiod's death is "highly formulaic" (35, 52–56). She admits that she has not chosen to "determine the historical veracity of the details in the tradition" (6).

7. Hilary Mantel, *Wolf Hall* (London: Fourth Estate, 2009), 93.

8. Manuel Schonhorn, "'Here Comes the Son': A Shandean Project," in *The Age of Projects*, ed. Maximillian Novak (Toronto: University of Toronto Press, 2008), 272–296.

9. Otto Rank, *The Myth of the Birth of the Hero* (New York: Nervous and Mental Disease Publishing, 1913); Joseph Campbell, *The Hero with a Thousand Faces* (Princeton: Princeton University Press, 1968).

10. Seneca, *De brevitate vitae* 19, translated as "On the Shortness of Life," in Moses Hadas, *The Stoic Philosophy of Seneca* (Gloucester: Peter Smith, 1965), 44–73, esp. 72. Also Seneca, *Epistulae Morales ad Lucilium*, 62.2. For these citations, see Morford, *Stoics and Neostoics*, 54–55; for Muretus, see 60n4.

11. Ernst Robert Curtius, *European Literature and the Latin Middle Ages*, trans. Willard Trask (1948; repr., New York: Harper, 1963), 177.

12. For the Loeb editor, see Horace, *Satires*, trans. Fairclough, 208. See also Pope, *Imitations of Horace*, 248, and *The Poems of Jonathan Swift*, ed. Harold Williams, 3 vols.

(Oxford: Clarendon Press, 1958), 1:197–202. Also Pope, *Imitations of Horace, Satire II, vi,* 255, ll. 63–82.

13. Jason Lewis Saunders, *Justus Lipsius: The Philosophy of Renaissance Stoicism* (New York: Liberal Arts Press, 1955), 62–63. See also John Hale, *The Civilization of Europe in the Renaissance* (New York: Atheneum, 1994), 213. On 602n45, Hale misprints Saunders's 62 for 22. Earlier, Lipsius, in *De Constantia* (1594), had written, "If I love quietnesse and rest, the Trumpets and ratling of armour interrupt me. If I take solace in my countrey gardens and farmes, the souldiers and mirtherers force me into the Towne," quoted in Andrew Shifflett, *Stoicism, Politics, and Literature in the Age of Milton* (Cambridge: Cambridge University Press, 1998), 29. In his edition of Pope's *An Essay on Man,* Maynard Mack cites John Stradling's translation of Lipsius's *De Constantia* (1598) as a "source," but the thought in Pope's lines is too conventional to consider as a source, and there is no indication that Pope read the book, even though it was a "best seller" of the seventeenth century. See Alexander Pope, *An Essay on Man,* vol. 3 of *The Twickenham Edition,* ed. Maynard Mack (1950; repr., London: Methuen, 1970), iv:139nn. ll. 119–120, iv:140–141n136.

14. The essential bibliography is Ferdinand van der Haeghen, *Bibliotheca Belgica,* vols. 15–17 (Ghent: Bibliothèque de l'Université de Gand, 1880–1890).

15. Reid Barbour, *English Epicures and Stoics: Ancient Legacies in Early Stuart Culture* (Amherst: University of Massachusetts Press, 1998), 196. Saunders writes that Lipsius "tried sincerely to reconcile the thoughts of the Great Stoics with the fundamental doctrines of Christianity" (15).

16. See Thomas Hyde, *Catalogus Impressorum Librorum Bibliothecae Bodleianae,* 2 vols. (1673–1674; repr., Oxford: Sheldonian Theatre, 1738). Hyde is also listed as the author of a 1674 catalog of the holdings of the Bodleian. Consult also E. S. Leedham-Green, *Books in Cambridge Inventories,* 2 vols. (Cambridge: Cambridge University Press, 1986), and H. M. Adams, *Catalogue of Books Printed on the Continent of Europe, 1501–1600 in Cambridge Libraries,* 2 vols. (Cambridge: Cambridge University Press, 1967).

17. I owe this reference to Christine Jackson-Holzberg of the Shaftesbury Project.

18. Sheridan's library auction catalog (1739) has been published in Dirk F. Passmann and Heinz J. Vienken's *The Library and Reading of Jonathan Swift: A Bio-bibliographical Handbook,* pt. 1: *Swift's Library,* 4 vols. (Frankfurt am Main: Peter Lang, 2003), 4:217–288. Sheridan also owned a 1652 (Amsterdam) edition of Lipsius's *De Constantia.* Pope has some jocular comments on Sheridan in *Correspondence,* 3:97–98, 101.

19. Frederick Ribble and Anne Ribble, *Fielding's Library: An Annotated Catalogue* (Charlottesville: Bibliographical Society of the University of Virginia, 1996).

20. Charles Whibley, *A Facsimile Reproduction of a Unique Catalogue of Laurence Sterne's Library* (London: Tregaskis, 1930), nos. 1932, 1933. Neither William Congreve nor Daniel Defoe appears to have possessed the *Physiologiae.* Caution is suggested concerning attribution of ownership. Interested readers may want to see *Sale Catalogues of Libraries of Eminent Persons,* ed. A. N. L. Munby, 9 vols. (London: Mansell & Sotheby-Parke-Bernet, 1971).

21. See Passmann and Vienken, *The Library and Reading of Jonathan Swift,* 2:1079–1087. Swift refers to Lipsius in *The Prose Writings of Jonathan Swift,* ed. Herbert Davis, 14 vols. (Oxford: Basil Blackwell, 1964), 4:216. The text is *A Proposal for Correcting the English Tongue.* See also William LeFanu, *A Catalogue of Books Belonging to Dr. Jonathan Swift . . . Aug. 1715* (Cambridge: Cambridge University Library, 1988). Passmann and Vienken discuss a 1744 catalog published in Dublin (4:347). Harold Williams, in *Dean Swift's Library* (Cambridge: Cambridge University Press, 1932), has some older commentary. Some interesting bits of information about Swift's library and holdings can be found in Dirk F. Passmann, "Jonathan Swift as Book-Collector: With a Checklist of Swift's Association Copies," *Swift Studies* 27 (2012): 7–68. I owe much of the above to, and I have learned much about Swift from, my friend James Woolley.

22. Pierre Bayle, *General Dictionary, Historical and Critical*, 10 vols. (London: James Bettenham, 1734), 7:102–109. The first English edition was published in 1710; the first French edition in 1697. Bayle's *Dictionary* was not among Pope's books, but there "is evidence that he knew [him]"; see Maynard Mack, "Pope's Books: A Bibliographical Survey with a Finding List," in *English Literature in the Age of Disguise*, ed. Maximillian E. Novak (Berkeley: University of California Press, 1977), 221, an indispensable article. His listings have been reprinted with very minor additions in *Collected in Himself: Essays Cultural, Biographical, and Bibliographical on Pope and Some of His Contemporaries* (Newark: University of Delaware Press, 1982), appendix A, "A Finding List," 394–460. Mack mentions many hundreds of titles that Pope remarks about in conversation with Joseph Spence that are not listed in Mack's library records (394). Pope mentions Bayle in his *Correspondence*, 2:302. Lipsius is not noted in Thomas Stanley, *The History of Philosophy, in Eight Parts* (London: Humphrey Moseley and Thomas Dring, 1656), 16–142. Pope owned Stanley's third edition (1701); see Mack, "Pope's Books," 296, no. 154. Pope mentions him in *Correspondence*, 1:323. For an appreciation of Lipsius's polymathic industry, illustrations of his scholarship and editorial work, and a fair appraisal of his moral and professional failings, see Anthony Grafton, "Portrait of Justus Lipsius," *The American Scholar* 56 (1987): 382–390. Grafton remarks about Lipsius and Tacitus in his *Defenders of the Text* (Cambridge: Harvard University Press, 1991), 39–40, and calls Lipsius "learned but overheated" (98), in *The Footnote: A Curious History* (Cambridge: Harvard University Press, 1997).

23. *The Spectator*, ed. Donald Bond, 5 vols. (Oxford: Clarendon Press, 1965), 1:43, no. 9 (10 March 1711). For Fielding, see *Tom Thumb and the Tragedy of Tragedies*, ed. L. J. Morrissey (Berkeley: University of California Press, 1970), I:i.10.

24. Swift, *On Good Manners and Good Breeding*, in *Prose Writings of Swift*, ed. Davis, 4:215–216. Swift's library catalog listed *The Annals and History of Cornelius Tacitus . . . Made English by Several Hands*, 2nd ed., 3 vols. (London: John Nicholson, 1716). Volume 1 contained "A Character of C. Cornelius Tacitus and his Writings By Justus Lipsius" (3–8); see Passmann and Vienken, *The Library and Reading of Jonathan Swift*, 2:1785. For their appreciation of Lipsius's editorial work on Tacitus, see 2:1789. For Swift's many mentions of Tacitus, see the index to *Prose Writings of Swift*, 14:340.

25. Saunders, *Justus Lipsius*, 14. "Up to the nineteenth century [Lipsius's] meticulously edited commentary on the text of Tacitus (1575) in the main consisted of comments by, and on, Lipsius." See Morford, *Stoics and Neostoics*, 143n22—Morford is quoting C. O. Brink.

26. Louis Moreri, *Great Historical, Geographical, and Poetical Dictionary*, 2nd ed., 2 vols. (London: Henry Rhodes, 1701), n.p.

27. Saunders, in *Justus Lipsius*, writes that "no mention of Stoicism in the seventeenth and eighteenth centuries was complete without some reference to Justus Lipsius" (220). Perhaps that requires a note on Pope and Stoicism. Pope does not mention Stoics or Stoicism in his *Correspondence*. There are passing mentions, but nothing of depth, in his poetry. What is evident is that he refuses to satirize Stoics or Stoic doctrine. Their extreme beliefs are always balanced by an extreme of another kind; there is no frontal attack, no point-blank denunciation. His citations are without rigor, and, while Stoics are not treated sympathetically, a harsh edge is never evident; see *An Essay on Man*, ii:67, ll. 101–102, and ii:53, ll. 5–6. "The general structure and theme of Pope's ethics are strongly Stoic" (xxxv). See also *Minor Poems*, vol. 6 of *The Twickenham Edition*, ed. Norman Ault and John Butt (1954; repr., London: Methuen, 1964), 41, 114. Pope mentions Chrysippus, one of the most important founders of the Stoic philosophy, but his citation comes directly from Chaucer's "Wife of Bath Prologue," which he is translating. For Pope and Stoicism, see A. R. Humphreys, "Pope, God, and Man," in *Writers and Their Background: Alexander Pope*, ed. Peter Dixon (London: Bell and Sons, 1972), 60–100, and Rebecca Ferguson, *The Unbalanced Mind: Pope and the Rule of Passion* (Brighton: Harvester, 1986), who distinguishes Pope from Horatian and Stoic thought.

28. For the comprehensive list and thoughtful commentary on Pope's books, his gifts to friends, bequests, and annotations, see Mack, "Pope's Books," 209–305. Pope and Sir William Trumbull "read together, and naturally borrowed books passed frequently back and forth between them"; they "talked of the classics in his retirement." See George Sherburn, "Letters of Alexander Pope, Chiefly to Sir William Trumbull," *Review of English Studies,* n.s., 9 (1958): 388–406, esp. 389. The editors of *Windsor-Forest* suggest that it was in Sir William Trumbull's library that he had "gained access to some of the old chronicles which were of great use in the poem." See *Pastoral Poetry and An Essay on Criticism,* vol. 1 of *The Twickenham Edition,* ed. E. Audra and Aubrey Williams (1961; repr., London: Methuen, 1969), 127. For the importance of Trumbull in Pope's education, see Maynard Mack, *Alexander Pope: A Life* (New Haven: Yale University Press, 1985), 104–109. The libraries of Pope's friends need study, for, as far as I know, little commentary has seen publication.

29. Pope, *Correspondence,* 1:270, 3:187.

30. Pope, *Correspondence,* 1:338. The Lipsius volume cited by Pope, to be described below, is *Epistolarum Selectarum Centuria Prima Miscellanea* (1605). There were many subsequent editions. It was reprinted in *Opera Omnia,* 4 vols. (Antwerp, 1637), 2:59–71. I wish to thank James Towe, archivist librarian, Chatsworth, for checking the third Earl of Burlington's library catalog of 1742.

31. Pope, *Correspondence,* 3:147, 54, 114. Mack, citing the Elwin and Courthope edition of Pope's *Works,* 10 vols. (London, 1887–1889), 8:278, notes that Pope wrote Swift in 1730 of "[Oxford's] new room to lodge books in"; see Mack's introduction to *An Essay on Man,* i:xiii. The Earls of Oxford and Burlington were two of the three nobles to whom Pope assigned the copyright of the *Dunciad Variorum;* see *Epistles to Several Persons,* vol. 3, pt. 2 of *The Twickenham Edition,* ed. F. W. Bateson, 2nd ed. (1951; repr., London: Methuen, 1961), 83n. For a beautiful analysis of a beautiful poem, see Geoffrey Tillotson, "Pope's *Epistle to Harley*: An Introduction and Analysis," in *Pope and His Contemporaries: Essays Presented to George Sherburn,* ed. James L. Clifford and Louis A. Landa (New York: Oxford University Press, 1949), 58–77.

32. *Catalogus Bibliothecae Harleianae,* 5 vols. (London: Thomas Osborne, 1743–1745). See also W. Jackson Bate, *Samuel Johnson* (New York: Harvest, 1979), 223–225.

33. Mack, "Pope's Books," 225. See his comments on Pope's "exact learning" and "fine memory" (223), and his reading with "care and intensity" (284). Pope's edition of Montaigne is *Essays of Seigneur de Montaigne. In Three Books. Tr. Charles Cotton, Esq.,* 3 vols. (London: T. Basset, 1685). Volumes 2 (1686) and 3 (1693) are noted in Mack, "Pope's Books," 274.

34. Mack, "Pope's Books," 281. This is the last of thirty marginal notes that Pope made in his *Montaigne.* Mack writes, "There is hardly a page that is not starred up and down with his marginal commas, and there are also far more explicit verbal comments in this than in any other books of his with which I am acquainted" (225). Montaigne is noted fifty-six times by his editors in *The Twickenham Edition,* none of which is pertinent to this study. Pope in his poetry simply mentions Montaigne twice: See *Satire II, i,* l. 52, and *Epistle I, i,* l. 281. I cite Montaigne in the text by volume, chapter, and page number.

35. Mack, "Pope's Books," 276. Pope is citing Lipsius, letter 50, first printed in *Epistolarum Selectarum Centuria Prima Miscellaneae* (Antwerp, 1586), and often reprinted (1590, 1601), and in *Opera Omnia,* 2:59–71. Cotton's *Montaigne,* volume 2, which I read in Columbia University's Rare Book and Manuscript Library, has multiple errors in printing. Chapter headings are misnumbered, gatherings disordered, and running titles in error. The reader should be wary.

36. See Henry Knight Miller, "The Paradoxical Encomium with Special Reference to Its Vogue in England, 1600–1800," *Modern Philology* 53 (1956): 145–178. Miller has some lesser comments in his *Essays on Fielding's Miscellanies: A Commentary on Volume One* (Princeton: Princeton University Press, 1961), 302–306. I thank my friend Irwin Primer for this citation.

37. Marcia L. Colish, *The Stoic Tradition from Antiquity to the Early Middle Ages* (London: Brill, 1990), 27. Pope's stance on the "half-reas'ning elephant" is explicitly made in *Essay on Man*, i:43, l. 222.

38. Maynard Mack, *The Garden and the City: Retirement and Politics in the Late Poetry of Pope, 1731–1743* (Toronto: University of Toronto Press, 1969), 5.

39. *Epistolarum ad Belgas, Centuria I* (Antwerp, 1605), 53; Morford, *Stoics and Neostoics*, 5, 11, 33n63, 33n68; and J. A. Van Dorsten, *Poets, Patrons, and Professors* (London: Oxford University Press, 1962), plate opposite 117.

40. Pope, *Correspondence*, 4:505–508, 517–518; Pope, *Minor Poems*, 366–372; Marjorie Nicolson and G. S. Rousseau, *"This Long Disease, My Life": Alexander Pope and the Sciences* (Princeton: Princeton University Press, 1968), 75.

41. Van Dorsten, *Poets, Patrons, and Professors*, 148, and Morford, *Stoics and Neostoics*, 11.

42. From Pope, *Imitations of Horace, Satire II, i*, ll. 125–132. See Mack, *The Garden and the City*, and Peter Martin, *The Gardening World of Alexander Pope* (Hamden: Archon Books, 1984).

43. David Fairer, *The Poetry of Alexander Pope* (Harmondsworth: Penguin, 1989), 111. "For Pope friendship was of first importance," in Tillotson, "Pope's *Epistle to Harley*," 73; *A Concordance to the Poems of Alexander Pope*, ed. Emmett G. Bedford and Robert J. Dilligan, 2 vols. (Detroit: Gale, 1974). Also Brower, in *Alexander Pope*, calls him "the poet of friendship" (182); Mack, *Alexander Pope*: "He had an unusual talent for friendship" (186). Wide-ranging is Emrys D. Jones, *Friendship and Allegiance in Eighteenth-Century Literature: The Politics of Private Virtue in the Age of Walpole* (Houndmills: Palgrave Macmillan, 2013).

44. Morford, *Stoics and Neostoics*, 52. Given Pope's epistolary manipulations, if he had known, he would surely have smiled to have learned that Lipsius's letters were "always carefully gone over, some corrected, others radically changed, and some undoubtedly destroyed." See Saunders, *Justus Lipsius*, 24.

45. Saunders, *Justus Lipsius*, 78.

46. I thank Richard Peterson for help with this translation.

PART III

Re-evaluating Literary Modes

CHAPTER 7

When Worlds Collide

ANTI-METHODIST LITERATURE AND THE RISE OF POPULAR LITERARY CRITICISM IN THE *CRITICAL REVIEW* AND THE *MONTHLY REVIEW*

Brett C. McInelly

Shortly after the publication of *The Crooked Disciple's Remarks upon the Blind Guide's Method of Preaching* (1761), a satirical attack on George Whitefield, the *Critical Review* published this short notice: "All we can collect from this performance is, that the crooked disciple is as waggish as the blind guide is absurd."[1] The review illustrates a recurring tendency found in the pages of the *Critical Review*, as well as in its counterpart, the *Monthly Review*, to call out what the reviewers perceived as "bad" writing while declaiming against the Methodists and their leaders: the author is "as waggish" as Whitefield is "absurd." Although attacking Methodism was tangential to the primary goal of both journals—to offer ostensibly impartial reviews of newly published books in an effort to establish critical standards for literary merit—both review journals generally concurred with much of the anti-Methodist sentiment that circulated in the public press, and they seized upon the popularity of their productions, and their platform, to expose the Methodists as a group of religious fanatics. When an anti-Methodist work rose to the reviewers' critical standards, these dual purposes were easily reconciled, inasmuch as they could praise both the medium and the message. However, when the message came packaged in a form that violated rules of literary and satiric decorum, the reviewers found themselves negotiating between their desire to regulate literary tastes and their impulse to undermine the Methodist revival.

The notice for *The Crooked Disciple's Remarks* illustrates one of the cruder strategies that both reviews employed to achieve their aims: they dismissed an author and his work as simply being of inferior rank while castigating the Methodists. However, examining both review journals indicates that reconciling the principal objective of the burgeoning genre of the review essay with a social agenda proved to be a more complex issue than this simple strategy suggests. What happened to the anti-Methodist critique, which had been espoused in poems, plays, and other literary types, when it was filtered through the critical apparatus of the review essay? How was the genre of the literary review shaped by extracritical considerations? The review journals inevitably contributed to the campaign to discredit Methodism by merely reporting on anti-Methodist works from a clearly partisan point of view and, in a number of cases, amplifying the negative sentiments expressed in the anti-Methodist literature. In other instances, however, hostility toward the revival and its participants was muted by the reviewers' fidelity to their standards for making literary judgments, particularly when a given anti-Methodist work violated those standards. The treatment of Methodism by both the *Monthly Review* and the *Critical Review* demonstrates, on one hand, the extent to which Methodism in the eighteenth century took shape in the crucible of public disputation, while, on the other, how the modern literary review essay emerged out of a simultaneous pull between reviewer opinion, whether about critical standards or about a social issue, and the inclination to codify rules for assessing literary merit and decorum.

Not unlike the Protestant Reformation, which was made possible, in large part, by the printing press, Methodism in eighteenth-century Britain became a media event and participated in the literary culture of the day from its beginnings in the late 1730s. George Whitefield utilized advertising media to publicize himself and his ministry (a fact routinely documented by biographers and religious historians).[2] Both Whitefield and John Wesley published extensively, including sermons, spiritual biography, devotional poetry, and hymnals. Wesley eventually owned and operated his own printing press to ensure the steady circulation of Methodist works among his followers, and in 1779, he launched the *Arminian Magazine*, which was published monthly. From its founding at Oxford in the 1730s, Methodism received a good deal of negative press, whether in religious polemic, satiric verse, dramatic script, or prose fiction, all of which set out to undermine the revival but simultaneously brought the movement, including its beliefs and practices, to the public's attention—even if in a negative light. Indeed, Whitefield may have been among the first public figures to recognize that even bad publicity is good publicity. As he observed in the wake of Samuel Foote's *Minor*, which satirized Whitefield in the figure of Dr. Squintum, which was performed to critical and popular acclaim on the London stage in 1760, and which spawned a number of spinoffs, including *The Crooked Disciple's Remarks*: "I am now mimicked and burlesqued upon the public stage. All hail such contempt!"[3] Not only did Whitefield see persecution as a badge of honor, something that galvanized Methodist faith and sense of community, but he readily acknowledged that anti-Methodist attacks raised public awareness of and perhaps even curiosity about the revival.

The anti-Methodist attacks also provided Whitefield and Wesley an opportunity to respond publicly to their critics, an opportunity they regularly seized upon in an effort to clarify their doctrinal positions and to refute criticism. As Whitefield insisted, "For what in an human Way can have a more natural Tendency to strengthen the Methodist's Hands than their having a publick Occasion to shew that they preach up the great Doctrines of the Reformation, and are thrust out of the Synagogues for no other Reason, than because they preach Articles of Faith."[4] Although both Wesley and Whitefield tended to ignore the more satiric attacks published against them, they routinely and publicly responded to their Anglican critics, who represented some of their staunchest antagonists. As I have argued elsewhere, Methodism, in large part, was thus constituted in the controversy that surrounded it—most of which materialized in print.[5] In short, both Methodists and non-Methodists alike experienced Methodism in and through the printed word to a significant degree.

Even in an age that witnessed the first daily newspapers, the proliferation of periodicals that touched on nearly every imaginable topic, and the publication of numerous other literary genres, including novels, plays, travel literature, biography, and sermons, the sheer output of anti-Methodist publications is impressive. Between 1732 and the end of the century, no fewer than 600 anti-Methodist titles appeared in print.[6] By comparison, John Sekora notes that between 1721 and 1771 about 460 books and pamphlets were published on luxury, which he identifies as "the greatest single social issue and the greatest single commonplace" of the eighteenth century.[7] Moreover, bibliographies of the anti-Methodist literature of the era include only a fraction of the anti-Methodist materials that appeared in the periodical press, and they do not include works that make peripheral and negative references to Methodism, such as Henry Fielding's *Shamela* (1741) and Tobias Smollett's *Humphry Clinker* (1771). No religious movement during the period, or perhaps even before, received such extensive treatment in the public press.

The extent to which Methodism participated in eighteenth-century literary culture ensured that works and ideas associated with the revival would make their way into the review journals that became popular at midcentury, first via the *Monthly Review* in 1749, and then via the *Critical Review*, which produced its first issue seven years later. Both journals began with the same intention, which was described on the title page of the first volume of the *Monthly Review*: "Giving an Account, with proper Abstracts of, and Extracts from, the New Books, Pamphlets, etc. as they come out."[8] In a longer advertisement, the creators of the *Monthly Review* further explained their rationale:

> When the abuse of title-pages is obviously come to such a pass, that few readers care to take in a book, any more than a servant, without a recommendation; to acquaint the public that a summary review of the productions of the

press, as they occur to notice, was perhaps never more necessary than now, would be superfluous and vain. The cure then for this general complaint is evidently, and only, to be found in a periodical work, whose sole object should be to give a compendious account of those productions of the press, as they come out, that are worth notice; an account, in short, which should, in virtue of its candour, and justness of distinction, obtain authority enough for its representations to be serviceable to such as would choose to have some idea of a book before they lay out their money or time on it. This is the view and aim of the present undertaking.[9]

The textual culture surrounding the Methodist revival and the world of review criticism naturally converged in the pages of the *Monthly Review* and the *Critical Review*. The writings of both Whitefield and Wesley, including their sermons and apologia, were regularly reviewed in both journals, as were Charles Wesley's hymns and the published writings of other Methodist leaders. The anti-Methodist literature, whether in the form of learned treatises by respected ecclesiastical figures, or in the form of Grub Street productions that crudely satirized Methodist belief and practice, was similarly well represented in both journals. As both pro- and anti-Methodist works found their way into print, they likewise found their way into the emerging genre of the literary review essay, adding yet another layer to eighteenth-century readers' experience of Methodism.

Before delving into how review literature contributed to the discourse about Methodism, we might more fully consider the objectives and the influence of these journals. While earlier periodicals included literary criticism and reviews of newly published books, the *Monthly Review*, as Antonia Forster explains, "was the first review journal in anything approaching the modern sense of the term."[10] Richard Steele and Joseph Addison included, and helped popularize, critical literary commentary in both *The Tatler* and *The Spectator*, and a variety of newspapers and periodicals printed notices of recently published books that included abstracts and excerpts prior to the advent of the *Monthly Review*. But the *Monthly Review* included critical commentary alongside lengthy summaries and excerpts, and as Walter Graham argues, because of the journal's "size, general quality, and long career as a periodical, the justice of calling [it] the earliest Review of importance must be granted."[11]

Another innovation introduced by the *Monthly Review* and continued by the *Critical Review* involved the types of works that each publication submitted to critical review. As Forster notes, "The *Monthly Review* dealt from its first number with imaginative literature instead of restricting itself, as had been the usual practice of its predecessors, to 'works of the learned'" (3). Both review journals included books that they deemed of high and of low quality in their efforts to shape literary tastes and the reading habits of their consumers. This inclusive approach helps account for the appearance of the full gamut of anti-Methodist publications, from deftly argued polemical pieces to more imaginative literary genres that included anti-Methodist poems, plays, and works of prose fiction, several of which, when judged on purely aesthetic grounds, are of poor quality, a point reviewers routinely made and one to which I will return later in this chapter. High culture thus mingled with Grub Street in the pages of both journals, thereby bringing the variety of the materials available in the marketplace to the attention of a book-buying public.

These review journals were undoubtedly successful in publicizing newly published books and pamphlets. As James Basker observes, both the *Monthly Review* and the *Critical Review* "printed 2,500 to 3,500 copies a month, and they were read in coffeehouses, reading societies, and homes everywhere."[12] These journals, Frank Donoghue similarly argues, "affected virtually everyone in the English reading public—these were the most popular magazines of the time, printed in very large numbers with each copy reaching several readers."[13] As consumers navigated a marketplace flooded with materials and made decisions about which books were worth their time and resources, both the *Monthly Review* and the *Critical Review* became what Basker describes as "a consumer's guide for what was, after all, the first mass-production industry in history" ("Criticism," 328).

Booksellers and authors became keenly attuned to the influence of these journals. Booksellers began quoting from both in their advertisements for their books, and authors who worried about how a negative review might affect sales, and perhaps their reputations, often responded in letters to their reviewers, which were printed, along with editorial responses from both journals. Like a number of her contemporaries, Frances Burney dedicated her first novel, *Evelina*, to the authors of both journals—and with good cause. She was a first-time author who recognized the inferior status of novels generally in the minds of the reviewers and in the hierarchy of literary genres at the time she was writing. "The extensive plan of your critical observations," Burney wrote, "which, not confined to works of utility or ingenuity, is equally open to those of frivolous amusement, . . . encourages me to seek your protection, since . . . it entitles me to your annotations. To resent, therefore, this offering, however insignificant, would ill become the universality of your undertaking; though not to despise it may, alas! be out of your power."[14]

However, gauging the actual impact of the review journals on the book-buying decisions of the reading public is difficult. One measurable metric is evident in the records of lending and other libraries. A number of these institutions subscribed to both the *Monthly Review* and the *Critical Review*, and they consulted these publications when deciding on which books to add to their collections. As Basker observes, the review journals "actually determined the contents of libraries, public and private, throughout the English-speaking world" ("Criticism," 329).

The *Monthly Review* and the *Critical Review* began as commercial ventures, but both framed their endeavors as a public service, noting what the *Critical*

Review described as "the severe task of reading every new production" and the "delicate task of directing the public taste with regard to literature."[15] As Donoghue documents, however, the reviewers often expressed frustration with the seeming futility of their efforts, because "large numbers of readers showed no signs of heeding the Reviews' disparagement of many kinds of 'bad' writing, including novels." In fact, there is compelling evidence that readers generally ignored reviewer recommendations, evidenced by the enduring popularity of novels despite the reviewers' regular derision of many of them. While both the *Monthly Review* and the *Critical Review* played an instrumental role in establishing and popularizing review literature, which became a firmly entrenched part of literary and popular culture by the early nineteenth century, Donoghue raises an important question: "We need to ask . . . why the conservative rationale from which review criticism sprang was not dislodged by the nascent laissez-faire consumer culture with which it seems so much at odds." Donoghue posits that "the Reviews answered a crucial need not merely by claiming to offer, hypothetically, an impartial and independent judgment about books, but by offering the consumers of those books an orderly and comprehensible way of participating in the literary culture of the day" (63). As he goes on to note, "Reading a Review and abiding by its recommendations were two very different and not necessarily related activities" (70–71).

To put it another way, these reviews democratized literary culture by inviting readers from a multiplicity of backgrounds into a critical conversation about books—and the scope of both review journals ensured that books about Methodism, and the ideas those books promulgated, became a part of that conversation. It is worth noting that the review journals burst onto the literary scene at a time when Methodism had evolved from the "Holy Club" at Oxford (a group of young men who met together regularly to study religious texts and to practice a regimented kind of religiosity) to an institution in its own right with a well-defined and highly organized structure that was particularly evident in the Wesleyan arm of the movement. As Richard Heitzenrater describes, "By 1750, the Methodists had a specific doctrinal identity expressed in the *Minutes* and the *Sermons*; a national organizational network featuring circuits of societies . . . with some centralized financing, led by set-apart preachers who met yearly in Conference; and a characteristic missional program that consisted of benevolent institutions as well as charitable activities."[16] Although the Methodists never represented more than 1 percent of Britain's total population during the eighteenth century, they laid the groundwork for its unprecedented growth in the nineteenth century—on both sides of the Atlantic.

Moreover, the tenor of the anti-Methodist criticism, which spiked in the late 1730s and early 1740s, had been so firmly established by midcentury that the accusations leveled at the Methodists in the polemical and satiric literature produced at that time seem redundant, if not clichéd. From the outset of the revival, the Methodists had been charged with religious enthusiasm and had been accused of being antinomians for emphasizing salvation by faith. In addition, lay participation, especially by women and members of the lower classes, led to accusations that Methodism disrupted social, political, and ecclesiastical order. Methodist preachers reportedly used their rhetorical acumen to prey on the pockets and petticoats of their followers, and the Methodists were criticized for having a sanctimonious and ascetic bent while masking their carnal appetites behind a seemingly pious exterior. Indeed, stereotypes of Methodists as over-zealous hypocrites became commonplace in much of mainstream culture, so much so that the term "Methodist" was used in a variety of contexts to convey a sense of unconventionality and extremism. As early as 1741, a writer in the *Champion* satirically described a group of *"Political Methodists . . .* lately sprung up" who claimed that *"Regeneration* is as necessary in *Politics as Religion.* That all Men in a State of *Patriotism* are in a State of *Reprobation."*[17] Methodism and the ideas associated with it oriented this writer and his readers to a way of see-ing people of a particular political persuasion as being as radical in their views as a group of religious enthusiasts.

The *Monthly Review* and the *Critical Review* likewise propagated such stereo-types, first, by publicizing anti-Methodist works, and, second, by explicitly expressing the reviewers' own disdain for the revival and its participants. Both journals exposed readers to literary works they would not have otherwise encountered in much the same way that movie trailers today expose moviego-ers to movies they might not actually see. The journals included longer notices, some of which extended for several pages, or even into subsequent installments of the journal, along with detailed abstracts and lengthy excerpts, all of which provided a comprehensive overview of a work's content. Noting the "heavy reli-ance on quoted material" by Tobias Smollett and other earlier reviewers, Basker observes that 70 to 80 percent of their reviews consisted of summary and extracts.[18] Frances Brooke, who between 1755 and 1756 published a weekly peri-odical titled *The Old Maid*, pulled heavily from the *Critical Review* in an issue of her journal devoted entirely to lambasting Whitefield and the Methodists. Although she claims to quote directly from "the printed discourses" of a Meth-odist divine for her evidence against the revivalists, she later reports, "The pas-sages I have quoted from this author are to be found in the *Critical Review*."[19] In other words, Brooke appears to have relied exclusively on the *Critical Review* for her information about the treatise she criticizes. The review in question runs for nearly six pages and consists of mostly quotation and summary, thereby pro-viding Brooke with ample material for her critique of the Methodists and their beliefs—without having to consult the primary source.[20]

In addition to publicizing anti-Methodist works, both journals actively par-ticipated in the campaign to discredit the Methodists. While the reviewers writ-ing for the *Monthly Review* purported to present impartial accounts of the books they reviewed and to leave judgment up to individual readers, the reviewers' opinions, whether about social issues or a work's quality, regularly surface in its pages. The reviewers' opinions became even more prominent after the *Critical Review* went into circulation because it offered even more biased reviews than the *Monthly Review*. The "competitive pressure from the *Critical Review*," Donoghue notes, "pushed the *Monthly* into more and more opinionated articles" (59). But even before the *Critical Review* went into circulation, reviewers for the *Monthly Review* hardly masked their views of Methodism. For example, one reviewer summed up the aim of Theophilus Evans's *The History of Modern Enthusiasm*, published in 1752, in a clearly partisan way: "to expel the venom of [the Methodists'] pernicious and heretical tenets." The reviewer goes on to concur with Evans, who he insists "justly observes, [that] it is in vain to reason with [enthusiasts], argument having been always thrown away upon this sort of people."[21] Another review states that "the methodists are justly chargeable with superstition," while another concludes that an author whose "pious discourses" are incoherently assembled "seems to have been pretty highly tinctured with methodism."[22]

The *Critical Review* was even more prejudicial in its treatment of Methodism, which is not surprising because it "was established under Tory and Church patronage" and took up a more conservative position on political and religious matters than those expressed in the *Monthly Review* (Graham, 213). Smollett, who served as general editor during the early years of the journal, was leery of religious enthusiasm and believed that Methodism disrupted social and political order, points of view he would later register in such novels as *Sir Lancelot Greaves* (1760–1761), *Humphry Clinker* (1771), and in his *History of England* (1766). When reporting on the religious currents of his day, Smollett explained that

> the progress of reason, and free cultivation of the human mind, had not . . . entirely banished those ridiculous sects and schisms of which the kingdom had been formerly so productive. Imposture and fanaticism still hung upon the skirts of religion. Weak minds were seduced by the delusion of a superstition styled Methodism, raised upon the affectation of superior sanctity, and maintained by pretensions to divine illumination. Many thousands of the lower ranks of life were infected with this species of enthusiasm, by the unwearied endeavours of a few obscure preachers, such as Whitefield and the two Wesleys.[23]

Smollett honed his anti-Methodist sensibilities while writing for and editing the *Critical Review*. Referring to the journal's attacks on Methodism, Frances Brooke applauded in particular the journal's "ingenious and judicious authors" who "have, with true wit and humour, exposed the folly of this prevailing and pernicious spirit of enthusiasm" (188). Brooke, in other words, does not so much credit the *Monthly Review* with bringing anti-Methodist works to the public's attention; rather, she acknowledges the reviewers' own efforts to ridicule the Methodists in clever and entertaining ways via their reviews.

Brooke's praise of the *Critical Review*'s treatment of Methodism appears well deserved. As one reviewer claimed, Methodists were not true Christians: "The absurdity of those doctrines which distinguish the Methodists from other sober Christians and members of the Protestant church, are in this pamphlet fairly and clearly refuted."[24] Another reviewer described the progress of Methodism in England by echoing a common charge leveled against the Methodists—that they were tainted with the same religious and political zeal that sparked the civil wars of the previous century: "A new sect of enthusiasts, that would have disgraced the canting age of Cromwell, when hypocrisy was in the zenith, hath of late years gained considerable ground."[25] Writing about a tract composed by an Anglican clergyman on original sin, the reviewer lauded the author's achievement by juxtaposing the author's style of writing with "the incoherent rant and rhapsody of a Methodist."[26] Disparaging remarks regarding the Methodists likewise turn up in reviews of works that have nothing to do with Methodism or its doctrines. A pamphlet entitled *A Description of the Storm That Happened in West Kent* is described as "a piece of unintelligible rhapsody, penned, as it should seem by the style, by some wild enthusiastic Methodist."[27]

As these last few examples suggest, the *Critical Review* defined Methodism in wholly negative ways and then incorporated the term into its critical discourse. The word "Methodist" came not only to signify an enthusiastic participant in the revival, but also to describe what the reviewers perceived as an incoherent and hyperemotional style of writing, a point of view that derived, in part, from stereotypes of Methodist religiosity. These stereotypes were usually characterized by excessive zeal and emotional outbursts, but the association of the term "Methodist" with a certain style of writing likewise derived from a critical assessment of works that were authored by the revivalists themselves. Of a monody written at the time of Whitefield's death by a devotee, a reviewer claimed that the "performance [was] as far removed from real poetry, as methodism from true devotion" and described the verse as "unconnected nonsense" with "a few instances of fanatic elegance and sublimity."[28] The *Critical Review* offered a similar assessment of Whitefield's collected works, published shortly after his death by John Gillies. After applauding the motives that undergirded Whitefield's ministry, when perusing his printed sermons, the reviewer struggled to explain Whitefield's popularity as a preacher: "His discourses contain some few serious and rational exhortations; but the greatest part of them is made up of trifling observations, ludicrous stories, incoherent effusions, and pitiful rhapsody."[29]

Reviews like these helped establish a critical baseline against which reviewers described and judged various kinds of publications, including nonreligious and religious works. Of a work entitled *The Sick Man's Companion*, which includes instructions for and examples of various kinds of prayers an individual might offer up while ill, a reviewer praised both the simplicity and the plainness of the prayers by comparing them to the Lord's Prayer as recounted in the New Testament: "In this excellent prayer there is nothing mean, intricate, or obscure; there are none of those mystical expressions, those enthusiastic rants, those rapturous flights of unhallowed love and spiritual concupiscence; with which some of our modern books of devotion abound." Such books are produced, the reviewer states, by "the fanatical brain[s] of Methodists and Moravians."[30] A foreign author whose *History of Ancient Greece* had been recently translated into English is likewise linked to the Methodists for including what the reviewer describes as "fantastical" expressions: "Had he been an Englishman, the judicious part of his readers would have not hesitated one moment in pronouncing him to have been a kind of methodist."[31] On the other hand, an author whom the reviewers identify as a Methodist but who "seems to have kept clear of the excesses with which many of that persuasion are chargeable" is described as "a moderate Methodist."[32]

The reviewers for the *Monthly Review* similarly associated what they characterized as verbal excess, evasion, and obfuscation with Methodism and the writings of its leaders. Describing Wesley as "a man who is so much master of his own, as well as of other men's, passions," a reviewer offered ironic praise of Wesley's rhetorical acumen in his rebuttal to the Bishop of Gloucester's attack on the Methodists:

> [Wesley's] tract is, indeed, a notable one; he stands his ground manfully, repels the learned Bishop's attacks with such . . . Jesuitical evasions, and shelters himself so snugly under the authority of the Scriptures, and of the Church of England, (which he well knows how to twist and turn to his purpose) that we doubt not this performance will fully answer the great end of preventing his dignified Antagonist from enticing the sheep out of his fold.[33]

A reviewer of one of Charles Wesley's collections of hymns likewise observes Charles's capacity to manipulate language and scripture to his advantage. One of the hymns, the reviewer insists, "will make the reader *stare*, at least, if not *admire*, at the dexterity with which a Methodist . . . can typify, turn, and twist the plainest passages of holy writ, to adapt them to their mystical system." Noting the indelicate ways in which Charles's hymns yoke earthly images with spiritual ideas, the reviewer goes on to accuse Charles of "Bathos," ending with this rebuke: "May we not ask these rhyming enthusiasts how they dare to take such liberties, and use such indecent freedom, with the holy word of God!"[34] Considering these critical assessments of the published writings of such prominent Methodist figures, we should not be surprised that an anonymously published poem charged with incongruously adapting its tropes and figures to its religious subject was thought to have been the production of "some devout Methodist."[35]

The purportedly nonsensical ways by which Methodists communicated their religious experiences and ideas fit into a broader critique of the Methodists themselves, a critique that portrayed them as unintelligent, illiterate, and uneducated. These labels routinely appear throughout the corpus of anti-Methodist publications. Such accusations, however, took on even greater significance in the context of the review journals because the journals set out with the express purpose of promoting literacy and learning. The reviewers thus went out of their way not merely to denounce the writings of the Methodists as illogical, but also to emphasize how Methodism appealed to the unenlightened and corrupted the rational faculties of its adherents. In response to one author's report that "almost all the inhabitants [of Wales] are either Methodists or Moravians," the *Critical Review* claimed, "Ignorance, we may observe, is the parent of fanaticism; and while the common people of Wales spend their lives in a kind of barbarism, . . . they will naturally become the dupes of every enthusiast, who appears amongst them with any extraordinary pretensions."[36] Of a piece intended to vindicate Methodist teachings and practices, a reviewer for the *Monthly Review* claimed that the work confirmed the suspicions of the author's friends, that his "intellect had suffered some detriment by, or since, his conversion to methodism."[37] A review of Walpole's *Anecdotes of Painting in England* in a later issue of the same journal includes this brief observation: "Nonsense may make an apprentice a catholic or Methodist."[38] The *Critical Review* referred to Methodist preachers as "illiterate reformers," and both journals published reviews of anti-Methodist works that the reviewers hoped might "open the eyes of the blind."[39] At least one reviewer, however, wondered whether such an effect was even possible when commenting on a tract intended to discredit Whitefield's sermons. The piece, the reviewer insisted, "might probably have very good effect [on Whitefield's followers], if they would read them with the same spirit of moderation, and deference to common sense, with which they are penn'd by their judicious author."[40]

The hostile sentiments and charges leveled at the Methodists that regularly appear throughout the pages of both journals placed them firmly in the anti-Methodist camp. Indeed, the reviewers made no effort to disguise their antipathy for the revival and its participants. Nonetheless, disparaging the Methodists remained a secondary concern, subordinated to the primary objective of refining literary tastes and regulating the reading practices of the journals' consumers; that is, reviewers were more interested in the means than the ends and in judging whether an author had executed his attack on Methodism in a manner that fit their definition of good writing. Reconciling the journals' primary objective with their secondary objective proved relatively simple and straightforward when reviewers were assessing anti-Methodist works that adhered to their critical standards. Commenting on Evan Lloyd's long satiric poem *The Methodist* (1766), the *Monthly Review* insisted that "religious follies" are, in fact, an appropriate target of satire, though "the application [of ridicule in such cases] requires the most skillful management," which the reviewer claimed Lloyd achieved.[41] The *Critical Review* likewise offered praise for Lloyd's satiric method, stating that "the author out-methodizes even methodism itself."[42]

However, when a work failed to meet reviewers' standards of literary merit, the reviewers, still eager to derail the revival, found themselves challenged: which do you spend your energy on, attacking a work's deficiencies, or attacking Methodists? To be sure, many reviewers managed still to weave anti-Methodist commentary into their negative judgments of a work's literary quality. For example, in a review of Nathaniel Lancaster's *Methodism Triumphant* (1767), a reviewer for the *Monthly Review* criticized Lancaster's application of the mock-heroic form to his subject matter at the same time he declaimed against the Methodists:

> The verse is Miltonic, and the style is the sublime, in which the Author has shewn his want of judgment; for that kind of style and measure will not adapt itself to any thing that lies between the extremes of the Great and Little. The battles of archangels, and the contests of mice and frogs, will equally bear to be described by it; but the absurd doctrines and extravagancies of fanaticism would be more effectually ridiculed in the farcical strain of Butler.[43]

The *Critical Review* likewise unfavorably compares Lancaster to Samuel Butler while still endorsing Lancaster's characterization of the Methodists: "If this writer possessed the wit and the judgment of Butler, he might have produced a poem on Methodism, equal to Hudibras. The field is rich and extensive. The journals of some of our saints-errant are full of curious speeches and ridiculous adventures, and would have furnished the poet with a variety of choice materials."[44] In other words, Lancaster did not fail in his intent—to ridicule the Methodists—but he failed in the execution of the mock-heroic form and a precedent established by a more capable author.

Reviewers employed an array of strategies as they navigated between their primary aim of defining literary standards and the seemingly pressing impulse to criticize Methodism. For example, a reviewer might dismiss a work on aesthetic grounds without including editorial commentary at all. The *Monthly Review* described *The Spiritual Minor* (1760), an anonymously published spinoff of Foote's popular play that offers up a hyperbolic and scathing critique of the Methodists' insistence on salvation by faith, as "a low and stupid imitation of Mr. Foote's Minor," thereby ignoring what seems to be the obvious question: Does the play transgress the rules of satiric decorum?[45] The *Critical Review*, by contrast, acknowledges this possibility by expressing its uncertainty regarding the play's accuracy in portraying Methodist beliefs while still allowing that the Methodists had not been unfairly charged:

> We are not authorized from any knowledge we have of the Methodist princi-
> ples, to say, that this dramatical satire against them is not overcharged. The
> question depends upon the single fact, whether that set believes that good
> works are entirely unnecessary to salvation, and that, "the greater sins we com-
> mit, the greater glory do we give; the mediation being rendered meritorious
> in proportion to the offences." If such are the sentiments and the creed of
> Methodism, it ought to be exterminated from civil society; and stronger pre-
> cautions taken against it than against the vending of arsenic, and other
> poisons.[46]

Curiously, this review, which I have quoted in its entirety, does not include any
commentary on the literary quality of *The Spiritual Minor* or on its satiric
method; rather, it speculates on the play's accuracy while suggesting that, "if"
accurate, Methodism be treated like a poisonous substance. The reviewer does
not directly address the consequences, literary or otherwise, of the author potentially misrepresenting Methodist teachings in his efforts to achieve comic or
satiric effect. Consequently, an opportunity to establish a benchmark for judging hyperbolic literary expressions, the sort of critical move that would have
aligned the review with the professed aims of the journal, was ultimately sub-
sumed by the anti-Methodist sentiment.

As several of the aforementioned reviews suggest, some more directly than
others, the reviewers' judgments were influenced by specific ideas of literary
decorum and social propriety. The sorts of questions that guided reviewers
ensured that a fissure opened up in the review literature between what seem to
be straightforward, negative attacks on Methodism and efforts to establish
standards for forming literary judgments: To what extent does a given work
comply (or not) with the rules of a specific literary genre? How does it compare
to other examples of the same genre? Is the satire judiciously applied? The *Critical Review*'s assessment of *The Spiritual Minor* at least raises the possibility that
the Methodists might be "overcharged," a potential breach of both literary rules
and social tact.

The *Monthly Review*'s critique of Richard Graves's *Spiritual Quixote* aptly
illustrates how the impulse to deride the revival was tempered by the principles
of literary judgment. The reviewer offers qualified praise for Graves's novel, which
represents the most sustained anti-Methodist work written during the eighteenth
century, covering nearly one thousand pages and four volumes when originally
published in 1773:

> There is something singular in this production, and it deserves to be distin-
> guished from the common trash of modern novels. The subject, however, is
> mean, and unworthy the talents of this Writer. The adventures of a frantic
> enthusiast (a Methodist preacher) cannot be supposed to afford the materials

of an entertaining romance. The Author is therefore obliged to have recourse
to an artifice, and to make his episodes atone for the poverty of his general
fable.[47]

The reviewer, to be sure, disparages the Methodists as "frantic enthusiast[s]," but
the disparagement is ultimately minimized by the claim that the subject matter
is inappropriately adapted to its form, namely, romance. Curiously, the review
focuses almost exclusively on a relatively minor episode, "the history of Mr. and
Mrs. Rivers," which is designated "by far the best part of this novel" and includes
a lengthy excerpt describing the Rivers' courtship, followed by this pronounce-
ment: "We have seldom read so natural and pleasing an account of the com-
mencement of an amour."[48] Though the novel deals at length with nearly every
commonplace associated with Methodism, from the ill consequences of religious
enthusiasm on individuals to the social corruptions Methodism purportedly
promoted, the review mentions these only to suggest that they do not conform
to the expectations associated with a type of romance, one that recounts the
stages of courtship and includes a series of emotional and other trials but eventually ends in marriage. The reviewer thus misses an opportunity that *The Spiritual Quixote* afforded—to lambast Methodism—as a result of his fidelity to his
definition of romance.

By contrast, the review of this same novel in the *Critical Review*, perhaps
indicative of its more pronounced anti-Methodist position, took full advantage
of the opportunity presented in *The Spiritual Quixote* to amplify the anti-
Methodist critique while making a case for the novel's literary merit. The
reviewer achieves this last objective by, not surprisingly, situating his review in
the context of the Quixote tradition, another kind of romance, inaugurated by
Cervantes, who set out to "expose the absurdities of romantic chivalry," and continued by the likes of Charlotte Lennox in *The Female Quixote*, which was
"designed to ridicule romantic love, and to shew the tendency that books of
knight-errantry have to turn the heads of their female readers."[49] By quixotic
standards, then, Graves's novel measures up: "The demolition of the devil and
all his works is a very proper object for the heroism of the methodistical Quixote. By the mere force of imagination, [Graves's hero] conjures up the powers of
darkness in an enlightened age." The review features a detailed summary of
Geoffry Wildgoose's adventures as an itinerant preacher, including a lengthy
excerpt describing his enthusiastic turn to Methodism and another passage that
"exhibits a ludicrous . . . and just description of a methodist meeting."[50] While
the *Monthly Review*'s efforts to define proper standards for a certain form of
romance steered the review away from anti-Methodist critique, the *Critical
Review*'s turn to Cervantes and the Quixote tradition opened the door to anti-
Methodist rhetoric and ensured that the negative ideas associated with Methodism expressed in the novel resonated throughout the review.

Nowhere is the gap between the impulse to ridicule Methodism and efforts to establish literary standards more evident than in those reviews of works that push the boundaries of satiric decorum. Beginning in the Restoration, writers and critics fixated on defining the means and ends of satire as well as on specifying the proper objects of satiric critique; both the *Monthly Review* and the *Critical Review* continued this conversation in their pages. Some of the works reviewed routinely took satiric exaggeration to excessive extremes, even in the eyes of an author who generally shared the author's antipathy toward Methodism. The *Monthly Review*'s critics were the first to cry foul when an author had, in their judgment, gone too far. An eclogue describing a disturbance at Norwich allegedly occasioned by an "illiterate" Methodist preacher's fraternizing with his female converts caused the reviewer at the *Monthly Review* to declare, "It is unfair . . . to attack a whole sect, on account of the frailty of an individual." Such "scandalous anecdotes," the reviewer further explains, undermine the author's satiric intent, because "stronger weapons are requisite wherewith to encounter Enthusiasm and Fanaticism; whose party is very potent."[51] Although the reviewer in this case hardly vindicates the Methodists, he implies that satire should be not only just but also severe to be effective.

The *Monthly Review*'s review of Foote's *Minor* similarly questions the propriety of Foote's method, which involved attacking Methodism via Mrs. Coal, a Methodist convert and follower of Dr. Squintum (Whitefield), who conveniently reconciles her profession as a procuress to her newfound faith in Methodism by deriding works of righteousness. In addition to inspiring a number of literary and dramatic spinoffs, *The Minor* spawned one of the most publicized and heated pamphlet wars "in the history of theatre," as commentators debated Foote's treatment of Methodism in the press, a debate in which the *Monthly Review* actively participated.[52] After claiming that Foote's play did not answer the ends of comedy, the reviewer at the *Monthly Review* reviewer criticized Foote's treatment of Whitefield in the figure of Squintum:

> The satire at the great Leader of the Methodists, seems to be extremely out of character. It is no less unjust to Mr. W—, than absurd, to suppose a man of his penetration, either conniving at, or being the dupe of, an old Bawd's hypocrisy. . . . We despise and abhor all enthusiastic flights, and high pretensions to extraordinary sanctity, as much as Mr Foote can do; but without entering into the enquiry whether or not these are proper objects of playhouse ridicule, it is most certain, that no man, or body of men, ought to be charged with more than they are guilty of.[53]

Israel Pottinger's sequel to *The Minor* was attacked in a similar vein for its satiric treatment of Whitefield, which, according to the *Monthly Review*, "is carried to such a height, as, in our judgment reflects the utmost disgrace upon Literature."[54] Of course, these reviews hardly vindicate Methodism, but they at least condemn certain strains of the anti-Methodist critique, and they do so via a commitment to prescribed standards for making literary judgments.

The Minor naturally fared much better in the *Critical Review*. After conceding that "absurdities" are seldom found in a "polite age," the reviewer credits Foote for producing a play that "deserves to be ranked among some of the best of our comedic productions. We are here served up with no dull stage cant; with no stale and hackneyed repartee; the wit is original, and the satire poignant." In other words, the play's satire on Whitefield answers the ends of comedy by exposing folly—in this case, religious hypocrisy on the part of Whitefield and his followers—in a fresh and humorous way. The reviewer's one criticism centers on Foote's borrowing from Molière and Farquhar, which is quickly excused, since "among comic writers nothing is so frequent as plagiarism."[55] Satiric decorum appears to have been less of an issue for this reviewer than originality, and by that standard, Whitefield and Methodism provided, at least from the reviewer's point of view, a singular set of follies and frailties that were suitable for comedic and satiric representation. Foote's play was, in fact, the first staged production to tap Methodism for extensive comedic effect.

The *Critical Review*'s reviewers, unlike those at the *Monthly Review*, appear to have been unwilling, or at least reluctant, to spare the Methodists from any kind of criticism—even when that criticism was poorly executed in their minds. Of a work published in support of Foote's treatment of Methodism, a reviewer writes, "Here a great deal of abuse is thrown out against the Methodists; how justly sounded, we will not pretend to determine. Though we are unwilling to countenance scurrility and dullness, it is with pleasure we observe several late attempts to bring this sect of enthusiasts into contempt." The reviewer thus justifies the ends while criticizing the means, a tack likewise taken in the very next review of a similarly intended piece: "the only difference [between the two being] in the execution . . . that this is jocularly dull, and the other solemnly stupid."[56] In declaiming against dullness, such reviews may well have detoured readers from reading these works. Nonetheless, the direct and concise statements leveled against the Methodists embedded in the critical commentary promoted by proxy the intended effect of these anti-Methodist works—namely, to disparage Methodism.

One work about which the review journals generally concurred was Christopher Anstey's *The New Bath Guide* (1766), which recounts in a series of poetic epistles a family of quality's visit to Bath and satirizes the quirks of fashionable society. One of these epistles includes the conversion of one of the family members, a romantic young woman named Prudence, to Methodism. Both journals agree that the letters, most of which are composed in rhyming couplets, contain wit and humor, and both journals offer almost wholly positive reviews, with the same exception: the epistle describing Prudence's conversion. Prudence explains how, in a dream, she is visited in her bed by an apparition that resembles a young

Methodist preacher whom she has encountered at Bath, and she not so indirectly suggests that the experience, which is accompanied by panting and convulsions, involves an erotic element. The *Monthly Review* claims that "there is an indecency in this letter for which the humour of it can by no means answer."[57] The *Critical Review* similarly concludes that the scene "suggests some ideas which, in point of delicacy, we cannot applaud," adding this caveat: "Yet we are inclined to excuse the facetious author, when we consider, that some of the mysteries of enthusiasm are reported, upon good authority."[58] Both reviews include lengthy excerpts from the poetic epistles, but Prudence's conversion is excluded and criticized for its pornographic nature. Even though the *Critical Review* slips in its customary jab at the Methodists by suggesting that Prudence's experience might not be exaggerated, the satire of Methodist conversion is ultimately muted by fidelity to standards for literary decency. These standards steered the reviewers for both journals to more meritorious features of the work and compelled them to criticize the work's treatment of Methodism as unseemly and not worthy the reader's attention.

The New Bath Guide was certainly not the first anti-Methodist work to draw explicit attention to the ways in which Methodists reportedly confused spiritual and sexual feelings. Charges of sexual impropriety among the Methodists tailed the revival from its beginning. While some readers during the period may well have been scandalized by such accounts, the reviewers' responses to Anstey's work were, I would argue, shaped as much by notions of literary propriety as by moral scruples. Put another way, a self-consciousness about a set of literary standards that included rules regarding satiric decorum and decency ensured that Anstey's satire of Methodist conversion would not go unquestioned. Those standards likewise checked the anti-Methodist sentiment that often filtered into the reviewers' editorial commentary.

We see just how notions of satiric decorum, especially when applied to sexually charged material, mitigated the reviewers' proclivities for deriding the Methodists in their treatment of *A Plain and Easy Road to the Land of Bliss* (1762), an imitation of Swift's *Tale of a Tub* that satirizes the doctrine of justification by faith and, like *The New Bath Guide*, eroticizes Methodist conversion. The *Monthly Review* referred to the piece as "a dull and indecent Satire on the Methodists" that "is not only contemptible for its stupidity: it is also a filthy, obscene thing,—for which the dirty Author ought to be washed in the horse-pond."[59] By comparison, a reviewer for the *Critical Review* found more to praise in *A Plain and Easy Road*, including its attitude toward Methodism, but similarly found fault with the author's manner: "The progress of this sect our author combats with all the force of strong irony, poignant wit, and genuine humour, sometimes however bordering upon indelicacy." While the reviewer ultimately recommends the piece to his readers, he qualifies the recommendation by "assuring him that were the irony sustained with more regard to propriety, . . . we should not scruple to equal it to any publication of the same nature since the days of Swift and Arbuthnot."[60]

The reviewer for the *Critical Review*, in customary form, offers up a more favorable review of *A Plain and Easy Road*'s satire on Methodism while still raising the same questions regarding moral and literary appropriateness that concerned the reviewer for the *Monthly Review*. As I observed previously, such discrepancies in the review journals' critiques of anti-Methodist works can partly be accounted for by the relative conservative social and political agenda that undergirded the *Critical Review*'s founding. Nonetheless, the two journals' shared hostility toward the revival was more a matter of degree than actual difference; that is, they tended to level the same charges against the Methodists, with the *Critical Review* usually taking up the more unequivocal position. Moreover, as is evidenced in their reviews of *The New Bath Guide* and *A Plain and Easy Road*, the reviewers shared many of the same criteria for forming literary judgments. The discrepancies between reviews were thus shaped as much by the urge to discredit Methodism as they were by fidelity to critical standards. Such discrepancies aptly illustrate how the modern literary review essay developed out of a pull between reviewer opinion and a desire to objectify critical standards. The two competing journals may have been pulled in slightly different directions, but both felt the pull nonetheless as they wrestled with their own anti-Methodist attitudes and their literary judgments.

Whatever lip service the review journals gave to neutrality, the reviewers' opinions inevitably filtered into their reviews—and that, as much as anything, characterizes the genre of the literary review essay as it developed in the eighteenth century. Moreover, those opinions extended well beyond what constituted good literature. This convergence of a highly politicized agenda to discredit Methodism with the desire to codify and remain true to a set of literary principles inevitably led to conflicts and compromises that played out in both review journals. While Methodism was inevitably affected by the literary culture that surrounded it, perhaps most dramatically in its public perception, Methodism and the antagonistic literature written in response to it likewise influenced one of the more significant literary developments of the eighteenth century: the modern review essay. Whether dealing with their own personal hostility toward Methodism or some other prejudice, reviewers grappled with their own biases and fidelity to their criteria for judging literary worth. This contest between reviewer opinion and standards of critical judgments has defined the modern literary review ever since.

NOTES

1. *Critical Review*, vol. 12 (London: A. Hamilton, 1762), 76.
2. See, for example, Harry Stout, *The Divine Dramatist: George Whitefield and the Rise of Modern Evangelicalism* (Grand Rapids: William B. Eerdmans, 1991); Frank Lambert,

"Pedlar in Divinity": George Whitefield and the Transatlantic Revivals (Princeton: Princeton University Press, 1994).

3. George Whitefield, *The Works of the Reverend George Whitefield, M.A.*, 7 vols. (London: Edward and Charles Dilly, 1771–1772), 3:262.

4. George Whitefield, *Some Remarks upon a Late Charge Against Enthusiasm* (n.p., 1744), 19.

5. See Brett C. McInelly, *Textual Warfare and the Making of Methodism* (Oxford: Oxford University Press, 2014).

6. See, for example, Clive D. Field, "Anti-Methodist Publications of the Eighteenth Century: A Revised Bibliography," *Bulletin of the John Rylands Library* 73, no. 2 (1991): 159–208.

7. John Sekora, *Luxury: The Concept in Western Thought, Eden to Smollett* (Baltimore: Johns Hopkins University Press, 1977), 66, 75.

8. *Monthly Review*, vol. 1 (London: R. Griffiths, 1749).

9. *Monthly Review*, vol. 1, 81.

10. Antonia Forster, *Index to Book Reviews in England, 1749–1774* (Carbondale: Southern Illinois University Press, 1990), 3.

11. Walter James Graham, *English Literary Periodicals* (New York: T. Nelson & Sons, 1930), 209.

12. James Basker, "Criticism and the Rise of Periodical Literature," in *The Cambridge History of Literary Criticism*, vol. 4, ed. H. B. Nisbet and Claude Rawson (Cambridge: Cambridge University Press, 2005), 316–332, quotation from 327.

13. Frank Donoghue, "Colonizing Readers: Review Criticism and the Formation of a Reading Public," in *The Consumption of Culture, 1600–1800: Image, Object, Text*, ed. Ann Bermingham and John Brewer (London: Routledge, 1995), 54–74, quotation from 58.

14. Frances Burney, *Evelina, or The History of a Young Lady's Entrance into the World* (1778) (New York: Norton, 1965), dedication.

15. *Critical Review*, vol. 3 (London: R. Baldwin, 1757), 384; *Critical Review*, vol. 8 (London: A. Hamilton, 1759), 271.

16. Richard P. Heitzenrater, *Wesley and the People Called Methodist* (Nashville: Abingdon Press, 1995), 180–181.

17. *Champion* 1 (1741): 23.

18. James G. Basker, *Tobias Smollett: Critic and Journalist* (Newark: University of Delaware Press, 1988), 66.

19. Frances Brooke, *The Old Maid* (London: A. Millar, 1764), 187–188.

20. The review from which Brooke quotes is of a work entitled *An Exposition of the Church Catechism* by T. Jones, who the reviewer speculates might have ties to the Methodists. See *Critical Review*, vol. 1 (London: R. Baldwin, 1756), 175–180.

21. *Monthly Review*, vol. 6 (London: R. Griffiths, 1752), 153–154.

22. *Monthly Review*, vol. 7 (London: R. Griffiths, 1753), 396; *Monthly Review*, vol. 9 (London: R. Griffiths, 1754), 233.

23. Tobias Smollett, *The History of England (1757–65)*, vol. 5 (Oxford: Talboys, 1827), 280.

24. *Critical Review*, vol. 10 (London: A. Hamilton, 1760), 243.

25. *Critical Review*, vol. 13 (London: A. Hamilton, 1762), 358.

26. *Critical Review*, vol. 22 (London: A. Hamilton, 1766), 264.

27. *Critical Review*, vol. 17 (London: A. Hamilton, 1764), 63.

28. *Critical Review*, vol. 31 (London: A. Hamilton, 1771), 75–76.

29. *Critical Review*, vol. 34 (London: A. Hamilton, 1772), 350.

30. *Critical Review*, vol. 23 (London: A. Hamilton, 1767), 192–193.

31. *Critical Review*, vol. 27 (London: A. Hamilton, 1769), 191.

32. *Critical Review*, vol. 15 (London: A. Hamilton, 1763), 368.

33. *Monthly Review*, vol. 28 (London: R. Griffiths, 1763), 235.

34. *Monthly Review*, vol. 38 (London: R. Griffiths, 1768), 52–53, 54–55.

35. *Monthly Review*, vol. 16 (London: R. Griffiths, 1757), 363.

36. *Critical Review*, vol. 24 (London: A. Hamilton, 1767), 396.

37. *Monthly Review*, vol. 8 (London: R. Griffiths, 1753), 139.

38. *Monthly Review*, vol. 26 (London: R. Griffiths, 1762), 245.

39. *Critical Review*, vol. 25 (London: A. Hamilton, 1768), 397.

40. *Monthly Review*, vol. 6 (London: R. Griffiths, 1752), 485.

41. *Monthly Review*, vol. 35 (London: R. Griffiths, 1766), 319–320.

42. *Critical Review*, vol. 22 (London: A. Hamilton, 1766), 77.

43. *Monthly Review*, vol. 37 (London: R. Griffiths, 1767), 395.

44. *Critical Review*, vol. 25 (London: A. Hamilton, 1768), 66.

45. *Monthly Review*, vol. 29 (London: R. Griffiths, 1763), 236.

46. *Critical Review*, vol. 16 (London: A. Hamilton, 1763), 74–75.

47. *Monthly Review*, vol. 48 (London: R. Griffiths, 1773), 384.

48. *Monthly Review*, vol. 48, 384, 387.

49. *Critical Review*, vol. 35 (London: A. Hamilton, 1773), 275.

50. *Critical Review*, vol. 35, 276, 281.

51. *Monthly Review*, vol. 29 (London: R. Griffiths, 1763), 227–228.

52. Jane Moody, "Stolen Identities: Character, Mimicry, and the Invention of Samuel Foote," in *Theatre and Celebrity in Britain, 1660-2000*, ed. Mary Luckhurst and Jane Moody (New York: Palgrave, 2005), 80.

53. *Monthly Review*, vol. 23 (London: R. Griffiths, 1760), 83.

54. *Monthly Review*, vol. 23, 392.

55. *Critical Review*, vol. 10 (London: A. Hamilton, 1760), 69 and 70.

56. *Critical Review*, vol. 10, 322.

57. *Monthly Review*, vol. 34 (London: R. Griffiths, 1766), 472.

58. *Critical Review*, vol. 21 (London: A. Hamilton, 1766), 373.

59. *Monthly Review*, vol. 26 (London: R. Griffiths, 1762), 236.

60. *Critical Review*, vol. 13 (London: A. Hamilton, 1762), 358–359.

CHAPTER 8

Swift, Dryden, Virgil, and Theories of Epic in Swift's *A Description of a City Shower*

David Venturo

SWIFT, DRYDEN, PARODY, AND IMPERSONATION

Jonathan Swift's satiric parodies and impersonations of John Dryden may have grown out of a personal insult. Dryden, poet laureate from 1668 to 1689 and England's leading poet and playwright after the death of John Milton in 1674, was Swift's second cousin once removed. Swift's admired grandfather, Anglican priest and royalist Thomas Swift (1595–1658), married Elizabeth Dryden, daughter of Nicholas Dryden. Sir Erasmus Dryden of Canons Ashby, a brother of Swift's great-grandfather Nicholas Dryden, was John Dryden's grandfather.[1] As the War between the Two Kings loomed in Ireland in 1689, pitting Protestant William against Roman Catholic James, the twenty-one-year-old Swift, working toward his master of arts at Trinity College Dublin, decamped for England, where he became personal secretary to retired diplomat Sir William Temple, who was on good terms with the new king, William of Orange (Temple had actually helped negotiate the marriage between William, then Prince of Orange, and Mary). After visiting his mother in Leicester, Swift joined Temple, possibly at his estate in Sheen, Surrey (having walked the intervening one hundred miles), but ultimately taking up residence at Temple's new home, Moor Park, in Farnham, Surrey, to which he moved in June 1689.[2] Temple's family was in mourning when Swift joined it. King William recently had appointed Temple's only surviving child, thirty-two-year-old John, secretary at war. Young Temple advised the king to free Irish Catholic brigadier general Richard Hamilton from the Tower of London so that he might travel to Ireland to negotiate Lord Tyrconnell's surrender. Unfortunately, Hamilton joined Tyrconnell's army, and John Temple, horrified by his gaffe, drowned himself in the Thames in April 1689. Except for two extended sojourns in Ireland, from 1690 to 1691, and 1694 to 1696, Swift spent most of the next decade with Temple, copying, editing, and translating, under his employer's watchful eye, Sir William's letters, essays, and memoirs, readying them for publication. Temple died at Moor Park in January 1699, having willed Swift responsibility for publishing his papers.

As Swift's most recent biographer, Eugene Hammond, points out, although Temple chiefly resided at his Moor Park estate, forty-two miles southwest of London, he retained the house at Sheen (thirty-five miles closer to London), kept a city house on Pall Mall, and sometimes stayed at his sister, Martha, Lady Giffard's townhouse on Dover Street in London. Thus, no matter where the Temples were living, Swift enjoyed ready access to King William's court and to London's literary and social scene. Even Moor Park, which Temple regarded as a retreat, was only a day's ride from the city. Through Temple's court connections, Swift met important people in the early 1690s, including Archbishop William Sancroft, the most eminent of the Seven Bishops; Bishop Francis Turner, Andrew Marvell's old nemesis and another of the Seven Bishops who confronted James over his prerogative, only later to become a Jacobite, and, despite political differences, a friend of Sir William Temple; and the new king of England, William III, whom Temple had known since the late 1660s, when he negotiated the Triple Alliance with Sweden and the United Provinces, secretly betrayed by Charles II for a French subsidy (Hammond, *Jonathan Swift*, 61, 61n18, 66–68).

In the early 1690s, Swift wrote a series of heroic, Pindaric odes, celebrating King William, deposed Archbishop William Sancroft, his employer, Temple, and the Athenian Society, a group of writers admired by Temple and fronted by journalist John Dunton, who, in the broadsheet *Athenian Mercury*, anonymously answered a wide range of questions that had been posed by readers. To his first cousin Thomas Swift, a grandson of Sir William Davenant, Swift wrote in 1692 that, when composing these odes, "I am Cowley to my self," citing the then popular poet who died in 1667, the same year Swift was born.[3] He could have easily substituted Dryden's name for Cowley's, since Dryden in the 1680s and 1690s eclipsed Cowley as the leading author of English Pindaric odes.

Sir William Temple seems to have been an indulgent employer who did not monopolize his young secretary's time. We know that Swift was an accomplished walker and that, from Moor Park, London was a two to three days' journey on foot. Swift would have stayed at Sir William's or Lady Giffard's townhouses while in London, and his friendship with Kilkenny School and Trinity College classmate William Congreve may have given him access to John Dryden. Congreve was on good terms with the former laureate. He contributed a translation of Juvenal's eleventh satire to the *Satires of Juvenal and Persius*, published late in 1692 (the title page lists the date as 1693), at Dryden's invitation and also wrote a commendatory poem that was prefixed to Dryden's Persius translations. Not long afterward, Swift wrote a poem praising Congreve's comedy, *The Double Dealer*, but when the play was published in December 1693 (the title page lists the date as 1694), Dryden's commendatory verses, which praised Congreve as his literary heir, were given pride of place and Swift's (if he ever presented them to Congreve) were not included. Beginning late in 1693, Congreve took lodgings with Jacob Tonson, Dryden's publisher. Later, Congreve helped with the contract negotiations for Dryden's Virgil project and reviewed the accuracy of the translation against the Latin, for which Dryden graciously thanked him in the *Dedication of the Æneis* (1697).[4]

That Swift's first cousin, Thomas Swift, was a grandson of Sir William Davenant also might have helped him gain access to Dryden. Dryden had succeeded Davenant as poet laureate, and had collaborated with him in adapting Shakespeare's *Tempest* for the Restoration stage. Moreover, Swift's kinship through his grandmother, Elizabeth Dryden Swift, widow of the Reverend Thomas Swift, whom Swift knew in Dublin when he was a boy, might have served as a means of introduction to Dryden (Hammond, *Jonathan Swift*, 22–23). Thus, it is plausible that, through his Congreve, Davenant, or Temple connections, or even through his own grandmother, Swift met Dryden at his favorite haunt—Will's Coffee House in London, and that Dryden, having read the young man's odes, shook his head and intoned, "Cousin Swift, you will never be a poet," offending Swift. Dryden buoyed the career of Swift's friend and classmate, Congreve, mentoring him as a playwright and poet, but we know of nothing Dryden did for Jonathan Swift.[5]

This encounter could mark the beginning of Swift's animus toward the man he called "my near Relation" in a 12 April 1735 letter to Thomas Beach, although Dryden's shape shifting—his willingness to change his political allegiances and religious affiliations in 1660 and again in 1688, while sanctimoniously defending his actions and his career as a poet and playwright—doubtlessly bothered Swift, independent of any offense given or taken (Swift, *Correspondence*, 4:88). In fact, Swift's most admired relative was his paternal grandfather Thomas Swift, who suffered for his unwavering royalism and Anglicanism during the Interregnum.

By the early 1690s, Swift probably knew Dryden's writing well. As Ian Higgins notes, "Swift's familiarity with Dryden's work bred parody," and his greatest parodies of Dryden are found in *A Tale of a Tub* and *The Battel of the Books* (217). Swift's debt to Dryden, though, goes deeper. His very decision to write parody may have been inspired by Dryden's discussion of it in his *Discourse Concerning the Original and Progress of Satire* (1693), where Dryden notes a kind of Greek invective satire called "silli" (from the Greek Σίλλοι) known for their "Scoffing and Petulancy." Timon of Phlius (ca. 320–230 B.C.) wrote silli ridiculing philosophers in mock-heroic hexameters. According to Dryden, from some fragments of Timon's silli, "We may find, that they were Satyrique Poems, full of *Parodies*," that is, of Verses patch'd up from great Poets, and turn'd into another Sence than their Author intended them. Such amongst the *Romans* is the Famous *Cento* of *Ausonius*; where the words are *Virgil*'s: But by applying them to another Sense, they are made a Relation of a Wedding-Night; and the Act of Consummation fulsomly [that is, obscenely] describ'd in the very words of the most Modest amongst all Poets. Of the same manner are our Songs, which are turn'd into Burlesque; and the serious words of the Author perverted into a ridiculous meaning. Thus in *Timon's Silli* the words are generally those of *Homer*, and the Tragick Poets; but he applies them Satyrically, to some Customs and Kinds of Philosophy, which he arraigns.[6]

Parody is thus an act of satiric, discordant ventriloquism—for Dryden, Swift, and other late seventeenth-century writers, a form of mock-Longinian imitation in which an author is imagined as writing in a new and inappropriate context. It has an element of drama about it, because one speaks not with one's own, but with another author's voice. Whether or not Swift was already an experienced parodist in 1693, this passage from Dryden's *Discourse* may have helped inspire *A Tale of a Tub* and *The Battel of the Books*. (The title of *The Mechanical Operation of the Spirit* may be indebted to a sentence in the first paragraph of Dryden's Preface to *Sylvæ* [1685], wherein Dryden wryly observes, "Many a fair Precept in Poetry, is like a seeming Demonstration in the Mathematicks; very specious in the Diagram, but failing in the Mechanick Operation.")[7] In these satires, Swift divested himself of the earnest voice of the Pindaric poet of his first years at Moor Park.

In "An Apology for the, &c.," prefixed to the fifth edition of *A Tale of a Tub* in 1710, Swift exasperatedly defends his satire from charges by writers such as William Wotton, of immorality and irreligion: "*There is one Thing which the judicious Reader cannot but have observed, that some of those Passages in this Discourse, which appear most liable to Objection are what they call Parodies, where the Author personates the Style and Manner of other Writers, whom he has a mind to expose.*"[8] Swift immediately cites Dryden as Exhibit A. Lecturing his *injudicious* readers, including, one assumes, Wotton, for failing to distinguish between the author and his impersonations, Swift calls attention to page 51 of his *Tale*'s present edition: "Dryden, L'Estrange, *and some others I shall not name, are here levelled at, who having spent their Lives in Faction, and Apostacies, and all manner of Vice, pretended to be Sufferers for Loyalty and Religion.*" Probably alluding to the *Discourse Concerning the Original and Progress of Satire* (1693), Swift explains, "*So Dryden tells us in one of his Prefaces of his Merits and Suffering, thanks God that he possesses his Soul in Patience: In other Places he talks at the same Rate, and* L'Estrange *often uses the like Style.*" Aggrieved by what his misreaders "*over-look'd*" but willing to point it out to them, Swift beautifully mimics Dryden aggrieved by his mistreaters but willing to forgive them (7). For years, Swift's Dryden has borne it all like a saint and a philosopher, despite suffering

From an Understanding and a Conscience, thread-bare and ragged with per-
petual turning; From a Head broken in a hundred places by the Malignants
of the opposite Factions, and from a Body spent with Poxes ill cured, by trust-
ing to Bawds and Surgeons, who, (as it afterwards appeared) were profess'd
Enemies to Me and the Government, and revenged their Party's Quarrel upon
my Nose and Shins. Fourscore and eleven Pamphlets have I writ under three
Reigns, and for the Service of six-and-thirty Factions. But finding the State
has no farther Occasion for Me and my Ink, I retire willingly to draw it out
into Speculations more becoming a Philosopher, having, to my unspeakable
Comfort, passed a long Life, with a Conscience void of Offence. (44)

Swift's parody of Dryden's sanctimonious, self-justifying doubletalk in *Discourse
Concerning Satire* has long been recognized. This passage is especially delightful because Swift's Dryden confesses truths that the real Dryden never willingly
acknowledged publicly, such as writing "under three reigns," that is, the Interregnum regime of Oliver Cromwell as well as the reigns of Charles II and James II.
But one of Swift's chief rhetorical strategies—to create in *A Tale of a Tub* a whole
book founded in parody—has been less appreciated. Indeed, Dryden's discussion of parody as a form of satire in his *Discourse* is perhaps one of the most
important seeds from which *A Tale of a Tub* grew. Dryden had been writing
lengthy critical prefaces to miscellanies featuring his translations of Ovid, Virgil, Horace, Theocritus, and Lucretius (as well as his own original poems) since
1680. After he was deprived of the offices of poet laureate and historiographer
royal in 1689, the Jacobite Dryden depended more than ever on his skills and
reputation as a translator. By the time Swift read Dryden's *Satires of Juvenal and
Persius*, probably when the book was published in 1693, he knew Dryden and
his "large comely Volumes" well (22). He alludes to *The Hind and the Panther*
(1687) as one of a number of "Types and Fables" in *A Tale of a Tub* and may have
used it as one of the inspirations for his allegory of the three brothers and their
coats (42–43). The later *Works of Virgil* (1697) further encouraged the zany, laby-
rinthine digressiveness of Swift's *Tale*. He also echoes "To the Memory of
Mr. Oldham" and some of Dryden's Pindaric odes, published in the 1680s, in
his own Pindarics.

Dryden is perfect for Swift's parody, because Dryden is constantly striving to
justify and aggrandize himself. In the prefaces to Juvenal and Persius and Virgil, the wily old poet casts himself as the suffering hero of his own life story. Especially in the last decade of his career, after he was deposed as poet laureate,
Dryden loved to depict himself as a Christian hero in the fallen Adam's manner: Milton's One Just Man. Old and sick, he endures the obloquy of his enemies, turns the other cheek, and holds steadfast to his cause. When he was
younger, he had determined, as he reveals to the Earl of Dorset, to write an epic
on King Arthur or Edward the Black Prince: "But being encourag'd only with

fair Words, by King *Charles* II, my little Sallary ill paid, and no prospect of a future Subsistance, I was then Discourag'd in the beginning of my Attempt; and now Age has overtaken me; and Want, a more insufferable Evil, through the Change of the Times, has wholly disenabl'd me."[9] He sounds like Milton in the complaint from the invocation to book seven of *Paradise Lost*:

> fallen on evil days,
> On evil days though fallen, and evil tongues;
> In darkness, and with dangers compassed round,
> And solitude. (7:25–28)

There is, however, a difference. Milton discovers that he is not really alone because the Holy Spirit—Urania—inspires and protects him. She, he declares rapturously, visits

> my slumbers nightly, or when morn
> Purples the east. (7:29–30)[10]

Dryden, too, has a muse of sorts, though made of less exalted stuff: the Earl of Dorset, who gave Dryden "a most Bountiful present" in his need and to whom Dryden now declares, "I Love you."[11] Dryden's attempts at pathos—to elicit sympathy while flattering and thanking his patron Dorset end in bathos. Swift's Dryden parodies merely exaggerate the old poet's apologias and deftly send him tumbling into Mikhail Bakhtin's "zone of . . . contact."[12]

If Dryden's presence haunts *A Tale of a Tub* and *The Battel of the Books*, in the latter of which Dryden schmoozes Virgil into exchanging his vastly better gear and horse for his translator's rusty armor and gimpy nag, it also pervades Swift's verse. Dryden was famous for perfecting the heroic couplet, combining the strength of Denham and the sweetness of Waller, as Pope observes in *An Essay on Criticism*, whereas Swift writes only occasionally in this poetic form and only once in mock-heroic style. Most of the time, Swift preferred the octosyllabic couplet. How, then, did Dryden help shape the poetic career of his cousin Swift? The paragraphs on versification near the end of Dryden's *Discourse Concerning Satire* may provide some insights. After a brief dalliance with the heroic couplet in the early 1690s, Swift first turned to what would become his signature verse form, the octosyllabic couplet, in "Verses Wrote in a Lady's Ivory Table-Book" (ca. 1697–1698), the very form Dryden unfavorably contrasted with the heroic couplet in his 1693 *Discourse*.

As Dryden prepares to conclude the *Discourse*, he turns to versification and apologizes for not having discussed Samuel Butler's *Hudibras* sooner. Although he commends the poem, he does so sparingly: "The choice of his Numbers is suitable enough to his Design, as he has manag'd it. But in any other Hand, the shortness of his Verse, and the quick returns of Rhyme, had debas'd the Dignity of Style." Octosyllabic couplets, Dryden complains, lack dignity. Moreover, they make it impossible to achieve the sublime. The rhymes return too quickly and the double rhymes are "not so proper for Manly Satire." Dryden complains that these rhymes, such as

> Then did Sir *Knight* abandon dwelling,
> And out he rode a Colonelling,

turn "Earnest too much to Jest, and give[] us a Boyish kind of Pleasure."[13] Though Dryden pretends to exclude Butler from his general criticism of burlesque, that is, octosyllabic satiric poets, he praises him faintly: "'Tis, indeed, below so great a Master to make use of such a little Instrument." Butler's tiny violin, it seems, squeaks too much. Furthermore, the pleasure we get from octosyllabic satire is not rational but forced: "It tickles aukwardly with a kind of pain, to the best sort of Readers; we are pleas'd ungratefully, and, if I may say so, against our liking. We thank him not for giving us that unseasonable Delight, when we know he cou'd have given us a better, and more solid."

Dryden goes on to complain that octosyllabic couplets are not roomy enough: "When the Rhyme comes too thick upon us; it streightens the Expression; we are thinking of the Close, when we shou'd be employ'd in adorning the Thought. It makes a Poet giddy with turning in a Space too narrow for his Imagination. He loses many Beauties without gaining one Advantage." The need to rhyme every eight, rather than every ten, syllables, he claims, forces the poet to sacrifice sense and embellishment to sound. By contrast, Dryden argues that "the Verse of ten Syllables, which we call the *English* Heroique," is more "Manly," more decorous. Drawing an analogy to tennis, Dryden prefers the baseline game: there is more power in long than in short volleys: "'Tis as in a Tennis-Court, when the Strokes of greater force, are given, when we strike out, and play at length."

For examples of satire written in the longer lines of heroic verse, not the shorter of burlesque, Dryden cites Allesandro Tassoni's *La Secchia Rapita* (1622) (The rape of the bucket or The stolen bucket) and Nicolas Boileau-Despréaux's *Le Lutrin* (1674, 1683) (The lectern). Of Tassoni's poem, which recounts a war fought over a bucket by the people of Bologna and Modena, Dryden notes that it is "written in the Stanza of Eight, which is their Measure for Heroique Verse." That is, Ariosto and Tasso wrote their epic poems in this stanza. "The Words are stately, the Numbers smooth, the Turn both of Thoughts and Words is happy. The first six lines of the Stanza seem Majestical and Severe: but the two last turn them all, into a pleasant Ridicule." The "Stanza of Eight," or ottava rima, rhyming abababcc with ten or eleven syllables per line, is perfect for mock-heroic since the closing couplet can be used succinctly to satirize what the poet has presented seriously in the first six lines. "*Boileau*," writes Dryden, "has model'd from hence, his famous *Lutrin*," a mock-heroic poem about a quarrel between the priest-treasurer and lay-precentor of the Sainte-Chappelle, the Holy Chapel in the courtyard of the royal palace on the Île de la Cité, about where in the chapel to place the lectern. Dryden emphasizes that Boileau read the burlesque poetry of his countryman, Paul Scarron, but rejected it as his model "with some kind of Indignation, as witty as it was, and found nothing in *France* that was worthy of his Imitation." As it happens, Boileau's *L'Art poétique* pointedly criticizes burlesque in canto one, lines 81–97. But, Dryden notes, "He Copy'd the *Italian* so well, that his own may pass for an Original." Scarron, a generation older than Boileau, was the author of *Le Virgile Travestie*, written in octosyllabic couplets, and transforming the high style and noble characters of Virgil's *Aeneid* into demotic vulgarians. Scarron laughs openly and heartily at Virgil's decorum and sublimity. By contrast, Boileau modeled his poem on Tassoni's: "He writes it in the *French* Heroique Verse," that is, rhyming alexandrine couplets, "and calls it an Heroique Poem: His Subject is Trivial, but his Verse is Noble." Dryden notices that Boileau "had *Virgil* in his Eye" when he wrote, "for we find many admirable Imitations of him, and some *Parodies*." Boileau cleverly dresses the low characters and petty events of his poem in the Virgilian high style. Dryden cites a passage from *Le Lutrin* that parodies a heartbreaking episode from book four of the *Aeneid*. In the middle of the night, as the precentor's wife catches him sneaking out of the house to adjust the lectern in the chapel without first making love to her, she scolds him in language that echoes Dido's denunciation of the faithless, departing Aeneas:

> Non, ton Pere a Paris, ne fut point Boulanger:
> Et tu n'es point du sang de Gervais Horloger:
> Ta Mere ne fut point la Maitresse d'un Coche:
> Caucase dans ses flancs, te forma d'une Roche:
> Une Tigresse affreuse, en quelque Antre écarté
> Te fit, avec son laict, succer sa Cruauté.

Most tellingly, Dryden praises Boileau for imitating the mock-heroic style of Virgil's "*Fourth Georgique*," on beekeeping: he "perpetually raises the Lowness of his Subject by the Loftiness of his Words; and ennobles it by Comparisons drawn from Empires, and from Monarchs." Thus, Virgil's bees are more than bees; by means of mock-high diction, he elevates them into sophisticated social creatures—a kind of elegant, miniature people. According to Dryden, "We see *Boileau* pursuing [Virgil] in the same flights; and scarcely yielding to his Master." "This," Dryden avers to Dorset, is "the most Beautiful, and most Noble kind of Satire. Here is the Majesty of the Heroique, finely mix'd with the Venom of [burlesque]; and raising the Delight which otherwise wou'd be flat and vulgar, by the Sublimity of the Expression." Thus, "Sublimity of . . . Expression"—the incongruous use of high or epic diction to describe low events and characters—is what constitutes the best satire for Dryden.

Dryden loves this "Sublimity of . . . Expression" and uses it himself in his finest satires, notably *Mac Flecknoe* and *Absalom and Achitophel*. "Sublimity of . . . Expression," however, might also describe Dryden's normal diction in much of his official, occasional poetry. A born public-relations man, Dryden resorts to a kind of Virgilian gloss whenever writing on behalf of the Stuarts—from *Astraea Redux* and *Annus Mirabilis*, to *Threnodia Augustalis* and *Britannia Rediviva*. Dryden's wont is to clothe Charles and James Stuart in Virgilian decorum, encomium, and high diction without calling attention to the disjunction between the real mundanity—sometimes the vulgarity and arrogance—of his subject and the loftiness of his words.

IMPERSONATION AND BURLESQUE IN "VERSES WROTE IN A LADY'S IVORY TABLE-BOOK"

By contrast, Swift rarely uses "Sublimity of . . . Expression." In only one poem, *A Description of a City Shower*, and to some extent in one other, *A Description of the Morning*, does Swift follow Dryden's prescription. For the most part, Swift prefers what Butler loved and Dryden scorned: the burlesque style and burlesque or octosyllabic couplet. Swift, however, did not begin as a burlesque poet. The Pindaric odes and the heroic couplets of the early 1690s came first, and Swift had trouble with them. In both forms, Swift is prolix and slow. The lines lack the energy—the lively dynamics—of the octosyllabic verse. Furthermore, the young poet takes his conventions too seriously. For example, he is surprisingly respectful of and deferential to the convention of the muse in the Pindaric odes and in the heroic couplets of "To Mr. Congreve." He treats her almost as if she were real, rather than a poetic fiction. From the start, though, Swift shows the "Kind of Knack at Rhyme" for which he later became famous.[14] In the "Ode to Sir William Temple," he perfectly rhymes "Delays" and "Peace" (the long "a" sound in "peace" may be an Irishism or simply reflect late seventeenth-century English pronunciation), and in the "Ode to Dr. William Sancroft," "miss'd" and "Christ" (both probably with a dipthongy /ɔɪ/).[15] He is also painfully earnest about his satiric intentions, telegraphing them with solemn vows:

> *"My hate, whose lash just heaven has long decreed*
> *Shall on a day make sin and folly bleed."*[16]

There is no playfulness, irony, or understatement; no impersonation or wit. By 1697, however, Swift had found himself. In *A Tale of a Tub* and *The Battel of the Books*, the ingénue had become a ventriloquist. As a poet, Swift discovered the octosyllabic couplet. The "Verses Wrote in a Lady's Ivory Table-Book" (ca. 1697–1698) reflects the same characteristics as Swift's *Tale* and *Battel*. The poem is packed with satirical impersonations. The diary or memo book, whose pages are made of ivory, which makes it easy to erase anything written on them, speaks to its readers in its own voice:

> PERUSE my Leaves thro' ev'ry Part,
> And think thou seest my owners Heart,
> Scrawl'd o'er with Trifles thus, and quite
> As hard, as sensless, and as light:
> Expos'd to every Coxcomb's Eyes,
> But hid with Caution from the Wise. (ll. 1–6)[17]

The lady and her friends who write in the table book think their secrets are safe, but the book gives up its contents to any inquisitive reader and passes judgment on the writers, to boot! *I am an emblem*, the table book declares, *of my owner's cool and trifling heart*. The table book alternates, contrapuntally revealing comments by the lady's suitors and the lady herself, a line at a time; no one comes out looking good. The suitors never rise above the verbal trappings of the beau monde's courtship clichés. Some cannot even spell. The lady's entries, by contrast, are all practical: they deal with makeup, breath fresheners, perfume, and fashion—that is, the physical disguises and embellishments of contemporary courtship:

> Here may you read (*Dear Charming Saint*)
> Beneath (*A new Receit for Paint*)
> Here, in Beau-spelling, (*tru tel deth*)
> There in her own (*far an el breth*)
> Here (*lovely Nymph pronounce my doom*)
> There (*A safe way to use Perfume*)
> Here, a Page fill'd with Billet Doux;
> On t'other side (*laid out for Shoes*)
> (*Madam, I dye without your Grace*)
> (Item, *for half a Yard of Lace*). (ll. 7–16)

A decade and a half before Pope's *Rape of the Lock*, Swift offers his own more acidic view of the fashionable world of London's beaux and belles. Pope follows Boileau and Dryden in creating a "heroi-comical" poem that slyly laughs at both Queen Anne's London and the grand, elegant, slightly dated edifice of Virgil's *Aeneid*. Moreover, Pope's young courtiers get to banter with one another, turning war into courtship and courtship into war, their speech charged with double entendre. It is all, for the most part, light and playful. By contrast, the table book judges rather sharply the kind of people who inscribe it:

> Who that had Wit would place it here,
> For every peeping Fop to Jear.

> To think that your Brains Issue is
> Expos'd to th' Excrement of his,
> In power of Spittle and a Clout
> When e're he please, to blot it out;
> And then to heighten the Disgrace
> Clap his own Nonsence in the place.
> Whoe're expects to hold his part
> In such a Book and such a Heart,
> If he be Wealthy and a Fool
> Is in all Points the fittest Tool,
> Of whom it may be justly said,
> He's a Gold Pencil tipt with Lead. (ll. 17–30)

Instead of Pope's compliment to Belinda, Swift closes his poem with a slap at the lady and her suitors. No sensible person would write in the table book, whose contents can be pried into and erased by any "peeping Fop." Besides, the lady's heart is as changeable as the stuff scrawled on the book's pages. Spit and a bit of cloth can eliminate anything that's been written; any fool can then "clap"—a low word meaning "to impose suddenly and forcefully, to thrust"—his own rubbish in the same space. The poem ends with a stinging, complementary conceit. If the table book is an emblem for the lady, then a pencil—but not just any pencil—is the emblem for her ideal husband: he must be rich and foolish—incapable of understanding the lady's venality or the import of what's written in her table book: a "Gold Pencil tipt with Lead."

Dryden, Boileau, and Pope all use "Sublimity of . . . Expression" to create an alternative world of mock-heroic. Its tissue of heroic language makes it as unreal—as fantastic in its own way—as Bakhtin's idealized world of epic firsts and bests.[18] (Though, of course, its mockery also exposes its subject matter to the zone of contact and its parody also reflects satirically on epic and heroic poetry.) By contrast, Swift's lean octosyllabic couplets, shorn of all inessential modifiers, leave no room for a Virgilian edifice. Quite the contrary: they strip away illusion and reveal the unseemly truth about the world of fashionable court-ship. If Dryden felt constrained or "streighten[ed]" by the octosyllabic couplet, Swift was liberated by it.[19] Swift's octosyllabic couplets are taut and vigorous. They reveal Swift's doubts about sublimity and his dislike of clutter. If expression is the dress of thought, Swift, like his Houyhnhnms and Brobdingnagians, keeps his simple and unpretentious. Like Thomas Hobbes and John Locke, he recognizes the dangers to truth posed by rhetorical flourish—the dangers of embellishment, or what one might call, remembering the pompous name and titles of the Lilliputian emperor, the "Mully Ully Gue" effect. Swift embraces what Johnson, writing of Samuel Butler, terms "contempt of ornaments."[20]

MOCK-HEROIC AND MOCK-GEORGIC IN
A DESCRIPTION OF A CITY SHOWER

Only in *A Description of a City Shower* did Swift write a Virgilian mock-heroic poem, following—to some extent—Dryden's prescription about the "Sublimity of the Expression." Its mock-heroism also resembles *The Rape of the Lock*'s. Both are poems that tell stories. With its detail and careful plotting, Pope's mock-epic anticipates, as Blanford Parker has noticed, the courtship novels of Jane Austen.[21] Swift's *Description of a City Shower* tells in detail the story of the effects of a London rainstorm, using Virgil's first georgic as its parodic model. In addition, Swift parodies the story of the Trojan Horse and the fall of Troy from book two of the *Aeneid*. Although Swift's parodies of Dryden's translations of Virgil have long been recognized, his parodies of Virgil independent of Dryden have largely gone unnoticed. What begins as a playful parodic imitation of the first georgic ends as a layered parody of that georgic and of the *Aeneid*. Swift's poem laughs at Virgil as much as it does at Dryden.

In the *Discourse Concerning Satire*, Dryden defines parodies as, "verses patch'd up from great Poets, and turned into another Sence than their Author intended them."[22] In *A Description of a City Shower*, Swift parodies Virgil and Virgil's translator, John Dryden. Irvin Ehrenpreis in his biography of Swift helpfully lists many of the passages from Dryden that Swift parodies, as well as others from Samuel Garth's *Dispensary* and Richard Blackmore's *Prince Arthur* and *King Arthur*.[23] Dryden had insisted in his *Discourse* that the noblest kind of satire used heroic versification and diction to clothe low subject matter. In his fourth georgic, Virgil, according to Dryden, raises "the Lowness of his Subject by the Loftiness of his Words."[24] Dryden, writing for decades on behalf of the Stuart monarchy, had become a master of styles of poetic diction; as Samuel Johnson later noted, Dryden invented what eighteenth-century poets called "poetic diction": "Those happy combinations of words which distinguish poetry from prose."[25] He had also perfected the end-stopped couplet and the art of turning or pointing his couplets—what in the *Discourse* Dryden calls "beautiful Turns of Words and Thoughts."[26] Both Swift and Pope were keenly aware of Dryden's accomplishment.

For Swift, though, as much as he claims to admire the Ancients, there is something that he finds quaint and dated about their work. In order to remedy this problem, Swift, like many of his contemporaries, decided that he had to bring their work into the present. This translation across time and space, of course, became known as "imitation," and was linked to renewed interest in the ancient Greek critic, Longinus. To be inspired by the spirit of another author and to write as that author would, were he living in one's own time, became a common pursuit for writers beginning in the 1670s. We find this effort to contemporize the past reflected in both Swift's poetry and prose. (With his disdain of pretension,

Swift almost certainly never took seriously the metaphysics of inspiration or emulation that Longinus articulated in Περί ὕψους [On the sublime].) In *A Description of a City Shower*, Swift transfers Virgil's georgics from the countryside of ancient Rome to the urban landscape of contemporary London. He also cleverly updates the story of the Trojan Horse and the sack of Troy, bringing them to London. This was not the first time Swift attempted such historical translation. In *A Tale of a Tub*, Swift took the history of the pre-Reformation Roman Catholic Church and contemporized it by recasting the three brothers in his story as Restoration roués. Through Longinian sleight of hand, Swift turned ecclesiastical history into Restoration comedy. In *A Description of a City Shower*, Swift uses mock-heroic diction, while only occasionally raising "the Lowness of his Subject by the Loftiness of his Words."[27]

Swift's *Description* begins as a very precise, specific, and topical parody. Written between 10 October and 13 October 1710 and published in Richard Steele's *Tatler* no. 238 on Saturday, 17 October, the poem chiefly parodies and satirizes lines 311–334 of Virgil's first georgic, and lines 419–458 of John Dryden's translation of that poem.[28] The date of composition is important because it reflects a significant element of the poem's humor. Virgil and Dryden describe a violent autumn storm and the damage that its winds and rain inflict on the fall harvest. It causes the rivers to swell and the sea to heave, while Jove himself terrifies beasts and human beings with a dazzling display of lightning. "Terra tremit" (l. 330), notes Virgil: "The earth itself shivers."[29] Swift describes a London squall and its aftermath. We know that his poem is set in the fall because he refers to "Triumphant Tories and desponding Whigs." The parliamentary general election had begun on 2 October and continued until 16 November, but by 13 October, it was obvious that the Tories, bolstered by the unpopularity of the War of the Spanish Succession, supported for years by the Whig Junto, and the backlash to the impeachment of the high-flying Tory clergyman, Henry Sacheverell, would decisively defeat the Whigs. In the summer of 1710, Queen Anne already had begun to replace the Whig Junto with a Tory ministry. Swift himself changed from Whig to Tory that fall, after Robert Harley, in his first meeting with Swift, promised "he would do his utmost" to extend Queen Anne's Bounty from clergymen in the Church of England, to the impoverished clergymen of the Church of Ireland (Hammond, *Jonathan Swift*, 386). By November, Swift had become chief propagandist for the Tory *Examiner*.[30]

In four tight verse paragraphs, Swift reconceives the storm in the first georgic as a London squall. The poem could be a short story or a piece of mock-news reporting, rather like *The Battel of the Books*. Swift keeps the poem's events up to the minute with the opening adverbs of paragraphs two, three, and four: "MEAN while," "NOW," and "NOW" (ll. 13, 31, 53).[31] Moreover, Swift's use of detail is common to both genres. In the first paragraph, the narrator, following

Virgil, lists some signs—"sure Prognosticks" (l. 2)—that a storm looms. In the second paragraph, we see the squall blow up: the sky darkens, rain begins to fall, and the wind gusts, tossing and mixing rain and dust. Alert pedestrians start scurrying for shelter. In the third verse paragraph, the skies open and a torrent falls. Everyone heads for cover and finds a place to stay dry, waiting for the storm to pass. Finally, in the fourth verse paragraph, the "Kennels" (l. 53) or gutters (which ran down the middle of London's streets in Swift's time) swell with water and sweep an array of refuse to Fleet Ditch, the city's fetid, open sewer.

The diction of Swift's poem, of course, does not always come directly from Virgil, but is often mediated through John Dryden's translation, *Works of Virgil* (1697), which Swift had already ridiculed in *A Tale of a Tub* and *The Battel of the Books*. Swift's love of mundane details coupled with a deft mixture of high, middle, and low diction, sometimes reflecting Dryden's mock-heroic "Sublimity of the Expression," distinguishes the poem. Furthermore, in contrast to Virgil's, Swift's poem is focused very much on the physical world—not the metaphysical. Virgil combines his weather prognostics with advice on placating the gods to keep the weather fair and mild. For Virgil, the gods are *always* present in the natural world. When the terrible storm erupts in the first georgic, Jove is there. Here is Dryden's attempt to capture the metaphysical grandeur and sublimity of the storm:

> The Father of the Gods his Glory shrouds,
> Involv'd in Tempests, and a Night of Clouds.
> And from the middle Darkness flashing out,
> By fits he deals his fiery Bolts about.
> Earth feels the Motions of her angry God,
> Her Entrails tremble, and her Mountains nod;
> And flying Beasts in Forests seek abode:
> Deep horrour seizes ev'ry Humane Breast,
> Their Pride is humbled, and their Fear confess'd. (ll. 444–452)[32]

Swift eliminates Virgil's gods—his metaphysical realm—except for a few joking references and concentrates on physical aspects of the weather. There is no propitiation of Jove. Moreover, he reduces and tames the storm. Swift's squall is never terrifying or sublime. Instead, it is mundane and annoying: just another inconvenience for the inhabitants of London. Even the hints of Noah's or Deucalion's flood are risible.

The diction of Swift's first verse paragraph is earthy and direct. Storms are presaged by physical pain: a decaying tooth rages, aches (pronounced "AITCH-es") throb, a corn pulses. The "Sink" (l. 5)—we might call it a sewer or cesspool—is especially foul smelling in humid weather. Swift uses low diction—"double Stink" (l. 6)—to emphasize how bad it is. The gerund "Sauntring" perfectly captures the aimlessness of foolish "*Dulman*" in the coffeehouse, complaining about foul weather and his bad mood (l. 11). The cat stops playing. Only once does Swift rise to mock-high diction: the Latinate verb "depends" (l. 3) is positively Miltonic. A simple "approaches" would do but is not sufficiently portentous.

The second verse paragraph mixes low- and mock-high diction in a characteristically Swiftian way. The opening couplet of the second verse paragraph simply announces that the South Wind brings a dark cloud with it. But it does so grandiloquently:

> MEAN while the South rising with dabbled Wings,
> A Sable Cloud a-thwart the Welkin flings. (ll. 13–14)

Swift's diction in these lines is designedly stilted; the syntax, twisted. He represents the South Wind as a kind of giant bird with wet, bespattered wings that somehow tosses a vast cloud across the sky ("sable" is mock-high diction for the more common "black" or "dark"). By Swift's time, the Middle English "welkin" (sky) was strictly a poeticism. Spenserian revivalists were poised to take up its cause. Dryden used the word "welkin" in his poetry only twice: once in his Chaucerian imitation, "The Cock and the Fox" (1700), and once in the posthumously published pastoral, "On the Death of Amyntas" (1704). In the next couplet, Swift deflates the mock-high diction, comparing the "Sable Cloud" disgorging its rain to someone who vomits after overindulging in alcohol,

> That swill'd more Liquor than it could contain,
> And like a Drunkard gives it up again. (ll. 15–16)

Swift had used a similar conceit less cleverly in his "Ode to Sir William Temple" almost twenty years earlier to satirize scholars pontificating in polite company:

> And sick with Dregs of Knowledge grown,
> Which greedily they swallow down,
> Still cast it up, and nauseate Company. (ll. 47–49)[33]

The maid, "Brisk *Susan*" (l. 17), snappily pulls her laundry from the clothesline before it can get wet. The drizzle reminds the speaker of another

> Sprinkling which some careless Quean
> Flirts on you from her Mop, but not so clean.
> You fly, invoke the Gods; then turning, stop
> To rail; she singing, still whirls on her Mop. (ll. 19–22)

Some years before John Gay's *Trivia, or the Art of Walking the Streets of London* (1716), Swift calls attention to a common urban pedestrian hazard. Another maid (the speaker angrily puts her down as a "careless Quean"—"a bold or impudent woman"), leaning out of an upstairs window, has spattered him with dirty water from her mop. Swift clearly loves the details. The woman is not using an ordinary mop, but a new kind of labor-saving device popular in the early eighteenth century. This is a *"whirling* mop"—also mentioned in *A Description of the Morning*—hollow-handled with a crank at the end. Instead of wringing this mop by hand, the user twirled it by turning the crank. The water, dispersed by centrifugal force, flew everywhere. The speaker, annoyed, turns "To rail" at the woman, but she ignores him, safely ensconced (we presume) several floors above him. The speaker's comic invocation of the gods in this vignette—probably to curse the woman—is the closest (along with Dulman's damning of the climate) that Swift comes to the metaphysical world of Virgil's gods in his georgics.

The mingling of rain and dust that follows is both georgic and mock-epic or mock-heroic, because Swift's description of the swirling wind, water, and dust evokes the close combat of battle. The dust, aided by the wind, seeks to avoid being turned by its enemy, rain, into mud. ("Confus'd" is a mock-high diction Latinism from the verb "confundere," "to mix together.") Swift cannot resist continuing the martial conceit with a joke about a "needy poet" and his threadbare coat:

> Ah! where must needy Poet seek for Aid,
> When Dust and Rain at once his Coat invade;
> His only Coat, where Dust confus'd with Rain,
> Roughen the Nap, and leave a mingled Stain. (ll. 27–30)

This invasion by rain and dust does not result in bloodshed; the "Stain," rather, is caused by mud, which also spoils the "Nap," or smooth, tight fibers on the surface of the poor poet's "only Coat."

The third verse paragraph is the poem's most spectacular. The drops of rain become a "Flood" or "Deluge" falling in sheets—"contiguous Drops" (ll. 31–32). Swift may be playfully evoking Noah's and Deucalion's floods as well as the rainstorm in the first georgic, and perhaps the rain that drives Dido and Aeneas into the cave where they begin their romantic affair in the *Aeneid*. In Dryden's translation of the first georgic,

> whole sheets descend of slucy Rain,
> Suck'd by the spongy Clouds from off the Main. (ll. 437–438)[34]

Using mock-high diction, Swift describes the town as *"Devoted"* (l. 32)—that is, "doomed." The word is Miltonic; a variant of it appears in book nine of *Paradise Lost*.[35] In addition, Dryden uses "devoted" in book two of his *Aeneid* translation when Sinon, whose lies persuade the Trojans to accept the great wooden horse as tribute, also pretends that he was to be sacrificed to the gods and speaks of his "devoted," that is, "doomed" "Head" (2:132).[36] Despite these echoes, however, Swift's poem scarcely hints at moral or theological judgment. Instead, women soaked by the rain crowd into shops, haggling over goods but buying nothing. They already have what they came for: shelter. A law student—the "Templer" (l. 35)—nattily dressed but broke, probably stands under an awning, pretending to hail a coach until the rain stops and he can walk to his destination.

The "Sempstress" (l. 37) hitches up her skirts to keep them out of the ever-present mud, and scurries ahead. She carries an oiled umbrella, an unusual piece of rain gear in the early eighteenth century. Swift's poem, written and published in October 1710, is very topical. "Triumphant Tories, and desponding Whigs," divided by the ongoing political campaign and parliamentary election, unite to "save their Wigs," perhaps their most expensive and important fashion accessory (ll. 41–42).

Swift follows with a brilliant mock-epic simile based on the story of the Trojan Horse from book two of the *Aeneid*. Here, he comes closest to the mock-heroic praised by Dryden in his *Discourse*, rising from mock-georgic to mock-epic. Here, Swift elevates and complicates the genre of his poem:

> Box'd in a Chair the Beau impatient sits,
> While Spouts run clatt'ring o'er the Roof by Fits;
> And ever and anon with frightful Din
> The Leather sounds, he trembles from within.
> So when *Troy* Chair-men bore the Wooden Steed,
> Pregnant with *Greeks*, impatient to be freed,
> (Those Bully *Greeks*, who, as the Moderns do,
> Instead of paying Chair-men, run them thro'),
> *Laoco'n* struck the Outside with his Spear,
> And each imprison'd Hero quak'd for Fear. (ll. 43–52)

This conceit turns on one of Swift's favorite rhetorical devices, the riddle: in this case, how is a modern sedan chair like the Trojan Horse? Swift probably knew the episode from Virgil by heart, and returned to it even more spectacularly fifteen years later in the closing chapter of *Gulliver's Travels*. In the poem, the "Box'd" beau, the contemporary equivalent to the Greek soldiers enclosed in the horse, is first "impatient" and then afraid as he hears ominous sounds coming from outside (ll. 43–46). (Swift cleverly inverts "impatient beau" to "beau impatient," aping Latinate or Miltonic syntax.) Rainwater pours from overflowing spouts onto the leather roof (and sides) of the sedan chair. The beau "trembles"—perhaps fearful of getting his natty outfit wet. Then, as he moves from tenor to vehicle (beginning at line 47), Swift briefly flirts with the heroic. He wittily transforms the sedan chair into the Trojan Horse:

> the Wooden Steed,
> Pregnant with *Greeks*, impatient to be freed.

Here, Swift perfectly captures the heroic diction of Virgil and Dryden and the tension of Virgil's narrative, as the Greek soldiers, secreted inside the great horse, "impatient[ly]" anticipate their escape from their confines and the impending fight. Swift also plays with the gender of the horse. At first, it is a "Wooden Steed." "Steed" derives from Old English "stéda," "a stud-horse, stallion."[37] Swift, however, inverts the horse's gender. With the metaphor of pregnancy, Swift's figurative speech outdoes his cousin Dryden's. Virgil uses versions of the word "uterus" five times (in lines 20, 38, 52, 243, 258) in this episode to describe the hollow place within the horse that shelters the Greek soldiers.[38] Dryden, however, never embraces the metaphoric challenge; he never presents the Trojan Horse as a great mare, ready to give birth to live warriors. Instead, he translates "uterus" as "hollow Side," "dark Abode," "hollow sides," "hollow Fabrick," "hollow Belly," "dark Abodes," and "dark abodes" (2:23, 26, 49, 58, 67, 337). Only when he describes the horse as "Big with Destruction" (2:312) does Dryden hint at Virgil's powerful pregnancy metaphor.[39]

As grand as this metaphor is, however, Swift has already undercut it by comparing the Trojans who carried the horse, "Pregnant with *Greeks*," into the city to eighteenth-century "Chair-men." The pathos and tragedy of Troy evaporate when these figures from the distant epic past are translated to the urban landscape of Swift's London—brought into Mikhail Bakhtin's zone of contact. The Greek warriors are also diminished, transformed into contemporary bullies or ruffians, who would sooner kill a sedan-chair carrier (the equivalent of a modern taxi-driver) than pay the owed fare. These crimes were part of urban lore from the era of John Wilmot, Earl of Rochester, in the 1670s, to Swift's own day. Indeed, Swift has reduced the sack of Troy to a robbery and a murder. In the lines

> (Those Bully *Greeks*, who, as the Moderns do,
> Instead of paying Chair-men, run them thro') (ll. 49–50)

Swift may also be competing with or mocking Dryden by his use of parentheses. (Dryden was adept at inserting parentheses to interrupt a narrative to build suspense.) In the closing two lines of the simile, Swift returns to the heroic mode:

> *Laoco'n* struck the Outside with his Spear,
> And each imprison'd Hero quak'd for Fear. (ll. 51–52)

Neither the fear ascribed to the beau in the chair nor to the Greeks inside the horse is found in Virgil or Dryden. Where, then, did Swift get it? When Laocoön hurls the great spear ("ingentem . . . hastam") at the side of the horse and warns his countrymen not to take the supposed gift into the city, the spear sticks quivering ("tremens") in the wood (2:50, 52).[40] Moreover, in the first georgic, when Jove tosses lightning bolts during the autumn storm, the earth trembles ("terra tremit").[41] Despite the analogy, hinging on the adverb "So," Swift emphasizes a qualitative difference between the beau and "each imprison'd Hero." The beau is "Box'd in a Chair." The description is low and undignified, the beau reduced to an object in a container. He anticipates Gulliver in his traveling case in Brobdingnag, also diminished to something slightly less than human. By contrast, "each . . . Hero" is "imprisoned." A prison suggests a grim institution from which it is difficult to escape. In addition, the beau "trembles," whereas the hero "quakes." Swift has elevated the diction and increased and dignified the fear as we move from beau to hero. The beau trembles either because he fears for his clothes or is jostled as he is carried in the coursing rain. By contrast, "each . . . Hero" quakes because he fears discovery before he can climb down from the horse to fight. One worries for fashion's sake; the other, lest he not live up to his heroic aspirations.

Swift captures in this mock-epic simile how epic similes tell a story within a story. In this case, the trembling beau is almost lost in the quaking Greek hero, but he never quite disappears. The beau remains the tenor—the thing itself—in the simile, and the hero only the figurative vehicle. In the end, Swift laughs at the ridiculous disproportion between the London beau and the Greek soldier. He also, however, enjoys remodeling, updating, and miniaturizing Virgil. Although Swift was almost forty-three years old, his boyish lèse majesté is palpable. His Brobdingnagian imagination shrinks Virgil to Lilliputian proportions and eliminates the temporal gap between classical Rome and contemporary London altogether. Swift, in a hearty fit of laughter, mocks both the Moderns and the Ancients.

The fourth, and closing, verse paragraph also mixes mock-georgic and mock-epic. Once the cascading rain falls, it must flow somewhere. Its force, as Virgil and Dryden recognized in the first georgic, can be awesome and destructive:

> The lofty Skies at once come pouring down,
> The promis'd Crop and golden Labours drown.
> The Dykes are fill'd, and with a roaring sound
> The rising Rivers float the nether ground;
> And Rocks the bellowing Voice of boiling Seas rebound.   (ll. 440–444)[42]

The water collects, overflows the dykes and riverbanks, and rushes to the sea, sweeping away everything in its path, accompanied by terrifying sounds. Both humankind and nature are at its mercy. Neither man-made dykes nor natural riverbanks can contain it. In his *Description*, Swift transforms Virgil's earnest lesson of the sublimity of nature and the power of the gods into a mock-epic or mock-heroic catalog. When Swift writes

> NOW from all Parts the swelling Kennels flow,
> And bear their Trophies with them as they go:
> Filth of all Hues and Odours seem to tell
> What Street they sail'd from, by their Sight and Smell (ll. 53–56)

he evokes the massive catalog of ships from book two of the *Iliad* (ll. 494–759) and Virgil's analogous, more modest naval catalog from book ten of the *Aeneid* (ll. 230–307). The Homeric and Virgilian catalogs, of course, offer sweeping surveys of the geopolitical origins of the Greek and Trojan forces and their allies. Swift, perhaps following the mock-heroic, micro-geographic scope of Dryden's *Mac Flecknoe*,

> Rows'd by report of Fame, the Nations meet,
> From near *Bun-Hill*, and distant *Watling-street* (ll. 96–97)

shrinks his catalog and survey to a few small districts of seedy, smelly London.[43] Instead of ships carrying troops from various city-states, Swift imagines gushing sewers bearing refuse from different areas of the metropolis to a single, putrid destination.

Swift mixes high and low diction in his closing paragraph. "Swelling Kennels," of course, are sewers swollen with refuse and rainwater, running down the middle of the street. After the squall, the waters gather force. "Trophies" and "Filth of all Hues and Odours" refer to the same things, though one would scarcely know it. "Trophies" is high diction, a word that is part of the epic lexicon. Trophies are objects gathered by the victors after they have been dropped in battle by defeated troops as they turn to flee. They mark the spot where those turnings took place. Indeed, "trophy" derives from the Greek word τροπαῖος, "of turning or change," from τροπή, "turning, putting to flight, defeat," and is related to the English word "trope," a turn or figure of speech.[44] But the trophies in this case are various kinds of "Filth" or refuse, chiefly decaying animal and plant matter swept into the gutters and carried away by the rain.

If descriptions of leaders and generals distinguish the city-states of various legions of soldiers as they sail to battle, "Hues and Odours" distinguish the places of origin of London's refuse. "Sight and Smell" will tell us where they came from. Much of the garbage comes from Smithfield, known in Swift's time for its butcher shops and cattle and sheep pens. It must have stunk terribly even in the cold of winter. Streams of offal from Smithfield and waste from the parish of St. Sepulchre's Church conjoined at Snow Hill Ridge. These in turn flowed to Fleet Ditch, a fetid river that was still above ground at Holborn Bridge in Swift's time. This sewer emptied into the Thames. Swift uses mock-epic language to track the rush of waters; the diction swells with the reeking flow:

> They, as each *Torrent drives, with rapid Force*
> From Smithfield, or St. Pulchre's *shape their Course,*
> And in *huge Confluent* join at Snow-Hill Ridge,
> *Fall from the Conduit prone* to Holborn-Bridge. (ll. 57–60; emphasis added)

The italicized phrases ring with power and sublimity, even as they occur in prosaic urban settings. The rushing water is breathtaking, although the locales through which it flows are not. At last, the gathering torrent plunges downward like a waterfall: "*prone* to Holborn-Bridge."

While Swift's paradigm for the torrent derives from Virgil's first georgic, it also has other sources, especially book two of the *Aeneid*. Epic similes describing the sack of Troy may have inspired Swift, especially one in the middle of a famous passage from book two, lines 298–317. Here, Aeneas recalls awaking to the sounds of a city under siege. He climbed to the roof of his father's house and surveyed the scene. He likens the terrible man-made conflagration he witnessed to natural disasters of fire and water. Here is Dryden's translation:

> Thus when a flood of fire by Winds is born,
> Crackling it rowls, and mows the standing Corn:
> Or Deluges, descending on the Plains,
> Sweep o're the yellow Year, destroy the pains
> Of lab'ring Oxen, and the Peasant's gains:
> Unroot the Forrest Oaks, and bear away
> Flocks, Folds, and Trees, an undistinguish'd Prey:
> The Shepherd climbs the Cliff, and sees from far,
> The wastful Ravage of the wat'ry War. (ll. 406–414)[45]

The power of these forces, as they

>   bear away
> Flocks, Folds, and Trees,

is similar to that of Swift's flowing kennels. In addition, Aeneas's memory of the Trojan Horse, as it stood towering in the midst of the city, pouring forth armed men, as Sinon encouraged the flames, may have inspired Swift:

> arduus armatos mediis in moenibus adstans
> fundit equus victorque Sinon incendia miscet
> insultans. (2:328–330)[46]

> [The horse, standing tall in the middle of the
> city's walls, pours out armed men, and conquering
> Sinon insolently spreads flames.]

In 1735, Swift claimed that the triplet unwinding into an "Alexandrian"—a twelve-syllabled line—that closed *A Description of a City Shower* was a satire aimed at Dryden's profligate use of a device of which Swift disapproved: "They were the mere Effect of Haste, Idleness, and want of Money; and have been wholly avoided by the best Poets, since these Verses were written." This note appearing in George Faulkner's edition of Swift's *Works* was almost certainly written by the author, who echoed these sentiments in a 12 April 1735 letter to Thomas Beach.[47] The triplet, however, is much more than a satire on Dryden:

> Sweepings from Butchers Stalls, Dung, Guts, and Blood, ⎫
> Drown'd Puppies, stinking Sprats, all drench'd in Mud, ⎬
> Dead Cats and Turnip-Tops come tumbling down the Flood. ⎭ (ll. 61–63)

It also captures Swift's understanding of and ambivalence toward epic, especially Virgil's *Aeneid*. In fact, he parodied many lines of Dryden's translation of Virgil's *Works* in writing his closing triplet:

> Then, when the Fleecy Skies new cloath the Wood,
> And cakes of rustling Ice come rolling down the Flood. (*First Georgic*, 417–418)

> Then Plumes the Prey, in her strong Pounces bound;
> The Feathers foul with Blood come tumbling to the Ground. (*Aeneid*,
>   11:1067–1068)

and especially,

> His Mouth and Nostrils, pour'd a Purple Flood,
> And pounded Teeth, came rushing with his Blood. (*Aeneid*, 5:625–626)[48]

The first couplet above describes a thawing river; the second, a falcon seizing a dove in midair; the third, the aftermath of a boxing match during Anchises's funeral games. In all three cases, Dryden's translation accurately reflects Virgil's Latin, perhaps especially Dryden's description of the boxing match:

> ast illum fidi aequales, genua aegra trahentem
> iactantemque utroque caput crassumque cruorem
> ore eiectantem mixtosque in sanguine dentes
> ducunt ad navis. (5:468–471)[49]

> [(Dares's) loyal friends lead him to the ships, dragging
> him on wobbly knees, his head flopping from side
> to side, spitting gore and teeth from his bloody mouth.]

The offal of London's streets: dead cats and dogs, viscera and excrement swept from the floors of Smithfield's butcher shops, rotting fish, and decaying vegetables, do not differ much from stuff found in the interstices of Virgil's georgics and his *Aeneid*. Swift, in contrast to Dryden, perceives much less of a distinction between the epic world of ancient Rome and contemporary London life. Dryden believes in the epic past and invests it in suitable linguistic garb. He loved Virgilian poetic diction and the challenge of creating an English equivalent. His achievement served him in translating Virgil and in his efforts to mythologize Charles II and James II—to elevate them above their often tawdry lives and circumstances. He also embraces mock-epic, believing it possible to clothe ordinary things and events in epic diction. He could transform Richard Flecknoe into Aeneas and John the Baptist as deftly as Charles Stuart into Augustus Caesar or King David. Dryden loved the resulting incongruity. For him, satire and encomium perfectly complemented one another. Swift, however, regarded epic itself as a mongrel genre, composed of a mixture of styles: high, middle, and low. To Swift, the epic world of firsts and bests was a lie. Consequently, *A Description of a City Shower* is both mock epic and itself a miniature epic—a distillation of epic. For Swift, Dryden's efforts to wall off high from low, epic from satire, the real from the ideal, are risible. Swift, like his Houyhnhnms and Brobdingnagians, regards rhetoric as a fig leaf, deployed to obscure the truth, not, as for Dryden, a means of establishing and maintaining order and decorum.[50] Swift liked to claim that *A Description of a City Shower* gave the lie to Dryden's heroic triplets and alexandrines. In fact, Swift's extraordinary mini epic (and mini georgic) did much more, calling the relevance and truthfulness of classical georgic and epic into question.

NOTES

1. James Anderson Winn, *John Dryden and His World* (New Haven: Yale University Press, 1987), genealogy chart between 12 and 13.

2. Eugene Hammond, *Jonathan Swift: Irish Blow-In* (Newark: University of Delaware Press, 2016), 50–55 (henceforth Hammond, *Jonathan Swift*).

3. Jonathan Swift, *The Correspondence of Jonathan Swift*, ed. David Woolley, 5 vols. (Frankfurt: Peter Lang, 1999–2014), 1:110 (henceforth Swift, *Correspondence*).

4. See the helpful headnote to "To My Dear Friend Mr. Congreve," in John Dryden, *The Poems of John Dryden*, ed. Paul Hammond and David Hopkins, 5 vols. (London: Routledge, 1995–2005), 3:326–328 (henceforth Dryden, *Poems*).

5. On Swift's disdain for Dryden, see Maurice Johnson, "A Literary Chestnut: Dryden's 'Cousin Swift,'" *PMLA* 67 (1952): 1024–1034; John R. Moore and Maurice Johnson, "Dryden's 'Cousin Swift,'" *PMLA* 68 (1953): 1232–1240; David Novarr, "Swift's Relation with Dryden, and Gulliver's *Annus Mirabilis*," *English Studies* 47 (1966): 341–354; J. V. Luce, "A Note on the Composition of Swift's Epitaph," *Hermathena* 104 (1967): 78–81; and Ian Higgins, "Dryden and Swift," in *John Dryden (1631–1700): His Politics, His Plays, and His Poets*, ed. Claude Rawson and Aaron Santesso (Newark: University of Delaware Press, 2004), 217–234. In addition, see the headnote to "To My Dear Friend Mr. Congreve," in Dryden, *Poems*, 3:326–328.

6. John Dryden, *Poems 1693–1696*, ed. A. B. Chambers and William Frost, vol. 4 of *The Works of John Dryden*, ed. E. N. Hooker and H. T. Swedenberg Jr. (Berkeley: University of California Press, 1974), 35, 548–549.

7. John Dryden, *Poems 1685–1692*, ed. Earl Miner, vol. 3 of *The Works of John Dryden*, ed. E. N. Hooker and H. T. Swedenberg Jr. (Berkeley: University of California Press, 1969), 3.

8. Jonathan Swift, *A Tale of a Tub and Other Works*, ed. Marcus Walsh, vol. 1 of *The Cambridge Edition of the Works of Jonathan Swift*, ed. Claude Rawson et al. (Cambridge: Cambridge University of Press, 2010), 7.

9. Dryden, *Poems 1693–1696*, 23.

10. John Milton, *Paradise Lost* (1667, 1674), ed. Alastair Fowler, 2nd ed. (London: Longman, 1998), 391.

11. Dryden, *Poems 1693–1696*, 23–24.

12. M. M. Bakhtin, *The Dialogic Imagination: Four Essays*, ed. Michael Holquist, trans. Caryl Emerson and Michael Holquist (Austin: University of Texas Press, 1981), 19–24.

13. Samuel Butler, *Hudibras*, ed. with intro. and commentary by John Wilders (Oxford: Clarendon Press, 1967), 1. All the Dryden quotations in this section are from *Poems 1693–1696*, 81–84.

14. Jonathan Swift, "Verses on the Death of Dr. Swift," in *The Poems of Jonathan Swift*, ed. Harold Williams, 2nd ed., 3 vols. (Oxford: Clarendon Press 1958), 2:563, l. 264 (henceforth Swift, *Poems of Swift*, ed. Williams).

15. Swift, *Poems of Swift*, ed. Williams, 1:28, ll. 71–72 in "Temple," and 1:39, ll. 160–161 in "Sancroft." In a couplet included in *On Poetry: A Rhapsody* in Pat Rogers's edition of Swift's poems and in an appendix to *On Poetry* in Sir Harold Williams's edition, Swift rhymes "Christ" and "ly'st." See Swift, *Poems of Swift*, ed. Williams, 2:658, and Jonathan Swift, *The Complete Poems*, ed. Pat Rogers (London: Penguin, 1983), 527, ll. 203–204.

16. Swift, *Poems of Swift*, ed. Williams, 1:47, ll. 133–134 in "To Mr. Congreve." The couplet is italicized in the first published edition of the poem (1789).

17. Swift, *Poems of Swift*, ed. Williams, 1:60–61.

18. Bakhtin, *The Dialogic Imagination*, 13–19.

19. Dryden, *Poems 1693–1696*, 82.

20. Samuel Johnson, *The Lives of the Poets* (1779–1781), ed. John H. Middendorf, vols. 21–23 of *The Yale Edition of the Works of Samuel Johnson*, gen. ed. Robert DeMaria Jr. et al. (New Haven: Yale University of Press, 2010), 21:225.

21. Blanford Parker, *The Triumph of Augustan Poetics: English Literary Culture from Butler to Johnson* (Cambridge: Cambridge University Press, 1998), 96–135.

22. Dryden, *Poems 1693–1696*, 35.

23. Irvin Ehrenpreis, *Swift: The Man, His Works, and the Age*, 3 vols. (Cambridge: Harvard University Press, 1962–1983), 2:384–387, 385n1.

24. Dryden, *Poems 1693–1696*, 83.

25. Johnson, *The Lives of the Poets*, 21:445.

26. Dryden, *Poems 1693–1696*, 84.

27. Dryden, *Poems 1693–1696*, 83.

28. Swift, *Poems of Swift*, ed. Williams, 1:136.

29. Virgil, *Georgics*, in Virgil, *Eclogues, Georgics, The Aeneid 1–6*, trans. H. Rushton Fairclough, rev. ed., Loeb Classical Library (Cambridge: Harvard University Press, 1978), 330. All prose translations of Virgil are my own.

30. James Anderson Winn, *Queen Anne: Patroness of Arts* (Oxford: Oxford University Press, 2014), 360–361, 536–537.

31. Swift, *Poems of Swift*, ed. Williams, 1:136–139.

32. John Dryden, *Poems: The Works of Virgil in English 1697*, ed. William Frost, vols. 5–6 of *The Works of John Dryden*, ed. E. N. Hooker and H. T. Swedenberg Jr. (Berkeley: University of California Press, 1987), 5:171.

33. Swift, *Poems of Swift*, ed. Williams, 1:27.

34. Dryden, *Poems: The Works of Virgil*, 5:171–172.

35. Milton, *Paradise Lost*, ed. Fowler, 521–222. Adam asks Eve when she returns from encountering Satan in the serpent, "How art thou lost, how on a sudden lost, / Defaced, deflowered, and now to death devote?" (9:900–901).

36. Dryden, *Poems: The Works of Virgil*, 5:383.

37. *Oxford English Dictionary*, s.v. "steed."

38. Virgil, *Eclogues, Georgics, Aeneid 1–6*, 294, 296, 310, 312.

39. Dryden, *Poems: The Works of Virgil*, 5:380–381, 389.

40. Virgil, *Eclogues, Georgics, Aeneid 1–6*, 296.

41. Virgil, *Eclogues, Georgics, Aeneid 1–6*, 102.

42. Dryden, *Poems: The Works of Virgil*, 5:171.

43. John Dryden, *Poems 1681–1684*, ed. H. T. Swedenberg Jr., vol. 2 of *The Works of John Dryden*, ed. E. N. Hooker and H. T. Swedenberg Jr. (Berkeley: University of California Press, 1972), 56.

44. *Oxford English Dictionary*, s.v. "trophy."

45. Dryden, *Poems: The Works of Virgil*, 5:391.

46. Virgil, *Eclogues, Georgics, Aeneid 1–6*, 316.

47. Jonathan Swift, *The Works of J[onathan] S[wift]*, 8 vols. (Dublin: George Faulkner, 1735–1769), 2:32; Swift, *Correspondence*, 4:88.

48. Dryden, *Poems: The Works of Virgil*, 5:169, 6:753, 5:507.

49. Virgil, *Eclogues, Georgics, Aeneid 1–6*, 476.

50. David Venturo, "Swift's Style, the Nakedness of the Houyhnhnms, and the Deceits of Rhetoric," *1650–1850: Ideas, Aesthetics, and Inquiries in the Early Modern Era* 18 (2011): 285–311.

CHAPTER 9

Tension, Contraries, and Blake's Augustan Values

Philip Smallwood

BLAKE'S PRECARIOUS EXCEPTIONALISM

"Blake was the human protest on behalf of life against the repression of creativity represented by the prevailing ethos of the eighteenth century," writes F. R. Leavis, author of a study of Blake and Dickens entitled *Nor Shall My Sword*.[1] It is easy to see how this view might arise. In his "Island in the Moon," probably composed in the same year as the death of Samuel Johnson (1784), Blake has his alter ego, the Epicurean philosopher Suction, engage in singsong banter with his interlocutor Quid, and has him refer slightingly to the state of blind, befuddled, incomprehension in terms of the bat with

> Leathern wing
> Winking & blinking, Winking & blinking, Winking & blinking, Like Doctor Johnson.[2]

As Blake's modern editor G. E. Bentley Jr. suggests, the "Leathern wing" may recall William Collins's "weak-eyed bat" from the "Ode to Evening" (ll. 9–10), but Blake may have also in mind at this point the famous satirically surreal print of 1782 by James Gillray depicting Johnson's head on an owl's body disrespectfully captioned "Old Wisdom Blinking at the Stars." And at the back of his mind he may also be recalling the nonsatirical original by Sir Joshua Reynolds, portraying an elderly Johnson straining shortsightedly to read a page of printed text and popularly, or affectionately, or derisively, known as "Blinking Sam" (1775?).[3] At any rate the raucous nonsense at Johnson's expense continues unchecked:

> QUID—"Oho" said Doctor Johnson
> To Scipio Africanus
> "If you don't own me a Philosopher
> Ill kick your Roman Anus."

This elicits the following edifying response from Suction:

> SUCTION—"A ha" To Doctor Johnson
> Said Scipio Africanus,
> "Lift up my Roman Petticoat
> And kiss my Roman Anus." (2:888–889)

Childish badinage, perhaps, and irreverence with respect both to Johnson's brutal adversarialism and to a scholastic culture fixated on the Roman classics. But it is clear in any event that Johnson symbolized a compound of culturally ridiculous and repellent qualities for Blake—again, not only philosophical but literary, aesthetic, and critical—qualities that with Johnson's departure from the scene in 1784, Blake saw his whole artistic career as aggressively pitched against.

"To Generalize is to be an Idiot" may be Blake's most celebrated stroke of unconscious logical self-detonation (in the marginalia to his copy of Sir Joshua Reynolds's *Works* of 1798): "This Man was Hired to Depress Art," writes Blake of Reynolds, promising "Proofs of this Opinion . . . in the following Notes" (2:1458, 1450).[4] But the point is taken, if not entirely excused, when one weighs in the balance the Shakespearean power that not only Reynolds but also Johnson invested in the appeal of the greatest art (literary or visual) to "general nature." That Johnson was himself aware of the portentous flavor of this concept and its openness to ridicule is suggested by the beginning of chapter 11 of Johnson's *Rasselas*, when the Prince of Abyssinia makes amiable fun of those who in chapter 10 are inclined to "aggrandize [their] own profession," and where in the "Dissertation on Poetry" he famously has Imlac insist that the duty of the poet is to discover "general and transcendental truths, which will always be the same."[5] "Natural Objects," Blake wrote in the 1826 marginalia to his copy of Wordsworth's poems of 1815, "always did & now do weaken, deaden & Obliterate Imagination in Me" (2:1511). Johnson insists on a broad horizon of complementary values held in tension whenever sound judgments of poetry are made.[6] Blake's mind-set requires the extreme, implacable specialization of mutually hostile criteria, and as the invisible worm that flies in the night in the howling storm must penetrate and corrupt the rose, so these values cannot cohabit, even in tension, except to destructive effect.

This turning of one's back on the past is a signature maneuver in Blake's self-fashioning and the projection of his self-worth; if he is not actually "blinking" or blinkered himself, then his mind is commonly directed inward, and Blake is consequently celebrated for the strangeness of his visionary landscapes, his circles of destiny, and the mythological, prophetic, and cosmic structures of "thought" outside the constraints of Johnson's "sublunary nature." Scholars of Blake's more occult intuitions have investigated these worlds of mind with minute attention to pattern and system; others have cataloged Blake's symbols and their remote, abstruse sources in legend, epic, or saga.[7] Blake presents his personal mission as having historical proportions, and his version of events, with himself leading the charge against such Augustans as Johnson, has been received as the way that English poetry went.

Among critics of this historical exceptionalism is John Wiltshire who, in an essay for the *Cambridge Quarterly* of 1971 devoted to "Blake's Simplicity," recalled T. S. Eliot's judgment that Blake presents the emotions "in an extremely simplified, abstract form."[8] Such an observation can point the way to Blake's re-enactment of Augustan ideals in the *Songs*, though by comparing Wordsworth's sense of the simple and abstract with Blake's, Wiltshire concludes that Blake's simplicity is subtractive or eliminative, something different but also something less. There is a cutting away of the world and a cutting off of the self that makes the simplicity of the "Innocence" poems seem remote from Wordsworth's *Lyrical Ballads*, but also from the decaying tradition that at its height produced the work of Pope and Dryden, and then transformed and deformed into the experimental verses of Gray's "Odes," or the sentimentalism, Gothicism, and "enthusiasm" of the brothers Warton. Doubtless the eighteenth-century sources of Blake's Gothic imagination, underpinned by the Burkean "sublime," might be better known.[9] This Blakean mode is reflected in his portrait of Pope (1800) with its backdrop imagery from "Eloisa to Abelard" and the "Elegy to the Memory of an Unfortunate Lady" (both 1717). Other examples include his illustrations to Gray's poems and those of Edward "Night Thoughts" Young. Yet through the impulse to "simplicity" voiced in the "Songs of Innocence," Blake also stands with the Augustan heirs of Boileau's *Traité du sublime* (1674). His poetry responds to a legacy of both the French and classical sublime and to the quotation from Genesis adapted for critical and aesthetic use by Boileau's *Longin*: "God said 'Let there be light,' and there was light." With the proviso that Wiltshire suggests, Blake's claim to originality recalls the broad terms of this poetic revolution.[10]

Were it not that he is traditionally judged a Romantic Poet, there would be few surprises in finding Blake a highly traditional one, nor, while himself a writer of quasi-satiric verses, does Blake in practice usurp the place that Milton and Shakespeare had in the imaginations of Dryden, Pope, and then Johnson. (One only has to think of the centrality of *Paradise Lost* to the creative and critical lives of all these writers.) Nor does he fight shy of poetical rhyme:

> Tyger, tyger, burning bright,
> In the forests of the night,

and so forth (1:185). Pope's chaos of warring abstractions in the *Dunciad* cannot be entirely severed from the temper of Blake's prophetic books, and the embattled isolation of their author links Blake with Pope, and via Pope, with the master of antagonist rhetoric, the contrarian author of England's Christian epic. Blake, moreover, stands squarely within a visual artistic tradition of responses to Milton. The creative reactions of the eighteenth-century satirical caricaturists, not least in the imaginative medium of Gillray's great satirical print *Sin, Death and the Devil* (1792), shape this milieu. The dramatic illustration to the problematic allegory from book 2 of *Paradise Lost* follows Fuseli's romanticized and unsatirical *Satan and Death Separated by Sin* of 1776 and, preceding both, William Hogarth's *Satan, Sin and Death* of 1767. Blake's own *Satan, Sin and Death* of 1808 rests on such antecedents and recalls them.[11]

ARGUING WITH THE AUGUSTANS

In his recent study *The Devil as Muse*, Fred Parker suggests that "much of Blake's visionary writing can be seen as an extraordinary mutation of eighteenth-century mock-heroic, which similarly finds its life in the relation between two opposing forms of consciousness," and with Pope's likeness of Belinda to the rising sun in *The Rape of the Lock* (1714–1717)—"Not with more Glories, in th'Etherial Plain,"— and so on—Parker places a passage from Blake's "Vision of the Last Judgment" affirming the priority of the world of Mind over the world of Nature:[12]

> Mental things are alone Real. . . . I assert for My Self that I do not behold the outward Creation & that to me it is hindrance & not Action; it is the Dirt upon my feet, No part of Me. "What" it will be Questioned "When the Sun rises do you not See a round Disk of fire somewhat like a Guinea? O no no I see an Innumerable company of the Heavenly host crying 'Holy Holy Holy is the Lord God Almighty!'" (2:1027)

For Parker, Pope's wit is "all about holding the balance between the power of art and beauty and the irreducible facts of life." In Blake, however, he suggests, "The perspective of imaginative vision is offered as pretty much overwhelming the other on contact." But Parker's appeal to the visionary also describes the Blake whose common ground with Augustan culture is necessary to the force of his arguments against its influence. Blake's mock-heroic mode reignites the contraries played out in this poetical movement. Pope's political defiance of his middle and later years, and his apocalyptic prophecies of universal dullness and nightmare darkness, "the night-world of dream-like complexities and metaphysical horror," as W. W. Robson conceives it, would have spoken powerfully to Blake's imagination whether or not he esteemed his mock-heroic source.[13] Like Pope, he appointed himself the great savior of art for his age. R. Paul Yoder has drawn attention to the lines that Blake inserted on the title page of his copy of Reynolds's *Works*:

> Degrade first the Arts if you'd Mankind Degrade.
> Hire Idiots to Paint with cold light & hot shade:
> Give high price for the worst, leave the best in disgrace,
> And with Labours of Ignorance fill every place. (2:1450)

And he observes that "Blake's couplets here nicely combine much of the criticism of taste expressed in Pope's *Epistles to Several Persons* with the bitter irony of the *Dunciad*," adding that "Blake's sentiments and fears about art and culture are much the same [as Pope's]—the sense that Art is crucial to human dignity, that certain fundamentals of representation must be observed, and that the public and political support for bad art contributes to the degradation of humanity."[14] For Blake, as for Pope, it is the traditional lament intoned by W. B. Yeats: "The beating down of the wise," and "great Art beaten down."[15]

Blake qualifies his hostility by distinguishing between what he emphatically does not disdain in the Augustan poets from those qualities that offended him as a fellow artist. The tone is absolutist as ever, but also defensively that of a man much misunderstood: "I do not condemn Pope or Dryden because they did not Understand Imagination but because they did not understand Verse. Their Colouring Graving & Verse can never be applied to Art" ("Public Address," 2:1036). Blake's Augustan values close the gaps that have to be kept open by historians looking for a new "Romantic" chapter in literary history, and his terms from the graphic arts—"Colouring," "Graving"—echo long-standing parallels between poetry and painting.[16] Blake's visualizing consciousness (as distinct from his visionary mental habits) means that he differs from some late eighteenth-century predecessors in refusing to deny Imagination to the greatest of the Augustans when otherwise more tentative critics such as Joseph Warton could equivocate.[17] Blake is meanwhile enough the beneficiary of an Augustan genealogy to seek a unity of form and content and to have, say, his own versions of the conflicted concepts, laden abstractions, and contrasting capitalized essences that strain the sinews of Johnson's poetry and prose. "Hope," "Fear," "Suspense," "Fate" jostle within the structures of Johnson's "Vanity of Human Wishes" (1749). The "mind-forg'd manacles" of Blake's "London" recall the mind-manacling of which Johnson writes, to dramatizing effect, when he talks of the attention enchained by literature.[18] And if Johnson's Juvenalian lament in "London" is out of kilter with Blake's in virtue of the contrasting personality of its author, the somber darkness of a civilization abandoned to contemporary moral and material chaos is common territory. Both Blake and Johnson, like Milton and like Pope, commit themselves to what Howard Erskine-Hill would call an "opposition culture." Blake's claims to radical originality, in the formation of which Pope and Johnson can play no part as kindred spirits, have been too easy to take at face value.

There may be vital differences to record—the comic spirit of Augustan writing, for example, is an instinct Blake only partially embraces. A jokey tone at the expense of artists and art critics pervades Blake's "Satiric Verses and Epigrams," as David V. Erdman has categorized them.[19] And there is gaiety and childlike lightness in some of the "Innocence" poems, if sometimes to the point where, except to Blakean devotees, such verses can seem candidates for satirical treatment themselves. This poet of would-be prophetic insights also has "an endearingly comic" side, which makes him, not so much ridiculous, according to Patrick Cruttwell, as "an outstanding specimen of the English Eccentric."[20] Yet his traditional association with the poets (if not with the prophets) contradicts the voice in the wilderness he assiduously cultivates. He makes fun of Pope's legacy as a classical translator and a rhymester:

> [*Who* cries all art is fraud (?) & Genius a trick
> And Blake is an unfortunate Lunatic *del*]
> Thus Hayley on his toilette seeing the Sope
> Says "Homer is very much improved by Pope."
> ("Public Address," 2:1040, and, with small changes, 1041)

We have seen that Blake has no inhibitions about making his own poems rhyme. Here, the practice is in the spirit of the best eighteenth-century light verse of Matthew Prior, Alexander Pope himself, or in extempore fashion by Samuel Johnson. In the darker poems of "Experience," the tone is hauntingly sardonic and as a social or political critic, Blake lacks the focused derision of the best of Johnson, Dryden, or Pope. Similarly, because it seems less under artistic control, Blake's madness is less productive of the most coruscating satire than is the comparable madness of Jonathan Swift. In their putative satire of ordered philosophical discourse, the chaotic ramblings of the "Island in the Moon" are Swiftian. But Blake's disorder of form is too destructive of the not-mad coherence and expressive intelligence necessary to convey the experience of madness to the sanity of the normal reader. Pope's wit and judgment, in his *Essay on Criticism*, "want each others' aid" in the delighted coupling of strife-torn opposites that remain, nevertheless, distinct, "like Man and Wife" (ll. 82–83, *Pope*, 1:248). Blake's contrarieties can sound by comparison tortured, pitiless, and agonized. Thus, in *Marriage of Heaven and Hell* (1790–1793?), Blake's contrasts are less pliant than Pope's difficult communion of natural antagonists. "Without Contraries is no progression," writes Blake, in a vehement, fundamentalist vein that both Pope and Johnson had sought in their various ways to complicate: "Attraction and Repulsion, Reason and Energy, Love and Hate, are necessary to Human existence" (1:77).

BLAKE'S DRYDEN

Blake's arguments with the Augustan past are not always original, though he often writes as if he had thought of them first. Blake cannot resist them because they energize his contrarian convictions—"I will assert that every Body of Understanding must cry out Shame on such Niggling & Poco Pen as dryden [*sic*] has degraded Milton with," he writes in his "Public Address," here with reference to Dryden's adaptation of *Paradise Lost* as *The State of Innocence* (2:1049). Doubtless the differences between Dryden and Blake should not be underestimated, and this negative comparison at the expense of Dryden is hardly novel. But while Blake addresses his criticism of Dryden to people of "Understanding," his reductively bald juxtapositions of intellectual concepts mark a retreat from the Augustan (and Miltonic) triumph of "reasoning in verse." "Of the simple and elemental passions that spring separate in the mind," wrote Johnson of Dryden, "he seems not much acquainted," and goes on to characterize the intellectual preoccupations of Dryden's poetry (Johnson, *Lives*, 2:148), rising to a comprehensive evaluation (Johnson, *Lives*, 4:64–66). When, however, Blake writes off Dryden with the verb "assert," his cheerleading of "shame" at Dryden's expense falls short of a reasoned critical judgment. The penalty for being the enemy of reason at the level of reason is that to Blake's "O yes it is," we can always reply "O no it isn't."

But even at the point of conflict and denial, the tortured sensibility of its most ardent antagonist makes common cause with the Augustan. If he rejects Augustan values at the level of nature and reason, the Restoration and eighteenth-century writers register as deep-level sources at crucial moments in Blake's poetry. Thus, the master musician in Dryden's second ode on St. Cecilia's Day, "Alexander's Feast" (1697), is portrayed as taking over mental and emotional control of the tyrant, and shown to choose

> a mournful Muse
>   Soft pity to infuse
> He sung Darius great and good,
>   By too severe a fate,
> Fallen, fallen, fallen, fallen,
>   Fallen from his high estate
>   And weltering in his blood. (ll. 75–79)[21]

The repetition of "fallen," the editors of the Longman Dryden suggest, may be prompted by biblical voices, those of Isaiah 21:9 or Revelation 14:8 or 18:2, for example (*Poems of Dryden*, 5:13n). But the music of the same sources is likely to have remained active in Blake's mind, both directly and indirectly, through the resonating and unbroken reputation of one of Dryden's most celebrated poems, here in the "Introduction" to the *Songs of Experience* of 1794:

> Hear the voice of the Bard!
> Who Present, Past, & Future, sees;
> Whose ears have heard,
> The Holy Word,
> That walk'd among the ancient trees,
>
> Calling the lapsed Soul,
> And weeping in the evening dew:

That might controll
The starry pole;
And fallen, fallen light renew! (1:174)[22]

With Dryden, Blake has joined the imagery of Pope, and he simultaneously taps into the rich stock of inspirational diction that, as Johnson had observed, the Augustan poet gave to poetical posterity: thus the phrase "starry pole" had made its earlier appearance in book 8 (l. 241) of Pope's *Iliad* (1715–1720):

> deep anguish stung Saturnia's soul;
> She shook her throne that shook the starry pole. ("Translations of Homer," *Pope*, 7:409)

The most sympathetic contemporaries of Blake could not ignore such allegiances. In what follows, we see how one of their number could document and reinforce them through the tagging of visual analogies.

BLAKE'S AUGUSTAN *EUROPE*

Recalling the poetic background, Blake's friend and fellow printmaker George Cumberland (1754–1848) inscribed plates from Blake's illustrations to his mythic-historical-revolutionary poem *Europe a Prophecy* (1794). In the illustrations to "Copy D" of the poem, Cumberland used passages from Edward Bysshe's *The Art of English Poetry* for his inscriptions—including lines from Sir Samuel Garth and Sir Richard Blackmore under the rubric of "Winds" and "Storms."[23] In the manuscript text of *Europe*, Blake refers to the sons of Enitharmon who "shook their bright fiery wings" (1:209), echoing touches evident within the image (figure 9.1). The long hair hanging vertically earthward from the head of the central female figure suspended horizontally in space reminds Cumberland of lines from Milton, from Shakespeare (*Henry VI*), but also from Nicholas Rowe's blank-verse tragedy of 1703, *The Fair Penitent*, and from book 4 of Pope's translation of the *Iliad* ("Copy D," plate 6, 1:209, and 709n).

At the top of this plate, and relying on Bysshe's poetic excerpts on planets, Cumberland inscribed "A Comet," and he inserted an extract from Pope: two couplets from book 4 of the *Iliad* (ll. 101–102 and 105–106). He positions the following inscription at the foot of his copy:

> As the Red Comet from Saturnius sent
> To fright the nations with a dire portent
> With sweeping Glories glides along in air
> And shakes the sparkles from its blazing hair. (*Pope*, 7:225)[24]

The comparison is with the flight of Minerva, dispatched by Jove to break the truce between Trojans and Greeks. Other details include the airborne species of

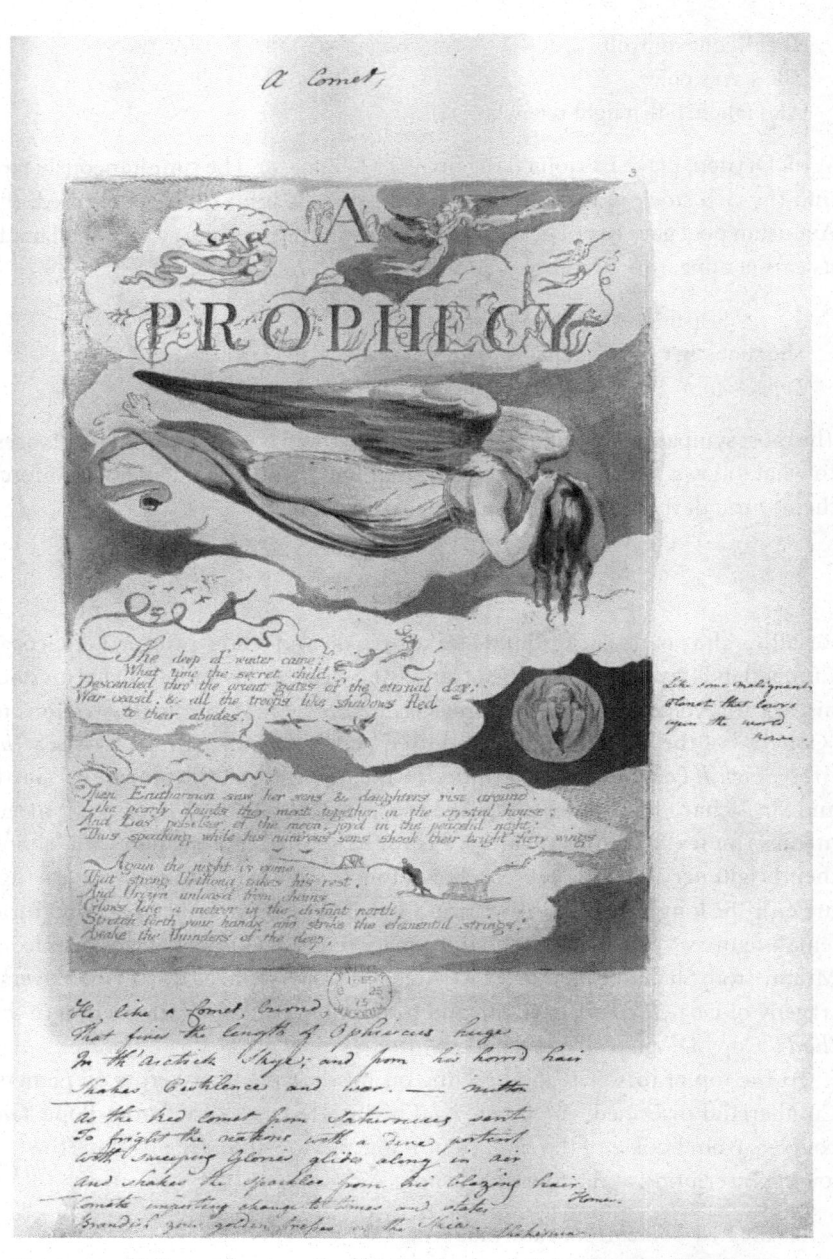

Figure 9.1. "A Comet," as inscribed by Cumberland. Reproduced © The Trustees of the British Museum.

supple conjoining forms. The visual effect takes us to the imaginative parallel universe of Pope's sylphs from *The Rape of the Lock* and reinforces the role that Pope played in Blake's visual creativity. So too does Blake's echo of Pope's most famous lines from the *Rape* on the gloriously detailed description of the heroine's "*Toilet.*" The lines appear in the course of Blake's abrasive notes-to-self on Reynolds:

> Some look to see the sweet Outlines
> And beauteous Forms that Love does wear;
> Some look to find out Patches, Paint,
> Bracelets & Stays & Powderd Hair. (2:1453)[25]

The plate that follows (1:210) expresses the poem's highest of heroic styles. The passage begins with the rousing

> The shrill winds wake!
> Till all the sons of Urizen look out and envy Los

to expand rhapsodically:

> Sieze [*sic*] all the spirits of life and bind
> Their warbling joys to our loud strings;
> Bind all the nourishing sweets of earth
> To give us bliss, that we may drink the sparkling wine of Los
> And let us laugh at war,
> Despising toil and care,
> Because the days and nights of joy in lucky hours renew. (1:227)

Mindful of Blake's poetic continuity with English Augustan traditions, Cumberland again annotates the illustration of airy bodies with lines from Bysshe, here under the heading of "Ghosts" ("Copy D," plate 7, 1:210 and 710n: figure 9.2). Of the three verses inscribed on the plate, the first describes the sufferings heaped on the damned in Dryden's translation of the sixth book of Virgil's *Aeneid* (1697). This is followed by a second and a third line not actually from the *Aeneid* but quoted from the eighth book of Ovid's *Metamorphoses*, the fable of "Meleager and Atalanta" (ll. 316–317) and translated in Dryden's *Fables, Ancient and Modern* (1700):

> Forms without body and impassive air, . . . (*Aeneid*, book 6, l. 409)
> Thin shades the sport of winds are toss'd
> O'er dreary plains, or tread the burning coast ("Meleager," ll. 316–317)

lines that Bysshe wrongly attributes in their entirety to "Dryden's *Virgil,*" and that Bentley's modern edition of Blake does not see fit to correct (1:710n).

Further inscriptions to the illustrations to *Europe* are entered from extracts found in Bysshe that the anthologist had plucked from the poet William Mason

Figure 9.2. "Ghosts," as inscribed by Cumberland. Reproduced © The Trustees of the British Museum.

(1724–1797) ("Copy D," plate 10), from Dryden's *Indian Emperor* (1665) ("Copy D," plate 9), from his opera *King Arthur* (1691) ("Copy D," plate 15), and from book 2 of his translation of Virgil's *Aeneid* ("Copy D," plate 11):

> Thus Deluges descending on the Plains
> Sweep o'er the yellow year &c. (1:710n)

Once again, Blake's visual imagination reflects poetical tastes that the eighteenth-century writers (and their Restoration predecessors) variously addressed in their time. The combinations of verbal and visual, and the interplay between them on the page, are the distinctive twin channels of Blake's art, but these relations have roots deep in the language and imagery of Augustan poetry and gain from the dynamic graphic traditions of eighteenth-century caricature that reflect and illustrate literature.

The Re-enactment of Augustan Revolt

"At length, for hatching ripe, he breaks the shell" is Dryden's line from his translation of book 3 of Chaucer's "Knight's Tale" in *Fables, Ancient and Modern*, rendering into modern English verse, at the moment of new birth, the great terminating consolation of Theseus on the cycles of existence—of which that moment of mortal beginning and becoming is part.[26] The same line is transfused into further life-affirming form in a caption Blake attached to his "Notebook" design, in *For Children: The Gates of Paradise* (1793), "Copy D," plate 8 (Library of Congress), 1:166. The design (figure 9.3) depicts a muscular winged babe incongruously breaking the prison of an enormous egg as he bursts with infant ferocity into a world of cloudy, overcast, skies—much in the spirit of revolt Blake himself enacts when he intervenes to illuminate literary history.

Blakean sympathy with past political subversion is attested likewise by a marginal note to Edmond Malone's editorial footnote in Blake's copy of Reynolds's *Works* regarding the most political of English Augustan poems. Here, Blake could mark the unfortunate turns of revolutionary ambition in lines quoted within Malone's footnote from Dryden's *Absalom and Achitophel* (ll. 51–52, 55–56). These "*may be applied*," Malone observed, "*to the ferocious and enslaved Republick of France*" (ciii). Reading of those who "began to dream they wanted liberty" and in the process

> led their wild desires to woods and caves
> And thought that all but SAVAGES were slaves,

Blake responded:

> When France got free Europe 'twixt Fools & Knaves
> Were Savage first to France & after: Slaves. (2:1459)

Figure 9.3. "At Length for Hatching Ripe He Breaks the Shell," as it appears at the foot of the original illustration. Courtesy of the Library of Congress.

So far as sense can be made of Blake's perfunctory disjointed couplet, he appears mindful of Dryden's irony: the libertarian self-delusion that passes for revolutionary fervor but concludes in tyranny is a shared understanding.

Finally, in the opening of *Vala or the Four Zoas* ("Night the First") (1796?–1807?), the Romantic visionary in Blake, committed to poetry's revolutionary power, can write of "the Song of the Aged Mother which shook the heavens with wrath. . . . Hearing the march of Long resounding strong heroic verse" (2:1073–1074). Again, Blake's terms resonate with all the wrathful melodrama of rejection. But they also directly recall the triplet from Pope's "Epistle to Augustus" (1737, ll. 267–269) that came to Johnson's mind, in his "Life of Pope," in his appreciative account of Dryden's own revolutionary versification:

> Dryden taught to join ⎫
> The varying verse, the full-resounding line, ⎬
> The long majestick march, and energy divine. ⎭

"Some improvements had been already made in English numbers," writes Johnson, "but the full force of our language was not yet felt" (lines as quoted by Johnson, "Life of Dryden" [1779], *Lives*, 2:153). Even in resistance to Augustan values, Blake's artistry is a consequence of which such innovating values are the cause, and he must re-enact Pope's homage to Dryden's own celebrated "energy," and to the energizing power of those two great Augustan poets whose work stands as the epitome of "strong heroic verse." From such a force of nature as Blake, the forces of the poetical past could not expect, and did not receive, a wholly fair-minded treatment.

NOTES

1. F. R. Leavis, "Literature and the University: The Wrong Question," in *English Literature in Our Time and the University: The Clark Lectures* (Cambridge: Cambridge University Press, 1969), 52. For further Leavisian commentary on Blake, see also Leavis's *Nor Shall My Sword: Discourses on Pluralism, Compassion, and Social Hope* (London: Chatto & Windus, 1972).

2. "An Island in the Moon," in *William Blake's Writings*, ed. G. E. Bentley Jr., 2 vols. (Oxford: Clarendon Press, 1978), 2:888. All subsequent quotations from Blake's work are taken from this edition, and unless otherwise indicated, are cited by volume and (where appropriate) page number.

3. For a detailed discussion of Gillray's satirical print and Reynolds's portrait of Johnson, see Philip Smallwood, *Johnson's Critical Presence: Image, History, Judgment* (Burlington: Ashgate, 2004), 102–107. See also Robert Folkenflik, "*Blinking Sam,* 'Surly Sam,' and 'Johnson's Grimly Ghost,'" in *Samuel Johnson: New Contexts for a New Century*, ed. Howard D. Weinbrot (San Marino: Huntington Library, 2014), 265–294.

4. The edition, in three volumes, by Edmond Malone of *The Works of Sir Joshua Reynolds* was published in 1798. Bentley suggests that the marginalia were composed in two periods, 1801–1802? and 1808–1809. Blake claimed to be offering "Proofs" of Reynolds's hostility to art in these marginal comments—but who, one is bound to ask, apart from himself, does Blake hope to convince?

5. Samuel Johnson, *Rasselas, Prince of Abyssinia* (1759), in *Rasselas and Other Tales*, ed. Gwin J. Kolb, vol. 16 of *The Yale Edition of the Works of Samuel Johnson*, Robert DeMaria Jr. et al., gen. eds. (New Haven: Yale University Press, 1990), 46, 44. Except in the case of the *Lives of the English Poets* (1779–1781), subsequent references to Johnson's *Works* are to the Yale edition.

6. Johnson's compound of the "natural and the new" is applied in practice to crucial evaluations. One, on the metaphysical poets in the "Life of Cowley," is negative: "If by a more noble and more adequate conception that be considered as Wit, which is at once natural and new, that which, though not obvious, is, upon its first production, acknowledged to

be just,... to wit of this kind the metaphysical poets have seldom risen." Another, on *The Rape of the Lock*, where "New things are made familiar, and familiar things are made new," is positive. See Johnson, *Lives of the Most Eminent English Poets*, ed. Roger Lonsdale, 4 vols. (Oxford: Clarendon Press, 2006), 1:200, 4:71 (henceforth Johnson, *Lives*). Subsequent references to Johnson's *Lives* are to this edition.

7. See, in particular, Northrop Frye, *Fearful Symmetry: A Study of William Blake* (Princeton: Princeton University Press, 1947). The poet and critic Kathleen Raine, in *Blake and Tradition*, 2 vols. (Princeton: Princeton University Press, 1968), sees Blake as thoroughly traditional. But in Raine's account of Blake, his indebtedness is not to the earlier poets mentioned in the present essay but to the mystical writings of Swedenborg, Boehme, and others.

8. John Wiltshire, "Blake's Simplicity," *Cambridge Quarterly* 5 (1971): 211–222, quotation from 211.

9. See Edmund Burke, *A Philosophical Enquiry into the Origin of our Ideas of the Sublime and the Beautiful* (London: R. and J. Dodsley, 1757).

10. For Boileau's definition, see *Dissertation sur la Joconde. Arrest burlesque. Traité du sublime* (1662–1665?), ed. Charles H. Boudhors (Paris: Société Les Belles Lettres, 1966), 45–46.

11. See Blake's "Illustrations to Milton's *Paradise Lost*," William Blake Archive, the Butts Set (composed 1808), object 2, Butlin 536.2. Whatever their success as weird visualizations, Johnson in the "Life" has discussed at length the contradictions that arise when Milton depicts such allegorical personages in his poem: "To give them any real employment, or ascribe to them any material agency, is to make them allegorical no longer, but to shock the mind by ascribing effects to non-entity" (Johnson, *Lives*, 1:291).

12. Fred Parker, *The Devil as Muse: Blake, Byron, and the Adversary* (Waco: Baylor University Press, 2011), 86–87. All references to Pope are based on *The Twickenham Edition of the Poems of Alexander Pope*, ed. John Butt et al., 11 vols. in 12 (London: Methuen, 1939–1969) (henceforth *Pope*). The line from *The Rape of the Lock* is canto 2, line 1, *Pope*, 2:159. "Visions of the Last Judgment" is quoted from "Notebook" (1810).

13. W. W. Robson, *Critical Enquiries: Essays on Literature* (London: Athlone Press, 1993), 68.

14. R. Paul Yoder, "Blake's Pope," in *Romantic Generations: Essays in Honor of Robert F. Gleckner*, ed. Ghislaine McDayter, Guinn Batten, and Barry Milligan (Lewisburg: Bucknell University Press, 2001), 23.

15. W. B. Yeats, "The Fisherman," ll. 23–24, in *W. B. Yeats: The Poems*, ed. Daniel Albright (London: Dent, 1990), 197.

16. See Simon Jarvis's review of Steven Goldsmith's *Blake's Agitation: Criticism and Emotions*, "Eternal Great Humanity Divine-ist," *TLS*, 17 January 2014, 7: "Blake's denial that Rubens's and Titian's painting can be considered art is immediately extended to poetry: 'Nor can their Method ever express Ideas or Imaginations any more than Popes Metaphysical jargon of Rhyming.' Blake considered that Pope's (and Dryden's) handling of the heroic couplet had spiritual affinities with Venetian colouring. Both practices, he believed, falsely implied that invention could be separated from execution in the making of works of art." But then the point about the union of the two was Pope's own, as he had typically articulated in the *Essay on Criticism*.

17. See Joseph Warton, *Essay on the Genius and Writings of Pope*, 2 vols. (vol. 1, London: M. Cooper, 1756; vol. 2, London: J. Dodsley, 1782). While Warton had written that Pope's handling of the sylphs in the *Rape of the Lock* excelled anything in Shakespeare, he refused the term "imagination" to the poem, praising it as a symptom of Pope's technique: "It should, however, be remembered, that he was not the FIRST former and creator of those beautiful machines, the sylphs, on which his claim to imagination is chiefly founded. He found them existing ready to his hand; but he has, indeed, employed them with singular judgement and artifice" (1:244).

18. Johnson is writing of the human appeal of biography when he observes that "none can be more delightful or more useful, none can more certainly enchain the heart by irre-

sistible interest, or more widely diffuse instruction to every diversity of condition." See "Rambler 60," from *The Rambler*, ed. W. J. Bate and Albrecht B. Strauss, vol. 3 of *The Yale Edition of Samuel Johnson* (New Haven: Yale University Press, 1969), 219.

19. *The Poetry and Prose of William Blake*, ed. David V. Erdman (New York: Doubleday, 1965).

20. Patrick Cruttwell, "Blake, Tradition, and Miss Raine," *Hudson Review* 23 (1970): 133–142, quotation from 142.

21. "Alexander's Feast, or The Power of Music: An Ode in Honour of St Cecilia's Day" (1697), in *The Poems of John Dryden*, ed. Paul Hammond and David Hopkins, 5 vols. (Harlow: Longman, 2005), 5:13. Subsequent references to Dryden are taken from this edition. The poem was published in 1697 and included in *Fables, Ancient and Modern* (1700). It was a particular favorite of Samuel Johnson.

22. Though Blake's response to Dryden does not figure in their detailed account of the poem's eighteenth- and nineteenth-century reputation, the enduring appeal of Dryden's poem is extensively cataloged by Tom Mason and Adam Rounce, in "*Alexander's Feast: or the Power of Musique*: The Poem and Its Readers," in *John Dryden: Tercentenary Essays*, ed. Paul Hammond and David Hopkins (Oxford: Clarendon Press, 2000), 140–173.

23. Bysshe's poetical commonplace book went through nine editions from 1702 to 1762. In his "Notebook" for Sunday, August 1807, Blake relates, "My Wife was told by a Spirit to look for her fortune by opening by chance a book which She had in her hand; it was Bysshe's art of Poetry." He goes on to note that he was "so well pleased with her Luck" that "I thought I would try my own & opend the following," copying a passage from book 2 of Dryden's *Virgil* (ll. 963–964). With reference to "Copy D" of Blake's *Europe*, and to plate 5 of the eighteen-plate sequence accompanying the poem, see Bentley, *William Blake's Writings*, 1:709n. Bentley's transcription of the lines is taken directly from Cumberland's entry from Bysshe and he notes that the inscriptions in "Copy D" are not signed but can be identified as Cumberland's by the handwriting, which is identical to that of his letters of 1796 held in the British Museum Department of Manuscripts (1:707n). Bentley adopts Sir Geoffrey Keynes's assignment of a letter to each copy of an original work printed by Blake (1:xxxix).

24. The lines from the *Iliad* are identified simply as "Homer" by Cumberland, whose reference, adopted by Bentley, does not elaborate on the attribution of Bysshe, *Art of English Poetry* (1702), 7th ed., 2 vols. (London: A. Bettesworth, 1725), 1:63.

25. See *The Twickenham Edition of the Poems of Alexander Pope*, vol. 2, *The Rape of the Lock and Other Poems*, 3rd ed., ed. E. Audra and Aubrey Williams (London: Methuen, 1962): "Here Files of Pins extend their shining Rows, / Puffs, Powders, Patches, Bibles, Billet-doux" (ll. 137–138).

26. *Palamon and Arcite*, book 3, l. 1069, in *The Poems of John Dryden*, ed. Hammond and Hopkins, 5:184. Blake's Drydenian caption was first brought to my attention by Tom Mason of Bristol University, while the passage from which the line is taken appears in Bysshe. See Bentley, *William Blake's Writings*, 2:1713n.

Acknowledgments

This project began in a series of conversations between the coeditors, several of the contributors, and Greg Clingham, when we all were beginning to realize what the impact AMS Press's filing for bankruptcy would have on eighteenth-century scholarship. A highly regarded monograph series would shut down, seventeen scholarly annuals would have to find new homes (and many would not succeed in doing so), and the authoritative, and exemplary, bibliography of the field, *ECCB: The Eighteenth-Century Current Bibliography*, would grind to a halt. With Gabriel Hornstein's death, we had lost not only a friend and patron, but also hundreds of pages of scholarship annually, supporting and enhancing the careers of dozens of scholars. It also occurred to us that, although those in the field knew Gabe Hornstein well, those outside the circle, including many people reading and relying on that scholarship, would not know who he was and what he did. We know distinguished scholars by name. But we seldom know publishers. Without Jacob Tonson there is no Dryden or Pope; without Robert Dodsley there is no Gray's *Elegy Written in a Country Churchyard* or Johnson's *Dictionary*. We agreed that Hornstein's contributions to scholarship should be publicly acknowledged and celebrated.

Our thanks, of course, goes to the many contributors, who range from Manuel Schonhorn, who has perhaps known Gabriel Hornstein the longest, to Leah Orr, whose academic career was just beginning when Gabe died, but whose knowledge and interest in eighteenth-century book publishing made her a natural choice for this volume. Our thanks also to the anonymous reviewers at Bucknell University Press for their many helpful suggestions, and for help at key points from Michael Edson and Sharon Harrow. Finally, the editors would like to thank Greg Clingham, for his encouragement and enthusiastic support, every step of the way.

Bibliography

Adams, H. M. *Catalogue of Books Printed on the Continent of Europe, 1501–1600 in Cambridge Libraries.* 2 vols. Cambridge: Cambridge University Press, 1967.

Adler, Mortimer. *How to Read a Book.* New York: Simon and Schuster, 1940.

Allestree, Richard. *The Works Of the Learned and Pious Author of the Whole Duty of Man.* Dublin: P. Dugan, [1723].

Amis, Martin. *Money: A Suicide Note.* London: Penguin, 1985.

Anderson, James. *The Constitutions of the Free-Masons.* London, 1723.

Austen, Jane. *Northanger Abbey.* Edited by Barbara M. Benedict and Deirdre Le Faye. Cambridge: Cambridge University Press, 2006.

Backscheider, Paula R. "Frances Brooke: Becoming a Playwright." *Women's Writing* 23 (2016): 328–335.

Baker, David Erskine, Isaac Reed, and Stephen Jones, eds. *Biographica Dramatica; Or, A Companion to the Playhouse.* 3 vols. (1812). New York: AMS Press, 1966.

Bakhtin, M. M. *The Dialogic Imagination: Four Essays.* Edited by Michael Holquist, translated by Caryl Emerson and Michael Holquist. Austin: University of Texas Press, 1981.

Barbour, Reid. *English Epicures and Stoics: Ancient Legacies in Early Stuart Culture.* Amherst: University of Massachusetts Press, 1998.

Barclay, Robert. *The Anarchy of the Ranters.* Dublin: Elizabeth Sadleir, for Sam. Fuller, 1726.

Barker, Jane. *The Entertaining Novels.* 2nd ed. 2 vols. London: A. Bettesworth and E. Curll, 1719.

Basker, James. "Criticism and the Rise of Periodical Literature." In *The Cambridge History of Literary Criticism*, vol. 4, edited by H. B. Nisbet and Claude Rawson, 316–332. Cambridge: Cambridge University Press, 2005.

———. *Tobias Smollett: Critic and Journalist.* Newark: University of Delaware Press, 1988.

Bate, W. Jackson. *Samuel Johnson.* New York: Harvest, 1979.

Bayle, Pierre. *General Dictionary, Historical and Critical.* 10 vols. London: James Bettenham, 1734.

Beasley, Jerry C. *Novels of the 1740s.* Athens: University of Georgia Press, 1982.

Bedford, Emmett G., and Robert J. Dilligan. *A Concordance to the Poems of Alexander Pope*. 2 vols. Detroit: Gale, 1974.

Behn, Aphra. *Oroonoko: Or, The Royal Slave, a True History*. London: W. Canning, 1668.

Berland, Kevin J. H. "Frances Brooke and David Garrick." *Studies in Eighteenth-Century Culture* 20 (1990): 222–227.

———. "The True Pleasurable Philosopher: Some Influences on Frances Brooke's *History of Emily Montague*." *Dalhousie Review* 66 (1986): 286–300.

Blake, William. "Illustrations to Milton's *Paradise Lost*." William Blake Archive, the Butts set. http://www.blakearchive.org.

———. "An Island in the Moon." In *William Blake's Writings*, edited by G. E. Bentley Jr. 2 vols. Oxford: Clarendon Press, 1978.

———. *The Poetry and Prose of William Blake*. Edited by David V. Erdman. New York: Doubleday, 1965.

Boileau (Nicolas Boileau-Despréaux). *Dissertation sur la Joconde. Arrest burlesque. Traité du sublime* (1662–1665?). Edited by Charles H. Boudhors. Paris: Société Les Belles Lettres, 1966.

Bonnefons, Jean. *Pancharis, Queen of Love: Or; The Art of Kissing*. Dublin: [Elizabeth Sadleir?], Dominick Roach, 1723.

Bonnell, Thomas F. *The Most Disreputable Trade: Publishing the Classics of English Poetry, 1765–1810*. Oxford: Oxford University Press, 2008.

Boswell, James. *Boswell's Life of Johnson*. Edited by George Birbeck Hill, revised and enlarged by L. F. Powell. 6 vols. Oxford: Clarendon Press, 1934–1964.

Boulton, Richard. *An Essay on the Plague*. Dublin: John Harding, 1721.

Bradley, Richard. *The Plague at Marseilles*. Dublin: Elizabeth Sadleir, 1720.

The British Novelist. 4 vols. London: J. French, 1774.

The British Novelists. 50 vols. Edited by Anna Laetitia Barbauld. London: F. C. and J. Rivington, and others, 1810.

Brooke, Frances. *A Comic Opera in Two Acts*. 3rd ed. London: T. Cadell, 1783.

———. *The Old Maid*. London: A. Millar, 1764.

Brower, Reuben A. *Alexander Pope: The Poetry of Allusion*. Oxford: Oxford University Press, 1959.

Burke, Edmund. *A Philosophical Enquiry into the Origin of our Ideas of the Sublime and the Beautiful*. London: R. and J. Dodsley, 1757.

Burnet, Gilbert. *An Exposition of the Thirty-Nine Articles*. 3rd ed. Dublin: Elizabeth Sadleir, 1721.

Burney, Frances. *Evelina, or The History of a Young Lady's Entrance into the World* (1778). New York: Norton, 1965.

Butler, Isaac. *Advice from the Stars: or an Almanack . . . for . . . 1727*. Dublin: [Elizabeth Sadleir?], William Wilmot, for Mary Whalley, 1727.

Butler, Samuel. *Hudibras* (1663–1678). Edited with introduction and commentary by John Wilders. Oxford: Clarendon Press, 1967.

Butt, John. *Pope's Poetical Manuscripts: Warton Lecture of English Poetry, 1954*. London: The British Academy, 1954.

Bysshe, Edward. *Art of English Poetry*. 7th ed. 2 vols. (1702). London: A. Bettesworth, 1725.

Campbell, Joseph. *The Hero with a Thousand Faces*. Princeton: Princeton University Press, 1968.

Cerf, Bennett. *At Random: The Reminiscences of Bennett Cerf.* New York: Random House, 1977.

Cerf, Bennett, and Donald Klopfer. *Dear Donald, Dear Bennett: The Wartime Correspondence of Bennett Cerf and Donald Klopfer.* New York: Random House, 2002.

The Champion 1 (1741).

Chandler, W[illiam], A[lex]. Pyott, and J[o]. Hodges. *A Brief Apology In Behalf of the People, In Derision call'd Quakers.* Dublin: [Elizabeth Sadleir?], Sam. Fuller, 1727.

Charles, Katherine G. "Staging Sociability in *The Excursion*: Frances Brooke, David Garrick, and the King's Theatre Coterie." *Eighteenth-Century Fiction* 27 (2014–2015): 280–284.

Chomel, Noel. *Dictionaire Oeconomique: or, The Family Dictionary.* 2 vols. Dublin: [Elizabeth Sadleir?], J. Watts, and F. Davys, 1727.

Church of England. *The Book of Common Prayer and Administration of the Sacraments . . . Together with the Psalter.* Dublin: Elizabeth Sadleir, 1717.

———. *Report of the Committee of the Lower House of Convocation.* Dublin: Thomas Hume, 1717.

Cochrane, J. A. *Dr Johnson's Printer: The Life of William Strahan.* Cambridge: Harvard University Press, 1964.

Coffey, Charles. *Poems and Songs upon Several Occasions.* Dublin: Edward Waters, 1724.

Colish, Marcia L. *The Stoic Tradition from Antiquity to the Early Middle Ages.* London: Brill, 1990.

A Collection of Novels. 2 vols. London: R. Wellington, 1699.

A Collection of Pleasant Modern Novels. Vol. 2. London: Jacob Tonson, Richard Wellington, E. Rumbole, and J. Wild, 1700. Vol. 2 of *A Collection of Novels.* London: R. Wellington, 1699.

A Collection of Six New Delightful Novels. London: E. Tracy, 1710.

Collins, Charles. *Howell and Hoadly: or the Church of England Crucify'd between Two—.* Dublin: Elizabeth Sadleir, 1717.

Columbia Center for Oral History Research. "Bennett Cerf." In *Notable New Yorkers,* transcript 734.

Concanen, Matthew. *A Match at Foot-ball.* Dublin: [Elizabeth Sadleir?], 1720.

———. *Poems, upon Several Occasions.* Dublin: A Rhames, for E. Dobson, 1722.

The Critical Review. Vols. 1–3. London: R. Baldwin, 1756–1757.

The Critical Review. Vols. 8–35. London: A. Hamilton, 1759–1773.

Crouch, Nathaniel. *Surpizing Miracles Of Nature and Art.* 5th ed. Dublin: Elizabeth Sadleir for Sam Fuller, 1727.

Cruttwell, Patrick. "Blake, Tradition, and Miss Raine." *Hudson Review* 23 (1970): 133–142.

Cumberland, Richard. *De Legibus Naturæ Disquisitio Philosophica.* Dublin: Jacobi Carson, for Josephum Leatheley, and Patricium Dugan, 1720.

Cumpsty, Andrew. *A New Almanack for . . . 1714.* Dublin: Sarah Sadleir, 1713.

A Curious Collection of Novels. London: J. Billingsley, 1731.

Curtius, Ernst Robert. *European Literature and the Latin Middle Ages.* Translated by Willard Trask. 1948. Reprint, New York: Harper, 1963.

Davis, Lennard J. *Factual Fictions: The Origins of the English Novel.* New York: Columbia University Press, 1983.

de Bary, Wm. Theodore, ed. *Finding Wisdom in East Asian Classics.* New York: Columbia University Press, 2011.

Defoe, Daniel. *Farther Adventures of Robinson Crusoe, Being the Second and Last Part of His Life*. Dublin: Patrick Dugan, 1719.

———. *Farther Adventures of Robinson Crusoe, etc.* Dublin: J. Gill, J. Hyde, G. Grierson, R. Gunne, R. Owen, E. Dobson Jr., G. Risk, 1719.

———. *The Life and Strange Surprizing Adventures of Robinson Crusoe*. Dublin: J. Gill, J. Hyde, G. Grierson, R. Gunne, R. Owen, E. Dobson Jr., G. Risk, 1719.

DeMaria, Robert, Jr. *The Life of Samuel Johnson*. Oxford: Blackwell, 1993.

Donoghue, Frank. "Colonizing Readers: Review Criticism and the Formation of a Reading Public." In *The Consumption of Culture, 1600–1800: Image, Object, Text*, edited by Ann Bermingham and John Brewer, 54–74. London: Routledge, 1995.

Douglas, Anne, Countess of Morton. *The Countess of Morton's Daily Exercise*. Dublin: Andrew Crooke, 1723.

Drake, Christopher. "The Collision of Traditions in Saikaku's *Haikai*." *Harvard Journal of Asiatic Studies* 53 (1992): 5–75.

———. "Saikaku's Haikai Requiem: *A Thousand Haikai Alone in a Single Day*: The First Hundred Verses." *Harvard Journal of Asiatic Studies* 52 (1992): 481–588.

Drummond, John. "Frances Brooke's *Rosina*: A Lesson in Morality." In *New Windows on a Woman's World: Essays for Jocelyn Harris*, vol. 1, edited by Colin Gibson and Lisa Marr, 141–152. Otago: University of Otago Department of English, 2005.

———, ed. *Musica Britannica*. London: Stainer and Bell, 1998.

Dryden, John. *The Poems of John Dryden*. Edited by Paul Hammond and David Hopkins. 5 vols. London: Routledge, 1995–2005.

———. *The Works of John Dryden*. Edited by E. N. Hooker and H. T. Swedenberg Jr. 20 vols. Berkeley: University of California Press, 1956–2002.

Duncan, William. *The History of the Lives and Reigns of the Kings of Scotland*. Dublin: [Elizabeth Sadleir?], John Harding, 1721.

du Pin, Louis Ellies. *A New History of Ecclesiastical Writers*. 3 vols. Dublin: Grierson, 1722–1724.

Ehrenpreis, Irvin. *Swift: The Man, His Works, and the Age*. 3 vols. Cambridge: Harvard University Press, 1962–1983.

Ellis, Frank Hale. *Sentimental Comedy: Theory and Practice*. Cambridge: Cambridge University Press, 1991.

Elliston, Ebenezor. *The Last Farewell of Ebenezor Elliston*. Dublin: John Harding, for Elizabeth Sadleir, 1721.

Excerpts from "Life of a Sensuous Man": An Episodic Festschrift for Howard Hibbett. Episode 25. Translated by Christopher Drake. Hollywood: Highmoonoon, 2010.

Fairer, David. *The Poetry of Alexander Pope*. Harmondsworth: Penguin, 1989.

Ferguson, Rebecca. *The Unbalanced Mind: Pope and the Rule of Passion*. Brighton: Harvester, 1986.

Fiddes, Richard. *Theologica Speculativa*. Dublin: Hyde, Grierson, and Gunne, 1718.

———. *Theologica Speculativa*. Dublin: Hyde, Rhames, and Gunne, 1720.

Field, Clive D. "Anti-Methodist Publications in the Eighteenth Century: A Revised Bibliography." *Bulletin of the John Rylands Library* 73, no. 2 (1991): 159–208.

Fielding, Henry. *Tom Thumb and the Tragedy of Tragedies*. Edited by L. J. Morrissey. Berkeley: University of California Press, 1970.

Fiske, Roger. *English Theatre Music in the Eighteenth Century*. 2nd ed. Oxford: Oxford University Press, 1986.

Fleeman, J. D. Review of *Dr. Johnson's Printer: The Life of William Strahan* by J. A. Cochrane. *Review of English Studies* 16 (1965): 432–434.

Folkenflik, Robert. "*Blinking Sam*, 'Surly Sam,' and 'Johnson's Grimly Ghost.'" In *Samuel Johnson: New Contexts for a New Century*, edited by Howard D. Weinbrot, 264–294. San Marino: Huntington Library, 2014.

Forster, Antonia. *Index to Book Reviews in England, 1749–1774*. Carbondale: Southern Illinois University Press, 1990.

Franklin, Benjamin. *The Papers of Benjamin Franklin*. American Philosophical Society and Yale University. http://franklinpapers.org.

Frye, Northrop. *Fearful Symmetry: A Study of William Blake*. Princeton: Princeton University Press, 1947.

Genest, John. *Some Account of the English Stage from the Restoration in 1660 to 1830*. 10 vols. Bath: Carrington, 1832.

Gildon, Charles. *The Life And Strange Surprizing Adventures of Mr. D—De F—*. Dublin: Elizabeth Sadleir, for Patrick Dugan, 1719.

Gill, Joseph. *An Answer to a Pamphlet Sign'd by Oswald Edwards an Anabaptist*. Dublin: Elizabeth Sadleir, for Samuel Fuller, 1723.

Gordon, Thomas. *The Conspirators; or the Case of Cataline*. Dublin: Elizbeth Sadleir, 1722.

Grafton, Anthony. *Defenders of the Text*. Cambridge: Harvard University Press, 1991.

———. *The Footnote: A Curious History*. Cambridge: Harvard University Press, 1997.

———. "Portrait of Justus Lipsius." *American Scholar* 56 (1987): 382–90.

Graham, Walter James. *English Literary Periodicals*. New York: T. Nelson & Sons, 1930.

Griffith, Elizabeth. *Collection of Novels*. 3 vols. London: G. Kearsley, 1777.

———. *The History of Lady Barton*. 3 vols. London: T. Davies and T. Cadell, 1771.

———. *The Morality of Shakespeare's Drama Illustrated*. London: T. Cadell, 1775.

———. *The Story of Lady Juliana Harley*. 2 vols. London. T. Cadell, 1776.

Griffith, Elizabeth, and Richard Griffith. *Two Novels*. In *Letters*. 4 vols. London: T. Becket and P. A. de Hondt, 1769.

Gundry, David. *Parody, Irony, and Ideology in the Fiction of Ihara Saikaku*. Leiden: Brill, 2017.

Hadas, Moses. *The Stoic Philosophy of Seneca*. Gloucester: Peter Smith, 1965.

Haeghen, Ferdinand van der. *Bibliotheca Belgica*. Ghent: Bibliotheèue de l'Université de Gand, 1880–1890.

Hale, John. *The Civilization of Europe in the Renaissance*. New York: Atheneum, 1994.

Hammond, Eugene. *Jonathan Swift: Irish Blow-In*. Newark: University of Delaware Press, 2016.

Harley, Edward, second Earl of Oxford. *Catalogus Bibliothecae Harleianae*. Compiled and edited by Samuel Johnson and William Oldys. 5 vols. London: Thomas Osborne, 1743–1745.

Harrington, James. *The Oceana and His Other Works*. London: John Darby, 1700.

Harvey, Andrew. *An Exact Narrative of the Most Material Passages in the Late Dispute in Skinner's Alley: Between Oswald Edwards, Baptist, John Stoddard, Quaker*. Dublin: Elizabeth Sadleir, for Samuel Fuller, 1722.

Heitzenrater, Richard P. *Wesley and the People Called Methodist*. Nashville: Abingdon Press, 1995.

Henry, Matthew. *The Communicant's Companion*. Dublin: Elizabeth Sadleir, 1716.

Heylyn, Peter. *Cyprianus Anglicus: Or, The History of the Life and Death of The Most Reverend and Renowned Prelate William, . . . Lord Archbishop of Canterbury*. Dublin: James Carson, for John Hyde, and Robert Owen, 1719.

Hibbett, Howard. "Saikaku and Burlesque Fiction." *Harvard Journal of Asiatic Studies* 20 (1957): 53–73.

Higgins, Ian. "Dryden and Swift." In *John Dryden (1631–1700): His Politics, His Plays, and His Poets*, edited by Claude Rawson and Aaron Santesso, 217–234. Newark: University of Delaware Press, 2004.

Hoadly, Benjamin. *The Nature of the Kingdom, Church, of Christ. A Sermon . . . March 31st 1717*. Dublin: Elizabeth Sadleir, 1717.

———. *Remarks on the Present Conspiracy*. Dublin: Margaret Ffooks, 1723.

Hoffman, Michael. "Japan's First Pop Culture." *Japan Times*, 13 February 2011. https://www.japantimes.co.jp/news/2011/02/13/national/history/japans-first-pop-culture/.

Hooker, Richard. *The Lawes of Ecclesiastical Politie*. London: A Crooke, 1666.

———. *The Works Of the Learned and Judicious Divine, Mr. Richard Hooker, in Eight Books of Ecclesiastical Polity*. Dublin: Elizabeth Sadleir, 1720.

Horace. *Satires, Epistles, and Ars Poetica*. Translated by H. Rushton Fairclough. Loeb Classical Library. Cambridge: Harvard University Press, 1961.

Humphreys, A. R. "Pope, God, and Man." In *Writers and Their Background: Alexander Pope*, edited by Peter Dixon, 60–100. London: Bell and Sons, 1972.

Hunter, J. Paul. *Before Novels: The Cultural Contexts of Eighteenth-Century English Fiction*. New York: W. W. Norton, 1990.

Hyde, Edward, Earl of Clarendon. *History of the Rebellion . . . in Ireland*. 3 vols. Dublin: John Hyde, and Robert Owen, 1719.

———. *Lord Clarendon's History of the Grand Rebellion Completed*. Dublin: J. Leathley and P. Dugan, 1720.

Hyde, Thomas. *Catalogus Impressorum Librorum Bibliothecae Bodleianae*. 2 vols. (1673–1674). Oxford: Sheldonian Theatre, 1738.

Jarvis, Simon. "Eternal Great Humanity Divine-ist." *Times Literary Supplement*, 17 January 2014, 7.

Johnson, Charles. *The Masquerade*. Dublin: Elizabeth Sadleir, 1719.

Johnson, Claudia. "'Let Me Make the Novels of a Country': Barbauld's *The British Novelists* (1810/1820)." *Novel: A Forum of Fiction* 34 (2001): 163–179.

Johnson, Maurice. "A Literary Chestnut: Dryden's 'Cousin Swift.'" *PMLA* 67 (1952): 1024–1034.

Johnson, Samuel. *A Dictionary of the English Language* (1755). Edited by Gwin J. Kolb and Robert DeMaria Jr. Vol. 18 of *The Yale Edition of the Works of Samuel Johnson*. General editors Robert DeMaria Jr. et al. New Haven: Yale University Press, 2005.

———. *The Letters of Samuel Johnson*. Edited by Bruce Redford. 5 vols. Princeton: Princeton University Press, 1982.

———. *Lives of the Most Eminent English Poets* (1779–1781). Edited by Roger Lonsdale. 4 vols. Oxford: Clarendon Press, 2006.

———. *The Lives of the Poets* (1779–1781). Edited by John H. Middendorf. Vols. 21–23 of *The Yale Edition of the Works of Samuel Johnson*. General editors Robert DeMaria Jr. et al. New Haven: Yale University of Press, 2010.

Johnson, Samuel. *The Rambler.* Edited by W. J. Bate and Albrecht B. Strauss. Vols. 3–5 of *The Yale Edition of the Works of Samuel Johnson.* General editors Robert DeMaria Jr. et al. New Haven: Yale University Press, 1969.

———. *Rasselas and Other Tales.* Edited by Gwin J. Kolb. Vol. 16 of *The Yale Edition of the Works of Samuel Johnson.* General editors Robert DeMaria Jr. et al. New Haven: Yale University Press, 1990.

Jones, Emrys D. *Friendship and Allegiance in Eighteenth-Century Literature: The Politics of Private Virtue in the Age of Walpole.* Houndmills: Palgrave Macmillan, 2013.

Joseph, Betty. "Capitalism and Its Others: Intersecting and Competing Forms in Eighteenth-Century Fiction." *Studies in Eighteenth-Century Culture* 45 (2016): 157–173.

Keating, Geoffrey. *The General History of Ireland.* Dublin: J. Carson, 1723.

Keene, Donald. *World within Walls: Japanese Literature of the Pre-modern Era, 1606–1867.* New York: Columbia University Press, 1999.

Kivilo, Maarit. *Early Greek Poets' Lives: The Shaping of a Tradition.* Leiden: Brill, 2010.

Knapp, John. *An Almanack or Diary Astronomical.* Dublin: Elizabeth Sadleir, 1716; also 1717, 1718, 1721, and 1722.

Kris, Ernst, and Otto Kurz. *Legend, Myth, and Magic in the Image of the Artist.* New Haven: Yale University Press, 1974.

La Boissiere, Peter. *The Starry-Interpreter.* Dublin: [Elizabeth Sadleir?], J. Hyde, R. Gunne, R. Owen, and E. Dobson, 1720.

———. *The Starry-Interpreter.* Dublin: Elizabeth Sadleir, 1721; also 1722, 1727, [1728?].

[La Fayette, Marie-Madeleine]. *The Princess of Cleves.* London: W. Lane, 1780.

Lambert, Frank. *"Pedlar in Divinity": George Whitefield and the Transatlantic Revivals.* Princeton: Princeton University Press, 1994.

Law, William. *A Reply to the Bishop of Bangor's Answer.* London: William and John Innys, 1719. Dublin: Elizabeth Sadleir, 1719.

Leavis, F. R. "Literature and the University: The Wrong Question." In F. R. Leavis, *English Literature in Our Time and the University: The Clark Lectures.* 37–60. Cambridge: Cambridge University Press, 1969.

———. *Nor Shall My Sword: Discourses on Pluralism, Compassion, and Social Hope.* London: Chatto & Windus, 1972.

Lee, Nathaniel. *The Rival Queens.* 6th ed. Dublin: Elizabeth Sadleir, 1718–1719.

Leedham-Green, E. S. *Books in Cambridge Inventories.* 2 vols. Cambridge: Cambridge University Press, 1967.

LeFanu, William. *A Catalogue of the Books Belonging to Dr. Jonathan Swift . . . Aug. 1715.* Cambridge: Cambridge University Library, 1988.

Lefkowitz, Mary R. "Autobiographical Fiction in Pindar." *Harvard Studies in Classical Philology* 84 (1980): 29–49.

———. "Fictions in Literary Biography: The New Poem and the Archilochus Legend." *Arethusa* 9 (1976): 181–189.

———. *The Lives of the Greek Poets.* Baltimore: Johns Hopkins University Press, 1981.

———. "The Poet as Hero: Fifth-Century Autobiography and Subsequent Biographical Fiction." *Classical Quarterly* 28 (1978): 459–469.

Leupp, Gary P. *Servants, Shophands, and Laborers in the Cities of Tokugawa Japan.* Princeton: Princeton University Press, 1992.

Lewis, Thomas. *Oriines Hebrææ.* Dublin: P. Rider and T. Harbin, 1725.

Lipsiuis, Justus. *Epistolarum ad Belgas, Centuria I.* Antwerp, 1605.

————. *Epistolarum Selectarum Centuria Prima Miscellanea.* Antwerp, 1586.

————. *Opera Omnia.* 4 vols. Antwerp, 1637.

The London Stage, 1660–1800: A Calendar of Plays, Entertainments & Afterpieces, Together with Casts, Box-Receipts, and Contemporary Comment, Compiled from the Playbills, Newspapers and Theatrical Diaries of the Period. Edited by William Van Lennep, Emmett L. Avery, Arthur H. Scouten, George Winchester Stone Jr., and Charles Beecher Hogan. 11 vols. Carbondale: Southern Illinois University Press, 1960–1968.

Longinus. *Treatise on the Sublime . . . Translated . . . By Mr. Welsted.* Dublin: Elizabeth Sadleir, for Sam. Fuller, 1727.

Lucan. *Lucan's Pharsalia.* Translated by Nicholas Rowe. Dublin: James Cardon, for Joseph Leathley, 1719.

Luce, J. V. "A Note on the Composition of Swift's Epitaph." *Hermathena* 104 (1967): 78–81.

Mack, Maynard. *Alexander Pope: A Life.* New Haven: Yale University Press, 1985.

————. *Collected in Himself: Essays Cultural, Biographical, and Bibliographical on Pope and Some of His Contemporaries.* Newark: University of Delaware Press, 1982.

————. *The Garden and the City: Retirement and Politics in the Late Poetry of Pope, 1731–1743.* Toronto: University of Toronto Press, 1969.

————. *The Last and Greatest Art: Some Unpublished Poetical Manuscripts of Alexander Pope.* Newark: University of Delaware Press, 1954.

————. "Pope's Books: A Bibliographical Survey with a Finding List." In *English Literature in the Age of Disguise*, edited by Maximillian E. Novak, 209–305. Berkeley: University of California Press, 1977.

Mandelbrote, Giles. "Richard Bentley's Copies: The Ownership of Copyrights in the Late Seventeenth Century." In *The Book Trade and Its Customers, 1450–1900: Historical Essays for Robin Myers*, edited by Arnold Hunt, Giles Mandelbrote, and Alison Shell, 55–94. New Castle: Oak Knoll, 1997.

Manley, Delariviere. *The Power of Love.* Dublin: Patrick Dugan, 1720.

Mantel, Hilary. *Wolf Hall.* London: Fourth Estate, 2009.

Markley, Robert. *The Far East and the English Imagination, 1600–1730.* Cambridge: Cambridge University Press, 2006.

————. "Gulliver and the Japanese: The Limits of the Postcolonial Past." *Modern Language Quarterly* 65 (2004): 457–479.

Martin, Peter. *The Gardening World of Alexander Pope.* Hamden: Archon Books, 1984.

Mason, Tom, and Adam Rounce. "*Alexander's Feast:* or the *Power of Musique*: The Poem and Its Readers." In *John Dryden: Tercentenary Essays*, edited by Paul Hammond and David Hopkins, 140–173. Oxford: Clarendon Press, 2000.

McCarthy, William. *Anna Letitia Barbauld: Voice of the Enlightenment.* Baltimore: Johns Hopkins University Press, 2008.

McClain, James L. "Space, Power, Wealth, and Status in Seventeenth-Century Osaka." In *Osaka: The Merchants' Capital of Early Modern Japan*, edited by James L. McClain and Wakita Osamu. Ithaca: Cornell University Press, 1999.

McInelly, Brett C. *Textual Warfare and the Making of Methodism.* Oxford: Oxford University Press, 2014.

McMullen, Lorraine. "Double Image: Frances Brooke's Women Characters." *World Literature Written in English* 21 (1982): 356–363.

————. *An Odd Attempt in a Woman: The Literary Life of Frances Brooke.* Vancouver: University of British Columbia Press, 1983.

Melmoth, Wm. *The Great Importance of a Religious Life*. Dublin: M. Rhames, for S. Hyde, et al., 1735.

Mengel, Elias F. "Pope's Imitation of Boileau in *Arbuthnot*." *Essays in Criticism* 38 (1977): 295–307.

Messenger, Ann. *His and Hers: Essays in Restoration and Eighteenth-Century Literature*. Lexington: University Press of Kentucky, 1986.

Mettler, Susan. *Soldiers to Citizens: The G.I. Bill and the Making of the Greatest Generation*. New York: Oxford University Press, 2005.

Miller, Henry Knight. *Essays on Fielding's Miscellanies: A Commentary on Volume One*. Princeton: Princeton University Press, 1961.

———. "The Paradoxical Encomium with Special Reference to Its Vogue in England, 1600–1800." *Modern Philology* 53 (1956): 145–178.

Milton, John. *Paradise Lost* (1667, 1674). Edited by Alistair Fowler. 2nd ed. London: Longman, 1998.

Montaigne, Michel de. *Essays of Michael Seigneur de Montaigne*. Translated by Charles Cotton. 3 vols. London: T. Basset, 1685.

The Monthly Review. Vols. 1–38. London: R. Griffiths, 1749–1768.

Moody, Jane. "Stolen Identities: Character, Mimicry, and the Invention of Samuel Foote." In *Theatre and Celebrity in Britain, 1660–2000*, edited by Mary Luckhurst and Jane Moody. 65–89. New York: Palgrave, 2005.

Moore, John R., and Maurice Johnson. "Dryden's 'Cousin Swift.'" *PMLA* 68 (1953): 1232–1240.

Moreri, Louis. *Great Historical, Geographical, and Poetical Dictionary*. 2nd ed. 2 vols. London: Henry Rhodes, 1701.

Morford, Mark. *Stoics and Neostoics: Rubens and the Circle of Lipsius*. Princeton: Princeton University Press, 1992.

Moss, David, and Eugene Kintgen. *The Dojima Rice Market and the Origins of Futures Trading*. Cambridge: Harvard Business School, 2009.

Munby, A. N. L., ed. *Sale Catalogues of Libraries of Eminent Persons*. 9 vols. London: Mansell & Sotheby-Parke-Bernet, 1971.

Munter, Robert. *A Dictionary of the Print Trade in Ireland, 1550–1775*. New York: Fordham University Press, 1988.

———. *The History of the Irish Newspaper, 1685–1760*. Cambridge: Cambridge University Press, 1967.

Murphy, Arthur. *An Essay on the Life and Genius of Samuel Johnson, LL.D*. In *Johnsonian Miscellanies*, vol. 1, edited by G. Birbeck Hill, 353–488. New York: Harper & Brothers, 1897.

Nary, Cornelius. *The New History of the World*. Dublin: Edward Waters, for Luke Dowling, 1720.

National Archives. Servicemen's Readjustment Act. http://www.ourdocuments.gov/doc .php?doc=76.

Nicolson, Marjorie, and G. S. Rousseau. *"This Long Disease, My Life": Alexander Pope and the Sciences*. Princeton: Princeton University Press, 1968.

Nobuhiko, Nakai, and James L. McClain. "Commercial Change and Urban Growth in Early Modern Japan." In *The Cambridge History of Japan*, vol. 4, *Early Modern Japan*, edited by John Whitney Hall and James L. McClain, 519–595. Cambridge: Cambridge University Press, 1991.

Novarr, David. "Swift's Relation with Dryden, and Gulliver's *Annus Mirabilis*." *English Studies* 47 (1966): 341–354.

The Novelist's Magazine. London: Harrison and Co., [1780–1788].

O'Conner, Morgan [Murroghog]. *Poems, Pastorals, and Dialogues*. Dublin: S. Powell for J. Thompson, 1726.

"Opera Guide: NSW." *Theatre Australia* 6, no. 4 (December 1981): 65. https://issuu.com /libuow/docs/theatreaustralia1981dec1982jan.

Orr, Leah. *Novel Ventures: Fiction and Print Culture in England, 1690–1730*. Charlottesville: University of Virginia Press, 2017.

——. "Tactics of Publishing and Selling Fiction in the Long Eighteenth Century." *Huntington Library Quarterly* 81 (2018): 399–413.

Oxenford, John, and J. L. Hatton, eds. *English Ballad Operas*. London: Boosey & Hawkes, [1874].

Oxford Dictionary of National Biography. Oxford: Oxford University Press, 2004. http:// www.oxforddnb.com.

Parke, W. T. *Musical Memoirs*. 2 vols. London: Colburn, 1833.

Parker, Blanford. *The Triumph of Augustan Poetics: English Literary Culture from Butler to Johnson*. Cambridge: Cambridge University Press, 1998.

Parker, Fred. *The Devil as Muse: Blake, Byron, and the Adversary*. Waco: Baylor University Press, 2011.

The Particulars of an Indian Treaty at Conestogoe. Dublin: Elizabeth Sadleir, for Samuel Fuller, 1723.

Passmann, Dirk F. "Jonathan Swift as Book-Collector: With a Checklist of Swift's Association Copies." *Swift Studies* 27 (2012): 7–68.

Passmann, Dirk F., and Heinz J. Vienken. *The Library and Reading of Jonathan Swift: A Bio-bibliographical Handbook*. 4 vols. Frankfurt am Main: Peter Lang, 2003.

Philips, William. *Hibernia Freed*. [Dublin: Patrick Dugan], 1722.

Phillips, James W. *Printing and Bookselling in Dublin, 1670–1800: A Bibliographical Enquiry*. Dublin: Irish Academic Press, 1998.

Pittis, William. *Dr. Radcliffe's Life and Letters*. Dublin: [Elizabeth Sadleir?], for Pat. Dugan and W. Smith, [1724].

The Pleasant Companion. London: J. Brooks, 1734.

Plomer, Henry Robert. *A Dictionary of the Printers and Booksellers Who Were at Work in England, Scotland, and Ireland from 1668 to 1725*. Oxford: Oxford University Press for the Bibliographical Society, 1922.

A Poem To the whole People of Ireland Relating to M. B. Drapier. By A. R. Hosier. [Dublin]: Elizabeth Sadleir, 1726.

Pollard, M[ary]. *A Dictionary of Members of the Dublin Book Trade, 1550–1800, Based on the Records of the Guild of St Luke the Evangelist Dublin*. London: Bibliographical Society, 2000.

Pope, Alexander. *The Correspondence of Alexander Pope*. Edited by George Sherburn. 5 vols. Oxford: Clarendon Press, 1956.

——. *The Poems of Alexander Pope: A One-Volume Edition of the Twickenham Text with Selected Annotations*. Edited by John Butt. 1963. Reprint, London: Routledge, 1989.

——. *The Twickenham Edition of the Poems of Alexander Pope*. General Editor John Butt. 11 vols. in 12. London: Methuen, 1939–1969.

Price, Curtis, Judith Milhous, and Robert Hume. *Italian Opera in Late-Eighteenth-Century London*. 2 vols. Oxford: Clarendon Press, 1995.

Prior, Matthew. *The Turtle and the Sparrow*. Dublin: Elizabeth Sadleir, for Dominick Roach, 1723.

Pufendorf, Samuel, Freiherr von. *The Whole Duty of Man, According to the Law of Nature.* 4th ed. 1715. Dublin: Elizabeth Sadleir, for George Grierson, 1716.

Quarles, Francis. *Argalus and Parthenia.* Dublin: Elizabeth Sadleir, [1720?].

Raine, Kathleen. *Blake and Tradition.* 2 vols. Princeton: Princeton University Press, 1968.

Rank, Otto. *The Myth of the Birth of the Hero.* New York: Nervous and Mental Disease Publishing, 1913.

Reeve, Clara. *The Progress of Romance.* 2 vols. Colchester: W. Keymer and G. G. J. and J. Robinson, 1785.

Reynolds, Sir Joshua. *The Works of Sir Joshua Reynolds.* Edited by Edmond Malone. 3 vols. London: T. Cadell, Jun. and W. Davies, 1798.

Ribble, Frederick, and Anne Ribble. *Fielding's Library: An Annotated Catalogue.* Charlottesville: Bibliographical Society of the University of Virginia, 1996.

Richetti, John J., ed. *The Cambridge Companion to the Eighteenth-Century Novel.* Cambridge: Cambridge University Press, 1996.

———. *Popular Fiction before Richardson: Narrative Patterns, 1700–1739.* Oxford: Clarendon, Press, 1969.

Rigge, Ambrose. *A Brief and Serious Warning to Such as Are Concerned in Commerce.* Dublin: Elizabeth Sadleir, 1721.

Robinson, Colin. "The Trouble with Amazon." *The Nation*, 15 July 2010. https://www.thenation.com.artile/trouble-amazon/.

Robinson, John. *A Letter from the Lord Bishop of London.* Dublin: Elizabeth Sadleir, 1722.

Robson, W. W. *Critical Enquiries: Essays on Literature.* London: Athlone Press, 1993.

Rocket Opera: Past Performances. https://rocketopera.weebly.com/performances.html.

Rogers, Katharine M. *Feminism in Eighteenth-Century England.* Urbana: University of Illinois Press, 1982.

Rudd, Niall. "Variation and Inversion in Pope's *Epistle to Dr. Arbuthnot.*" *Essays in Criticism* 34 (1984): 216–228.

Ruggle, George. *Ignoramus, Comœdia coram Rege Jacobo.* Dublin: s.n., 1736.

Ryōi, Asai. *Ukiyo Monogatari (Tales of the Floating World).* Osaka, 1666.

Saikaku, Ihara. *Five Women Who Loved Love.* Translated by Wm. Theodore de Bary. Rutland: Charles E. Tuttle, 1956.

———. *Futokoro Suzuri (The Pocket Inkstone).* Osaka, 1687.

———. *Japanese Family Storehouse; Or the Millionaire's Gospel Modernised.* Translated by G. W. Sargent. Cambridge: Cambridge University Press, 1969.

———. *Kōshoku Gonin Onna (Five Women Who Loved Love).* Osaka, 1686.

———. *Kōshuku Ichidai Omna (The Life of an Amorous Woman).* Osaka, 1686.

———. *Kōshoku Ichidai Otoko (The Life of an Amorous Man).* Osaka, 1682.

———. *The Life of an Amorous Woman.* Translated by Kenji Hamada. 1963. Reprint, Rutland: Charles E. Tuttle, 2001.

———. *The Life of an Amorous Woman and Other Writings by Ihara Saikaku.* Translated by Ivan Morris. New York: UNESCO/New Directions, 1963.

———. *Nippon Eitaigura (The Eternal Storehouse of Japan).* Osaka, 1688.

———. *Saikaku Shokoku Hanashi (Saikaku's Tales from Various Provinces).* Osaka, 1685.

———. *Seken Munesan 'yō (This Scheming World).* Osaka, 1692.

———. *Some Final Words of Advice.* Translated by Peter Nosco. Rutland: Charles E. Tuttle, 1980.

———. *This Scheming World.* Translated by Masanori Takatsuka and David C. Stubbs. Rutland: Charles E. Tuttle, 1965.

Samuel Hayes's Catalogue. No. 332. [London: S. Hayes, 1785].

Saunders, Jason Lewis. *Justus Lipsius: The Philosophy of Renaissance Stoicism.* New York: Liberal Arts Press, 1955.

Schalow, Paul. "Ihara Saikaku and Ejima Kiseki: The Literature of Urban Townspeople." In *The Cambridge History of Japanese Literature*, edited by Haruo Shirane and Tomi Suzuki, with David Lurie, 415–423. Cambridge: Cambridge University Press, 2016.

Schonhorn, Manuel. "'Here Comes the Son': A Shandean Project." In *The Age of Projects*, edited by Maximillian Novak, 272–296. Toronto: University of Toronto Press, 2008.

Second Volume of Lackington's Catalogue for 1793. London: J. Lackington, 1793.

Sekora, John. *Luxury: The Concept in Western Thought, Eden to Smollett.* Baltimore: Johns Hopkins University Press, 1977.

A Select Collection of Novels. 6 vols. London: John Watts, 1720–1722.

Select Collection of Novels and Histories. 2nd ed. 6 vols. London: John Watts, 1729.

Sewell, George. *The Tragedy of Sir Walter Raleigh.* Dublin: [Elizabeth Sadleir?], G. Risk, 1719.

Shadwell, Charles. *The Works of Mr. Charles Shadwell.* 2 vols. Dublin: Dugan, Leathely, and George Risk, 1720.

Shakespeare, William. *Comedies, Histories, and Tragedies.* 4th ed. London: H. Herringman, for Joseph Knight and Francis Saunders, 1685.

Sherburn, George. "Letters of Alexander Pope, Chiefly to Sir William Trumbull." *Review of English Studies*, n.s., 9 (1958): 389.

Sheridan, Thomas. *The Intelligencer.* Edited by James Woolley. Oxford: Clarendon Press, 1992.

Shield, William. *Rosina: A Comic Opera.* London: Napier, [1783].

Shifflett, Andrew. *Stoicism, Politics, and Literature in the Age of Milton.* Cambridge: Cambridge University Press, 1998.

Shirane, Haruo. *Early Modern Japanese Literature: An Anthology, 1600–1900.* Abridged ed. New York: Columbia University Press, 2008.

Shively, Donald H. "Popular Culture: The Chōnin." In *The Cambridge History of Japan*, vol. 4, *Early Modern Japan*, edited by John Whitney Hall and James L. McClain, 706–769. Cambridge: Cambridge University Press, 1991.

Silverman, Al. *The Time of Their Lives: The Golden Age of Great American Publisher, Their Editors and Authors.* New York: St. Martin's Press, 2008.

Skinner, Thomas. *The Life of General Monk.* Dublin: Patrick Dugan, [1724].

Smallwood, Philip. *Johnson's Critical Presence: Image, History, Judgment.* Burlington: Ashgate, 2004.

Smith, Peter. *From Tyneside Village to Westminster Abbey: The Life, Times, and Music of William Shield, 1748–1829.* Gateshead: Gateshead Schools' Music Service, 2005.

Smollett, Tobias. *The History and Adventures of an Atom.* 2 vols. (1769). London: C. Cooke, [1795].

——. *The History of England (1757–65).* Vol. 5. Oxford: Talbooys, 1827.

Snape, Andrew. *A Letter to the Bishop of Bangor Occasiond by His Lordship's Sermon.* Dublin: Elizabeth Sadleir, 1717.

——. *A Second Letter to the Lord Bishop of Bangor.* Dublin: Thomas Hume, 1717.

Snape, Andrew. *A Sermon Preach'd before the Honourable House of Commons.* Dublin: J. Bowyer, 1717. Dublin: Elizabeth Sadleir, 1717.

Sonnenberg, Katarzyna. *At the Roots of the Modern Novel: A Comparative Reading of Ihara Saikaku's "The Life of an Amorous Woman" and Daniel Defoe's "Moll Flanders."* Krakow: Jagiellonian University Press, 2015.

South, Robert. *Thirty-Six Sermons and Discourses.* Dublin: Dugan and Leathley, 1720.

Sowter, John. *The Way to be Wise and Wealthy.* Dublin: [Elizabeth Sadleir?], Sam. Fuller, 1724.

The Spectator. Edited by Donald Bond. 5 vols. Oxford: Clarendon Press, 1965.

Sporting Life, 23 September 1861.

Stanley, Thomas. *The History of Philosophy, in Eight Parts.* London: Humphrey Moseley and Thomas Dring, 1656.

Stout, Henry. *The Divine Dramatist: George Whitefield and the Rise of Modern Evangelicalism.* Grand Rapids: William B. Eerdmans, 1991.

Sturmy, John. *Love and Duty: or, the Distress'd Bride.* Dublin: Elizabeth Sadleir, 1722.

Swift, Jonathan. *The Correspondence of Jonathan Swift.* Edited by David Woolley. 5 vols. Frankfurt: Peter Lang, 1999–2004.

———. *The Poems of Jonathan Swift.* Edited by Harold Williams. 2nd ed. 3 vols. Oxford: Clarendon Press, 1958.

———. *The Prose Writings of Jonathan Swift.* Edited by Herbert Davis. 14 vols. Oxford: Basil Blackwell, 1964.

———. *A Tale of a Tub and Other Works.* Edited by Marcus Walsh. Vol. 1 of *The Cambridge Edition of the Works of Jonathan Swift*, edited by Claude Rawson et al. Cambridge: Cambridge University Press, 2010.

———. *The Works of J[onathan] S[wift].* 8 vols. Dublin: George Faulkner, 1735–1769.

Tacitus. *The Annals and History of Cornelius Tacitus . . . Made English by Several Hands.* 2nd ed. 3 vols. London John Nicholson, 1716.

Taylor, Richard C. "James Harrison, *The Novelist's Magazine*, and the Early Canonizing of the English Novel." *Studies in English Literature 1500–1900* 33 (1993): 629–643.

The Theatre of Love, a Collection of Novels. London: W. Reeve, 1759.

Thompson, W[illiam]. *Mendico-Hymen Seu, Tuphlo-pero-gamia. The Beggar's Match.* Dublin: [Elizabeth Sadleir?], Tho. Hume, for Jer. and Sil. Pepyat, 1723.

Thomson, James. *The Seasons: A Hymn, a Poem.* London, 1730.

Tillotson, Geoffrey. "Pope's *Epistle to Harley*: An Introduction and Analysis." In *Pope and His Contemporaries: Essays Presented to George Sherburn*, edited by James L. Clifford and Louis A. Landa, 58–77. New York: Oxford University Press, 1949.

Todd, Janet. *Sensibility: An Introduction.* London: Methuen, 1986.

Toner, Anne. "Anna Barbauld on Fictional Form in *The British Novelists* (1810)." *Eighteenth-Century Fiction* 24 (2011): 171–193.

Totman, Conrad. *Japan before Perry.* Berkeley: University of California Press, 1981.

Trapp, Joseph. *The Real Nature of the Church or Kingdom of Christ: A Sermon.* 2nd ed. Dublin: H. Clements, 1717. Dublin: Elizabeth Sadleir, 1717.

van Dorsten, J. A. *Poets, Patrons, and Professors.* London: Oxford University Press, 1962.

Venturo, David. "Swift's Style, the Nakedness of the Houyhnhnms, and the Deceits of Rhetoric." *1650–1850: Ideas, Aesthetics, and Inquiries in the Early Modern Era* 18 (2011): 285–311.

Virgil. *Eclogues, Georgics, The Aeneid 1–6.* Translated by H. Rushton Fairclough. Rev. ed. Loeb Classical Library. Cambridge: Harvard University Press, 1978.

Ward, Edward. *Lord Clarendon's History of the Grand Rebellion Completed.* Dublin: Joseph Leathley and Dugan, 1720.

Warton, Joseph. *Essay on the Genius and Writings of Pope.* 2 vols. Vol. 1, London: M. Cooper, 1756; vol. 2, London: J. Dodsley, 1782.

Washburn, Dennis C. *The Dilemma of the Modern in Japanese Fiction.* New Haven: Yale University Press, 1995.

Wasserman, Steve. "The Amazon Effect." *The Nation,* 29 May 2012. https://www.thenation .com/article/amazon-effect/.

Watt, Ian. *The Rise of the Novel: Studies in Defoe, Richardson, and Fielding.* Berkeley: University of California Press, 1957.

Weinbrot, Howard D. *Britannia's Issue: The Rise of British Literature from Dryden to Ossian.* Cambridge: Cambridge University Press, 1993.

Whibley, Charles. *A Facsimile Reproduction of a Unique Catalogue of Laurence Sterne's Library.* London: Tregaskis, 1930.

Whitefield, George. *Some Remarks upon a Late Charge Against Enthusiasm.* N.p., 1744.

———. *The Works of the Reverend George Whitefield, M.A.* 7 vols. London: Edward and Charles Dilly, 1771–1772.

Wilkinson, Hazel. "Benjamin Franklin's London Printing, 1725–1726." *Papers of the Bibliographical Society of America* 110 (2016): 139–180.

Williams, Abigail. *The Social Life of Books: Reading Together in the Eighteenth-Century Home.* New Haven: Yale University Press, 2017.

Williams, Harold. *Dean Swift's Library.* Cambridge: Cambridge University Press, 1932.

Wiltshire, John. "Blake's Simplicity." *Cambridge Quarterly* 5 (1971): 211–222.

Winn, James Anderson. *John Dryden and His World.* New Haven: Yale University Press, 1987.

———. *Queen Anne: Patroness of Arts.* Oxford: Oxford University Press, 2014.

Wood, Thomas. *An Institute of the Laws of England.* Dublin: J. Watts, 1724.

Woodfield, Ian. *Opera and Drama in Eighteenth-Century England.* Cambridge: Cambridge University Press, 2001.

Woolley, James. "Poor John Harding and Mad Tom: 'Harding's Resurrection' (1724)." In *That Woman! Studies in Irish Bibliography; A Festschrift for Mary "Paul" Pollard,* edited by Charles Benson and Siobhán Fitzpatrick, 101–122. Dublin: Lilliput Press, for the Library Association of Ireland, 2005.

———. "Sarah Harding as Swift's Printer." In *Waking Naboth's Vinyard,* edited by Christopher Fox and Brenda Tooley, 164–177. Notre Dame: University of Notre Dame Press, 1995.

Yeats, W. B. *W. B. Yeats: The Poems.* Edited by Daniel Albright. London: Dent, 1990.

Yoder, R. Paul. "Blake's Pope." In *Romantic Generations: Essays in Honor of Robert F. Gleckner,* edited by Ghislaine McDayter, Guinn Batten, and Barry Milligan, 23–42. Lewisburg: Bucknell University Press, 2001.

Notes on Contributors

KEVIN L. COPE is Robert and Rita Wetta Adams Professor of English and Comparative Literature at Louisiana State University. His books include *Criteria of Certainty: Truth and Judgment in the English Enlightenment* (1990), *John Locke Revisited* (1999), and *In and After the Beginning: Inaugural Moments and Literary Institutions in the Long Eighteenth Century* (2007). He is the editor of *Enlightening Allegory: Theory, Practice, and Contexts of Allegory in the Late Seventeenth and Eighteenth Centuries* (1993) and *Compendious Conversations: The Method of Dialogue in the Early Enlightenment* (1992). He is the coeditor (with Robert C. Leitz III) of *Textual Studies and the Enlarged Eighteenth Century: Precision as Profusion*, and coeditor (with Cedric D. Reverand II) of *An Expanding Universe: The Project of Eighteenth-Century Studies: Essays Commemorating the Career of Jim Springer Borck* (2017, published by AMS Press). He is also the editor and founder of the annual *1650–1850: Ideas, Aesthetics, and Inquiries in the Early Modern Era*, as well as the editor of *ECCB: The Eighteenth-Century Current Bibliography*, both published by AMS Press.

JAMES E. MAY, professor emeritus of English at Pennsylvania State University, has, for over twenty-five years, surveyed rare book and manuscript sales for *The Scriblerian* and edited *The Eighteenth-Century Intelligencer*, the newsletter for the East Central American Society for Eighteenth-Century Studies. He has also been the contributing editor responsible for the bibliographical section of *ECCB: The Eighteenth-Century Current Bibliography* for nearly thirty years. He has written on bibliographical and textual problems in early editions of Oliver Goldsmith, George Lyttelton, Tobias Smollett, Jonathan Swift, and Edward Young. He is at present writing a descriptive bibliography of Edward Young (to 1775) and identifying the ornament stocks of early eighteenth-century Dublin and London printers.

BRETT C. MCINELLY is a professor of English at Brigham Young University, where he specializes in eighteenth-century British literature and culture. He has published numerous articles on the literary reception of Methodism in the eighteenth century and is the author of *Textual Warfare and the Making of Methodism* (2014). He served as the founding editor of AMS Press's *Religion in the Age of Enlightenment* and recently published a coedited volume (with Paul E. Kerry) titled *New Approaches to Religion and the Enlightenment* (2018).

LEAH ORR is an associate professor of English at the University of Louisiana, Lafayette. She is the author of numerous articles on fiction, the book trade, women writers, and the classical tradition in the long eighteenth century. Her book on the novel, *Novel Ventures: Fiction and Print Culture in England, 1690–1730*, was published in 2017.

CEDRIC D. REVERAND II is George Duke Humphrey Distinguished Professor Emeritus of English at the University of Wyoming. He has published extensively on seventeenth- and eighteenth-century literature, especially Dryden and Pope; he has also written on eighteenth-century art, architecture, and music. He has served as a contributing editor to *The Scriblerian* and was, for several years, one of the many contributing editors to AMS Press's *ECCB: The Eighteenth-Century Current Bibliography*. His recent publications include two books of essays: *Queen Anne and the Arts* (2015), which he edited, and *An Expanding Universe: The Project of Eighteenth-Century Studies: Essays Commemorating the Career of Jim Springer Borck* (2017, published by AMS Press), which he coedited with Kevin L. Cope. He is also the editor of *Eighteenth-Century Life*.

J. T. SCANLAN is a professor of English at Providence College. He has written on various aspects of the eighteenth century, including many essays on Samuel Johnson and on the law. His recent work on Johnson and the law has appeared in *Samuel Johnson After 300 Years* (2009); *Samuel Johnson in Context* (2011); and in *Impassioned Jurisprudence: Law, Literature, & Emotion, 1760–1848* (2015). He is a former president of the Northeast American Society for Eighteenth-Century Studies. He is also coeditor of *The Age of Johnson*, one of AMS Press's many scholarly annuals. He is currently writing a book on legal issues, *A Spirit of Contradiction: Law and Literature in Eighteenth-Century London*. In a more popular vein, he recently completed a comic-grim memoir about grad school at the University of Michigan and Yale, *Terminal Degree: My Quest for a PhD*. In the summertime, he writes on baseball, and has recently delivered essays at the National Baseball Hall of Fame in Cooperstown, New York.

MANUEL SCHONHORN is professor of literature and history emeritus at Southern Illinois University–Carbondale. His publications range from essays on Dryden, Defoe, Fielding, and Pope, to essays on Mark Twain and Nathaniel Hawthorne. He is the author of *Defoe's Politics: Parliament, Power, Kingship, and*

"Robinson Crusoe" (1991) and editor of Defoe's *General History of the Pyrates* (1972, repr. 1999). He is coeditor (with Maximillian Novak) of the ongoing *Stoke Newington Daniel Defoe Edition.*

PHILIP SMALLWOOD is emeritus professor of English at Birmingham City University (United Kingdom) and senior associate teacher in the English Department at Bristol University. He is the author of numerous articles and essays on Augustan literature and criticism together with several books, including, with AMS Press, *Critical Occasions: Dryden, Pope, Johnson and the History of Criticism* (2011). His *Johnson's Critical Presence* (2004) and (with Min Wild) *Ridiculous Critics: Augustan Mockery of Critical Judgment* (2014) are both *Choice* prizewinning volumes. He is coeditor (with Greg Clingham) of *Samuel Johnson After 300 Years* (2009) and (with Wendy James and David Boucher) of *The Philosophy of Enchantment* (2005), a collection of the previously unpublished critical and cultural writings from the 1920s and 1930s by the British philosopher R. G. Collingwood.

SUSAN SPENCER is a professor of English at the University of Central Oklahoma. She was the founding editor of AMS Press's annual *The Eighteenth-Century Novel* and, in 1998, worked with Gabe Hornstein to design AMS's first website. As a past president of both the South Central Society for Eighteenth-Century Studies and the Midwestern American Society for Eighteenth-Century Studies, she has worked to increase representation of Asian literature and culture in academic conferences. She is coauthor, with Nhu Nguyen, of "Sea and Mulberry: Hồ Xuân Hương, Nguyễn Du, and the Establishment of a Vietnamese National Literature," in *Citizens of the World: Adapting in the Eighteenth Century* (2015), edited by Kevin L. Cope and Samara Anne Cahill. Spencer is fascinated by Japan's Edo era, a period of intense isolationist policy when the nation's authors, cut off from outside literary influence, relied upon their own creative resources to come up with a vibrant vernacular literature that is unique to its time and place. This essay on Ihara Saikaku is her first publication in the field of Japanese literature.

LINDA V. TROOST, a professor of English at Washington & Jefferson College in Pennsylvania, has published on topics ranging from British musical theater, to Robin Hood, to zombies, but her major work has been on adaptations of the novels of Jane Austen. With Sayre E. Greenfield, she edited *Jane Austen in Hollywood* (2001), the first scholarly exploration of the Austen film phenomenon that started in the 1990s. She is a contributing editor to *The Scriblerian*; she has served on the editorial board of *1650–1850: Ideas, Aesthetics, and Inquiries in the Early Modern Era*; and she is the founding editor of *Eighteenth-Century Women*, both scholarly annuals that were published by AMS Press.

DAVID VENTURO is a professor of English at The College of New Jersey, author of *Johnson the Poet: The Poetic Career of Samuel Johnson* (1999), and editor of

AMS Press's *The School of the Eucharist . . . With a Preface Concerning the Testimony of Miracles* (2006). He writes about and teaches British literature, 1600–1850; poetry; baseball and American culture; and popular culture. He serves as editor for both *The Scriblerian* and *ECCB: The Eighteenth-Century Current Bibliography* (AMS Press). He is currently writing about epic, mock epic, growing skepticism about heroic ideals in seventeenth- and eighteenth-century literature, and the Beatles and their world.

Index